IMAGES
of America

HAVRE

ON THE COVER: Havre loves to have the opportunity to celebrate, and one of the biggest events was the Great Northern Stampede. The entire town celebrated in 1917, hosting a parade—with businesses putting out buntings for the occasion. The Great Northern Stampede held its events at the fairgrounds, then located in east Havre, near where Tilleman Hi-Line Dodge is currently located. Among the performers at the Great Northern Stampede events during its duration were "Long" George Francis and Marie "Buckskin Mary" Gibson. (Courtesy of Don Greytak.)

IMAGES
of America

HAVRE

Emily Ann Mayer

ARCADIA
PUBLISHING

ISBN 978-1-4671-3304-3

Published by Arcadia Publishing
Charleston, South Carolina

Printed in the United States of America

Library of Congress Control Number: 2015937263

For all general information, please contact Arcadia Publishing:
Telephone 843-853-2070
Fax 843-853-0044
E-mail sales@arcadiapublishing.com
For customer service and orders:
Toll-Free 1-888-313-2665

Visit us on the Internet at www.arcadiapublishing.com

This book is dedicated to Jamey Lammerding, the late Lou Lucke, and to my felines babies Skinny, Buddy, and Tux—but especially to Shorty, Smokey, and Pippie, who went to Rainbow Bridge in 2014, and to Mackie, who followed them in 2015.

Contents

Acknowledgments 6

Introduction 7

1. Old Downtown Havre 9
2. A Place to Call Home 43
3. Churches, Schools, and Government Buildings 59
4. People and Their Activities 101
5. In the Halls of History 119

ACKNOWLEDGMENTS

A publication such as this is not created alone. I am blessed by my family and many friends and colleagues who were instrumental in the success of this publication. I am indebted to the late Lou Lucke, whom I worked with shortly before his passing to fill in some of the gaps from our last book (even though I did not get as much material as I wanted); to Don Greytak, for his permission to use several of the enclosed images; and to Floyd Witt, Arvid Kristoffersen, Elsie K. Nelson, Randy and Laura Martin, Toni Hagener, and the people of Havre and Hill County, Montana.

Introduction

Millions of years before there was a Havre, Montana, dinosaurs of many different kinds roamed this area of the world. Both land and marine dinosaurs lived here, and the Badlands to the north of Havre showcase the many layers of paleontological history. Rare dinosaur discoveries, as well as evidence of prehistoric mammals in Hill County, have put us on the map as a valuable resource for those in this field of study.

Prehistoric peoples used the Havre area as a hunting ground for thousands of years. Evidence of the Besant, Avonlea, and Old Women's/Saddle Butte peoples at Wahkpa Chu'gn archaeological site behind the Holiday Village Mall showcases how they harvested and processed life-giving bison for their everyday needs. The Blackfeet, Gros Ventre, Assiniboine, Cree, and Chippewa tribes have all used what is now Havre as a place to live off what the land, water, and sky could provide.

As white settlers moved ever west, in 1879, after the Battle of the Little Big Horn (1876) in southwestern Montana and the Battle of the Bear's Paw (1877) just south of neighboring Chinook, Montana, it was decided a fort was necessary to keep the peace. Fort Assinniboine was constructed on the plains of Montana, about six miles south of present-day Havre. The construction of the fort brought not only Caucasian and African American troops but also civilians employed to perform various tasks at the military reservation. Some African Americans chose to stay in Havre after their tours of duty at Fort Assinniboine were over, and with other African Americans moving to Havre, they made up a small ethnic group in Havre. Most citizens today have never heard of them.

In September 1887, the St. Paul, Minneapolis, & Manitoba Railroad came through what is now Havre on its way south to Great Falls, Montana. Havre's plentiful supply of necessary water for the steam engines proved valuable to James J. Hill. With the railroad came people from all over the country, as well as immigrants, especially Chinese and Japanese workers. Of those who chose to stay in Havre, some worked at established businesses, while others owned laundries and restaurants.

For the area, there was no turning back. White settlers were coming, and they were going to stay. Havre's first businesses and homes were canvas tents, but soon wooden structures sprang up in the new settlement along the railroad tracks and Milk River, because everyone knows it gets cold up here, and it can last for months on end.

Havre's first permanent structures were of wood-frame design, typical of Western towns at the time. The downtown core quickly filled up with mercantile and drugstores, hardware stores, hotels, restaurants, saloons, and brothels. Havre was not known for refinement, and it was not unusual for the downtown to be quite active at all times of the day and night. Some of that activity resulted in a stay at the local jail for some, if anyone cared to catch them. Havre's reputation was so bad, James J. Hill threatened to move the division point out of Havre unless it cleaned up its act. Efforts were made to smooth the rough edges, at least for appearance's sake, but the vice continued nonetheless.

When the rules of the Homestead Act of 1862 were changed, allowing for more acres for a homestead claim and less time to prove up, a population boom resulted in Americans from all over the country and immigrants from foreign lands filing on a "free farm from Uncle Sam." Beginning about 1910, homestead shacks and other improvements required under the law dotted the prairie, towns sprang up, and Havre benefitted.

Residential housing was constructed to the north across the tracks and south and east of the downtown, eventually spreading to the west as development advanced. The oldest homes are found in the original townsite, part of the 36-block Havre Residential Historic District, which was placed in the National Register of Historic Places in 1989. Late Victorian–era homes are found in this location, but Craftsman, Bungalow, American Foursquare, Colonial, and Georgian homes were constructed as Havre grew over the years.

The great fire of 1904 changed downtown Havre forever. As most of the buildings were wooden, they quickly were consumed in a huge blaze on January 14 of that year, leaving only the concrete safe of one of the banks left. Most of the downtown area was destroyed, but the hardy businessmen of Havre quickly sprang into action. Many rebuilt their businesses aboveground, but some went underground, and a re-creation of some of those businesses can be seen at Havre Beneath the Streets. Construction had to be mostly of brick, stone, or concrete—definitely not solely of wood, for fear of a future fire.

With population comes civilization. As families settled in Havre, schools for the children were established. The worship needs of Havre were fulfilled with the construction of many churches, some with services in Norwegian or German, depending on the needs of the congregation. Local governments were established; Havre was incorporated as a city in 1893, and Hill County was created in 1912 by breaking away from the massive Chouteau County. Clubs and organizations were also established, and people found ways to entertain themselves with dances, music, and festivals. Everyone contributed to the construction of Havre's foundation, whether intentionally or not.

North central Montana can be a land of extremes. Very cold winters can follow very hot summers. Gully washers during the summer season can cause disaster to property and lives. Blizzards and subzero temperatures can hamper travel and commerce. And one cannot forget to mention the wind, which can be very strong and has been known to topple brick and stone structures. Flooding was a common occurrence in Havre prior to the construction of flood control levees and drainage systems in the 1950s and 1960s. Through it all, the people of Havre and Hill County have come together, helped each other out, and rebuilt homes and businesses.

Havre has changed over the years, but the downtown and Havre Residential Historic District, the east end, and north sides all have old businesses, churches, schools, and homes that people still use today. While not being all-encompassing—there simply was not the time or room for everything, thus leaving ample subjects for perhaps another volume—this book does offer a glimpse of how Havre started, where we have been, and where we will go, in a positive direction.

One

Old Downtown Havre

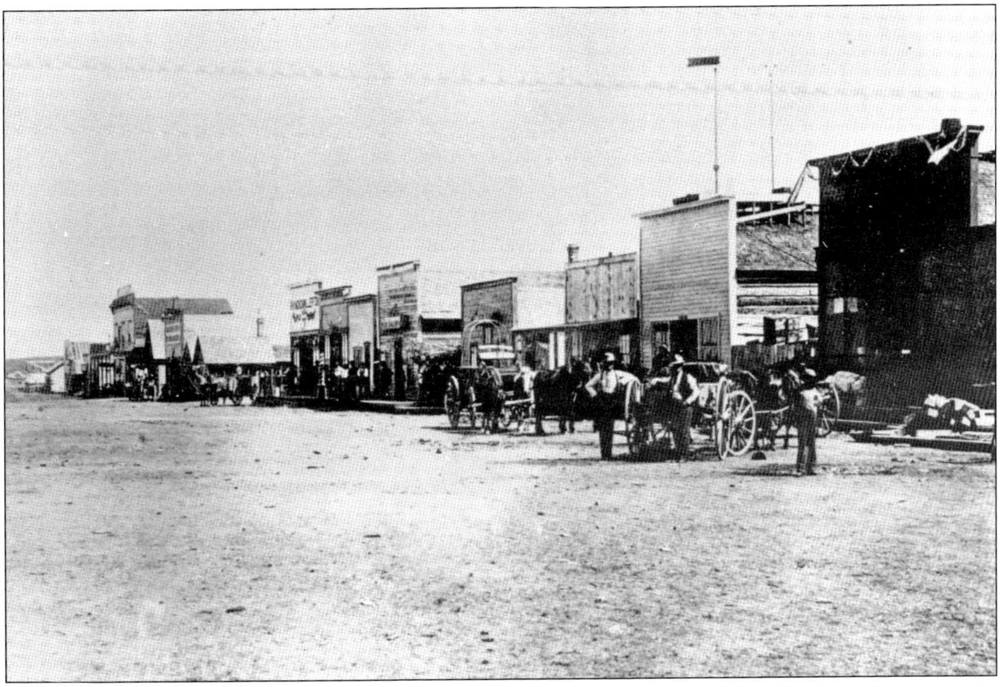

Havre started as a tiny settlement of canvas tents after the arrival of the St. Paul, Minneapolis & Manitoba Railroad in 1887. By the 1890s, Havre was a typical Western town with wooden buildings featuring false fronts, to give the appearance of taller structures. This is the south side of First Street, between Second and Third Avenues. The second building from the right has weather equipment on its roof. (Courtesy of Don Greytak.)

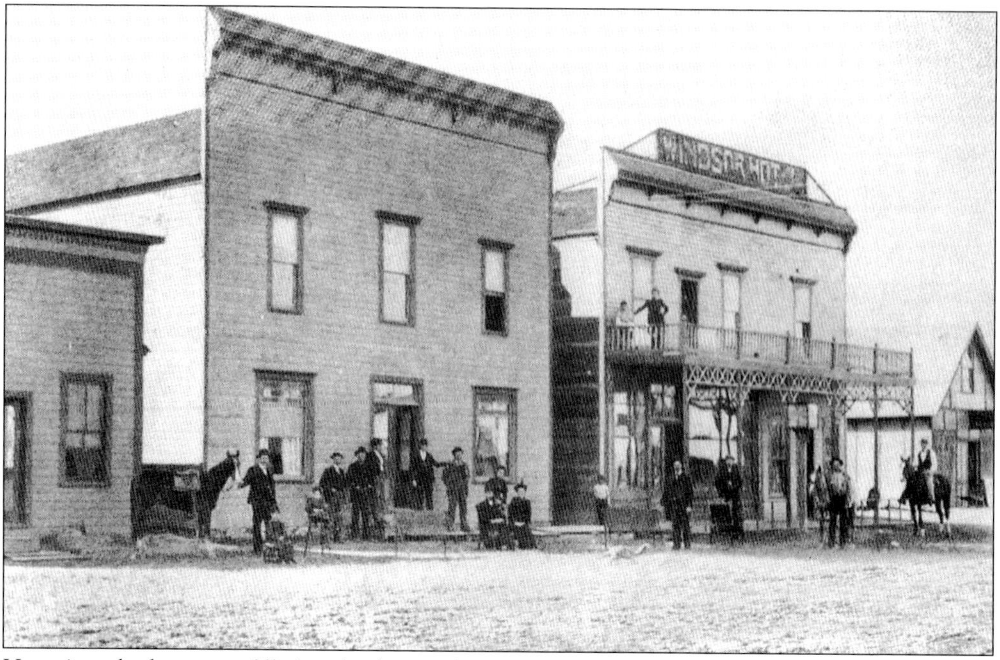

Havre's early days were filled with plenty of raucous activities in the downtown area. Shooting off firearms and brawls were not uncommon in Havre's youth. Despite the crude atmosphere, entrepreneurs saw promise in the fledgling city and set up shop. Some were extremely successful. Between Third and Fourth Avenues, First Street long held successful businesses such as the Windsor Hotel, which boasted "first class accommodations" in its advertising. (Courtesy of Don Greytak.)

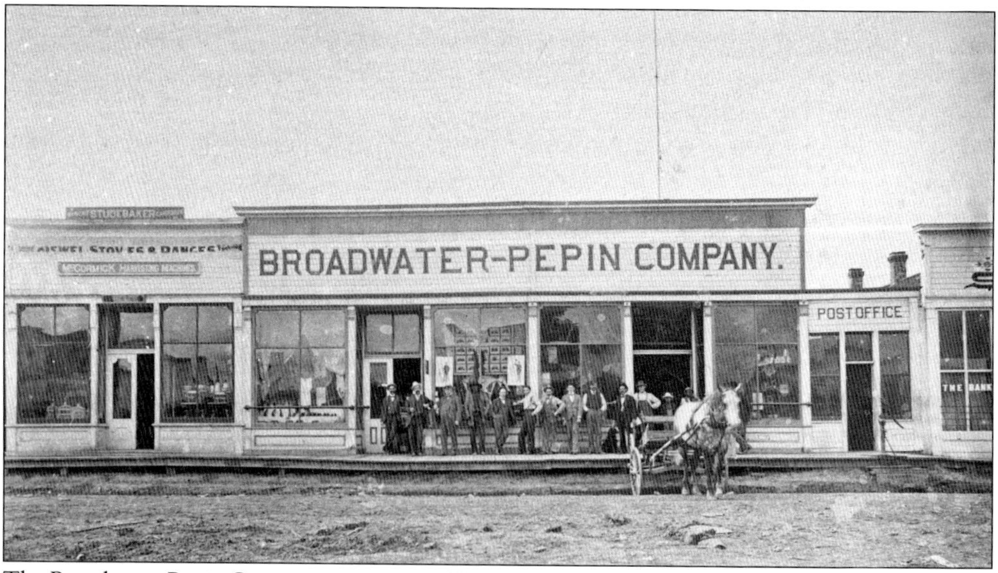

The Broadwater-Pepin Company was among Havre's most successful businesses. Founded by Edward Broadwater and Simon Pepin, the company started in a tent. In 1892, a wooden building was constructed next door to the post office to conduct the business of selling general merchandise. During its early days, Havre newspapers panned the post office for its lack of speed in getting the mail delivered. (Courtesy of Don Greytak.)

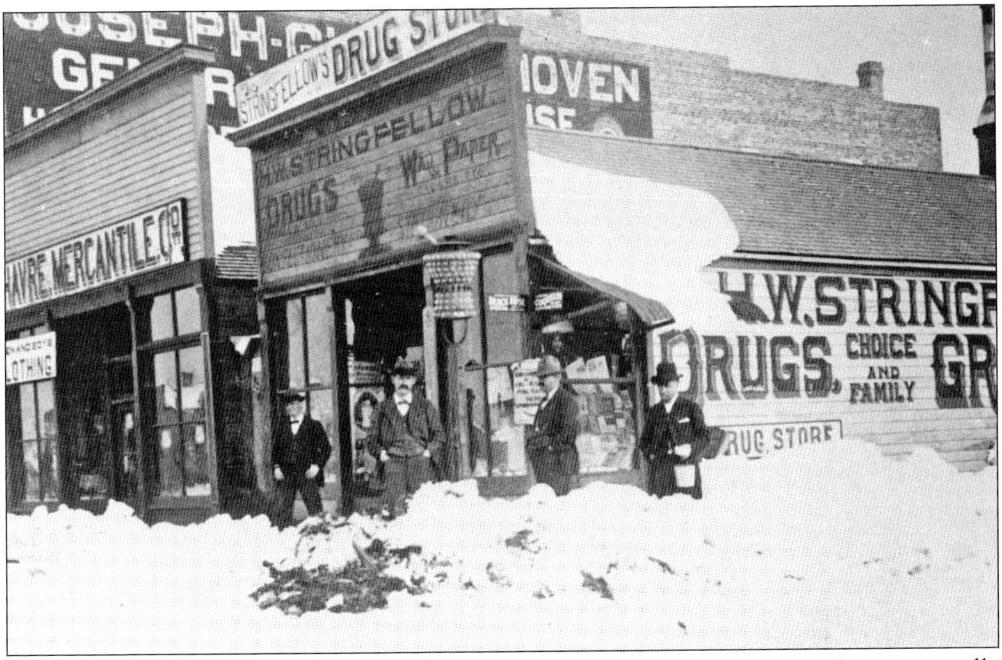

Henry Stringfellow came to Havre in 1892 and set up the first drugstore in town. It was originally located on the corner of First Street and Fourth Avenue but later moved to First Street and Third Avenue. After the great fire of 1904, Stringfellow branched out into the department store business, creating the Havre Commercial Company and relocating to the 200 block of Third Avenue. (Courtesy of Don Greytak.)

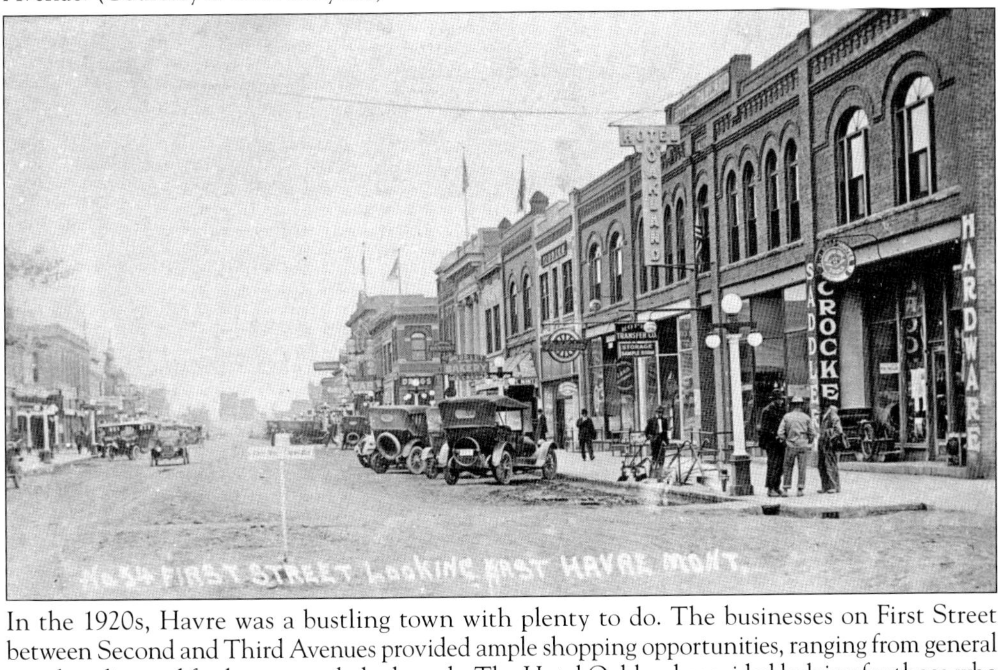

In the 1920s, Havre was a bustling town with plenty to do. The businesses on First Street between Second and Third Avenues provided ample shopping opportunities, ranging from general merchandise and fresh meats to baked goods. The Hotel Oakland provided lodging for those who needed it, and today it is honored by the Havre Jaycees during Halloween with their Haunted Hotel Oakland fundraiser to benefit the needy in Havre. (Courtesy of Don Greytak.)

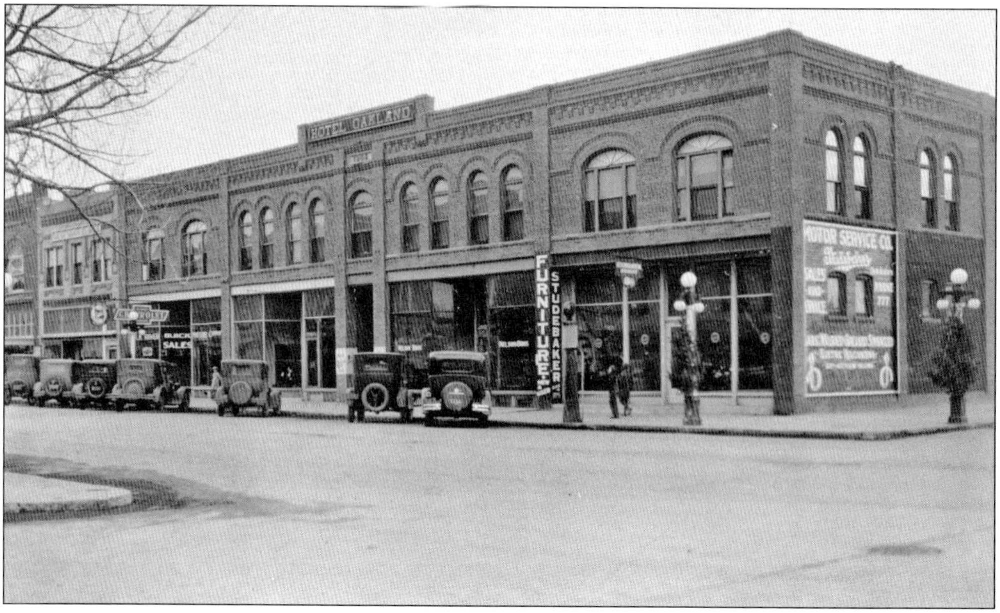

After the great fire of 1904, Edward Broadwater and Simon Pepin rebuilt their enterprise on First Street and Second Avenue. The Havre City Council passed an ordinance that stated new downtown buildings must be constructed mostly of brick, stone, or concrete to prevent another fire disaster. After Broadwater and Pepin closed their business, new establishments made the 1906 structure their home. The Motor Service Company was located below the building. (Courtesy of Don Greytak.)

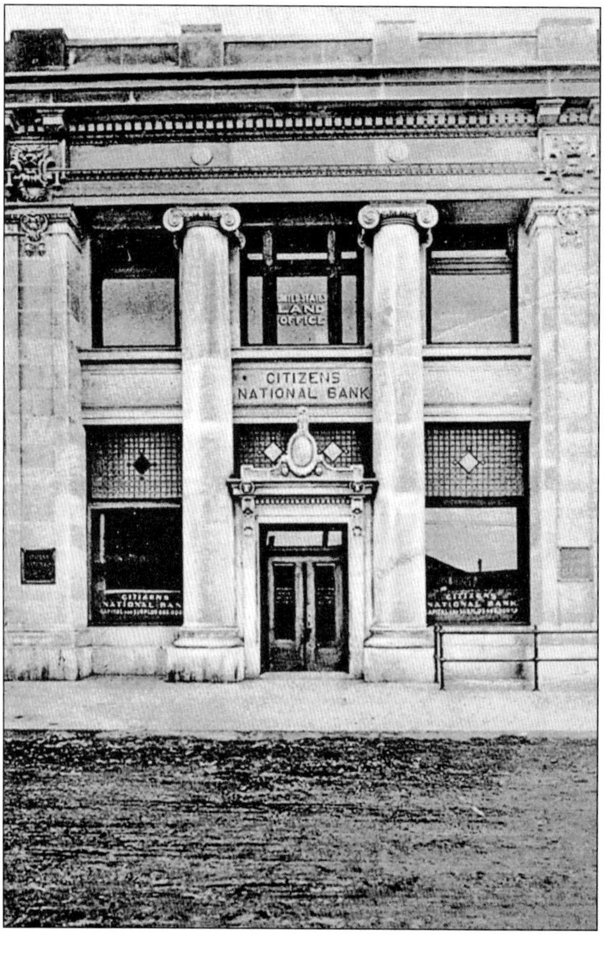

The Havre Citizens National Bank was a regal building on the south side of Havre's First Street between Second and Third Avenues. It was chartered on June 11, 1909, but voluntarily liquidated January 2, 1913. Banks in early Havre could be risky, and it was not uncommon for many to close their doors. Lack of population, cash, crop failures, and a shortage of professional bankers contributed to many bank failures. (Courtesy of High Line Heritage House.)

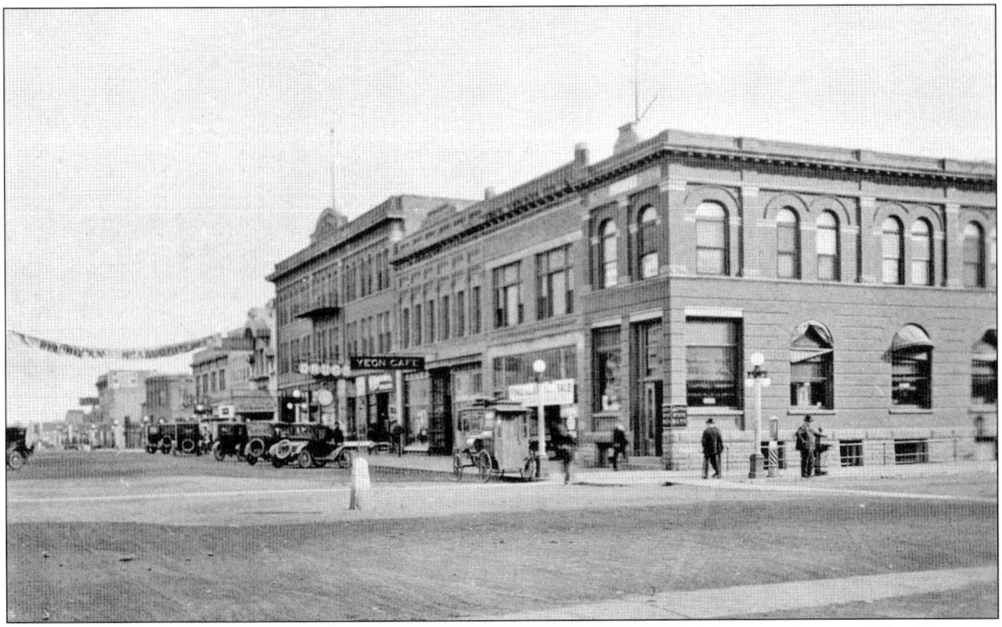

First Street between Third and Fourth Avenues also provided a busy business climate. The Security State Bank is on the corner, and the iron barrier indicates access to businesses underground. The Yeon Café was previously the Board of Trade Saloon; it switched to a café during Prohibition. The Havre Hotel, built with great fanfare in 1904, is in the middle of the block. (Courtesy of Don Greytak.)

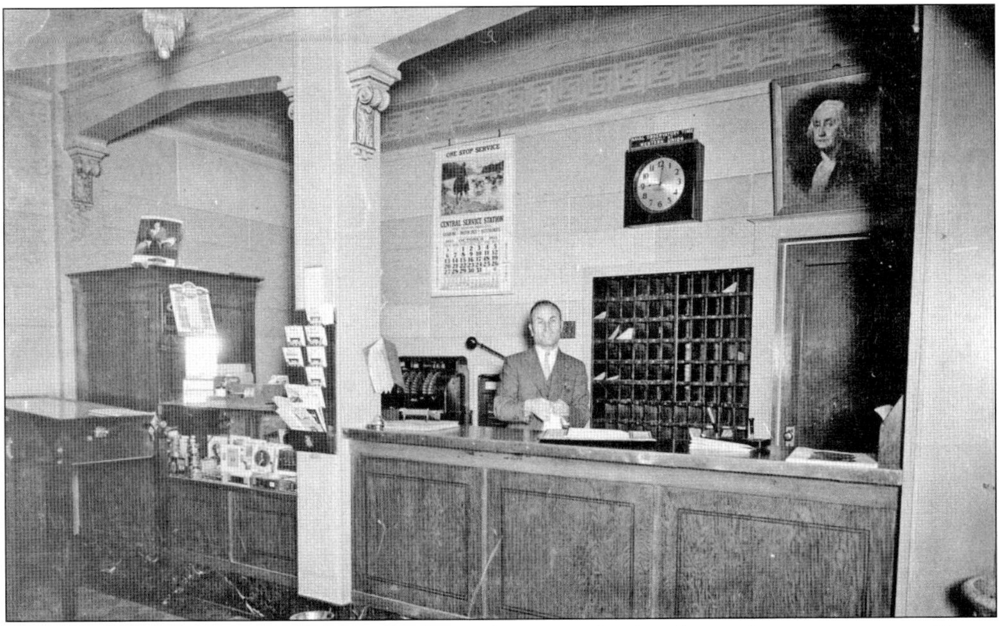

The register counter of the Havre Hotel was elegant and refined, a sophistication many Havre businesses wanted to project to give the image of a small town that had arrived. When guests signed in, they could expect only the best Havre had to offer, with well-appointed rooms, excellent service, and a lounge and restaurant to meet their needs and exceed their expectations. (Courtesy of Don Greytak.)

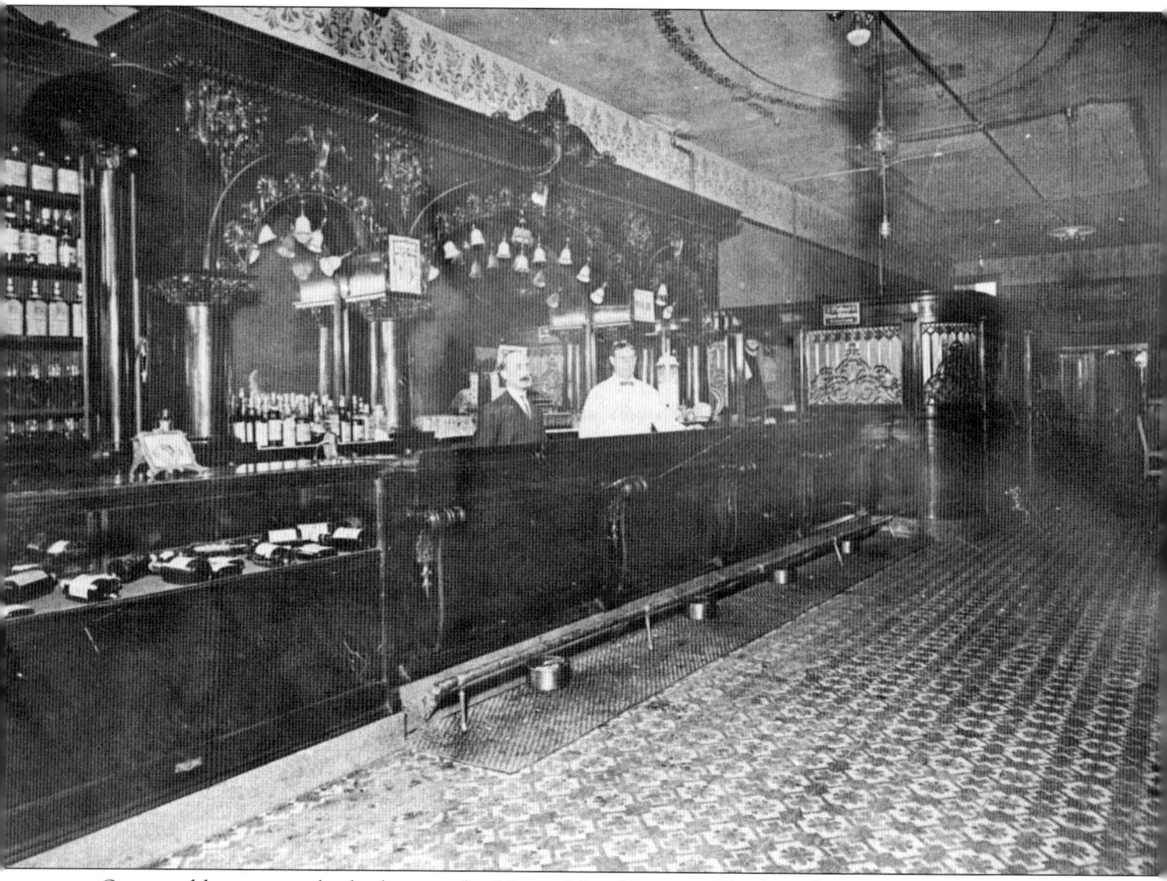

One could expect only the best at the Havre Hotel lounge. The best liquors could be enjoyed in the elegant surroundings of Havre's first-class drinking establishment, complete with a private area featuring stained- and leaded-glass panels. The Havre Hotel burned on October 8, 1975, due to a fire in the neighboring Downtowner Restaurant to the east, formerly the Orpheum Theatre. (Courtesy of Don Greytak.)

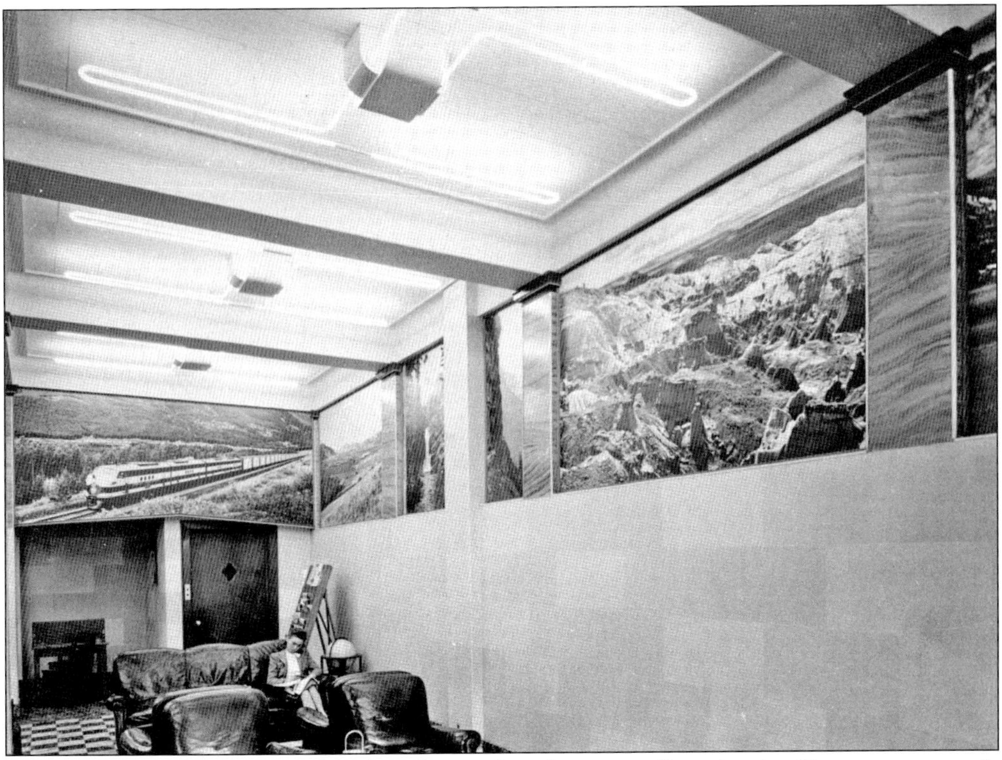

By the 1930s, the Havre Hotel had modernized its décor to reflect the Art Deco movement. It not only served as a first-class stop in Havre but also played an important role in promoting the area. Large sepia photographs showing off wonderful things about Havre, from ranching to the railroad, were placed in the waiting room area. Several of those images are found today at the Palace Bar in Havre. (Courtesy of Don Greytak.)

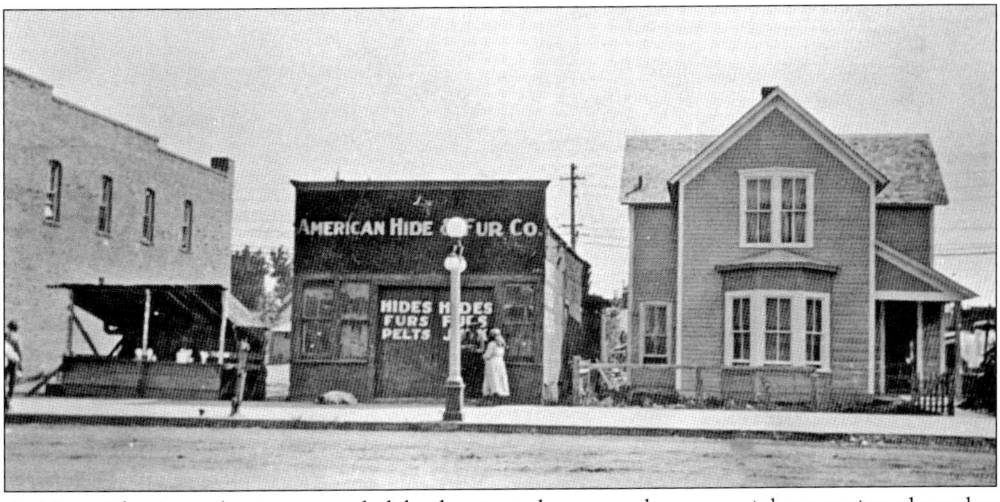

As Havre's business district expanded, both private homes and commercial enterprise adapted to fit the needs of a growing town. After the American Hide and Fur Company on the 400 block of First Street was razed, a brick building was constructed in 1956 by Bert Clikeman, who made a special accommodation for the bay window on the private residence by building around it. The alcove can still be seen today. (Courtesy of Don Greytak.)

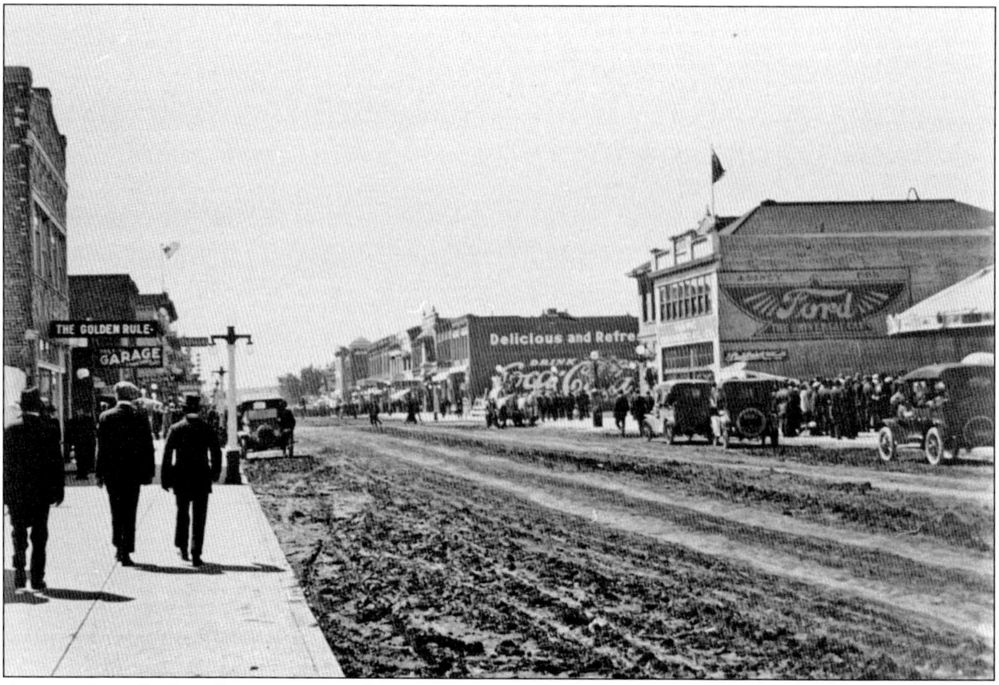

An unidentified gathering was taking place when this photograph was taken of First Street sometime in the 1910s. The Havre Commercial Company is seen to the right, and next to it is the 1908 city hall. To the left of the photograph is the Golden Rule, the precursor to the J.C. Penney Company. It is located in the Bramble Building, erected by local lawyer James Bramble. (Courtesy of Don Greytak.)

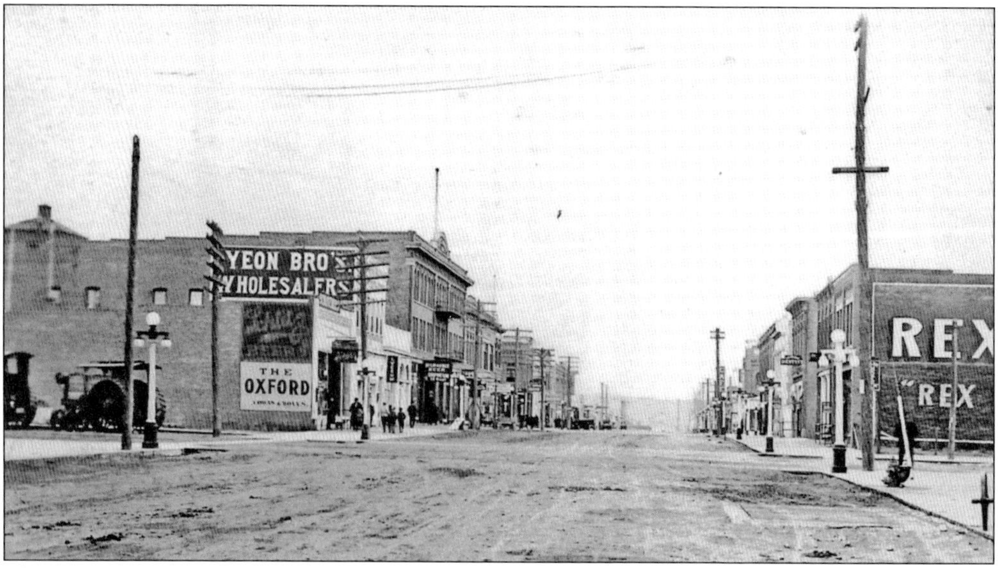

Electricity came to Havre in 1904, with the incorporation of the Havre Electric Company. Newspapers lauded the arrival of this technology, and businesses and many—but not all—residences were wired for electricity. In 1914, the Montana Power Company acquired all properties of the Havre Electric Company, which included the electrical distribution system, steam heating, and telephone system. (Courtesy of High Line Heritage House.)

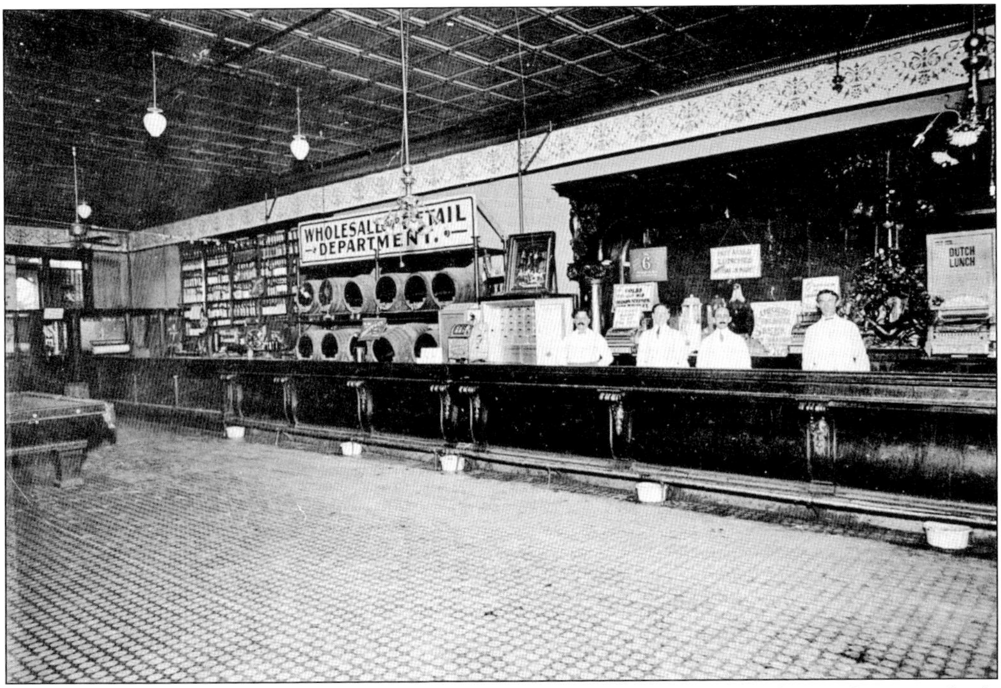

The Yeon Brothers Wholesale Liquor Store catered mostly to those purchasing liquor in high volume, such as saloons, and sold liquor "from half-pint to ten thousand gallons." It was located on the south side of First Street between Third and Fourth Avenues, on the ground floor of the Mansfield Hotel. The business also sold both hot and cold lunches both day and night. (Courtesy of Don Greytak.)

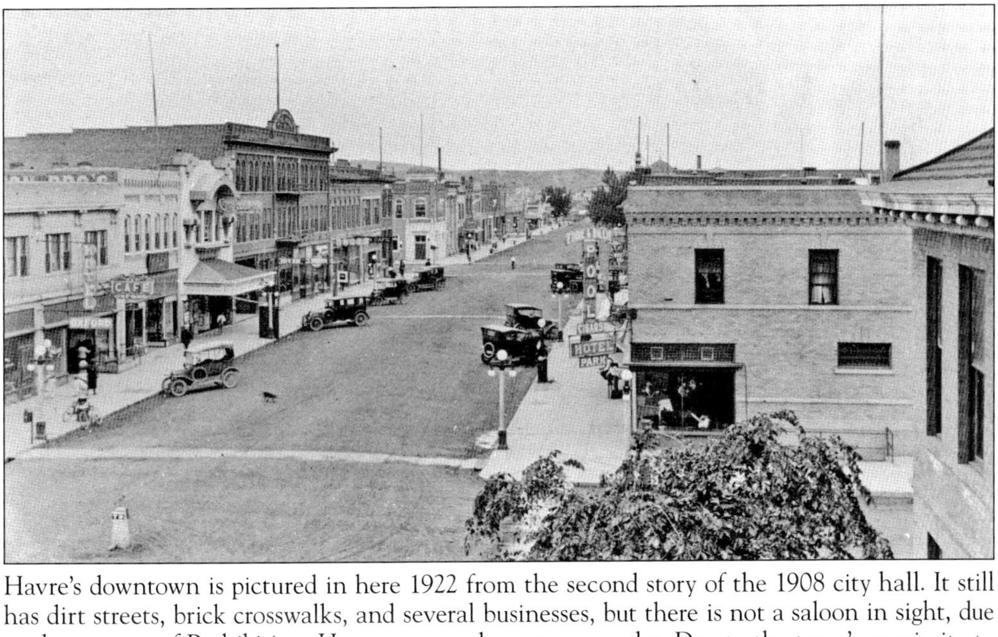

Havre's downtown is pictured in here 1922 from the second story of the 1908 city hall. It still has dirt streets, brick crosswalks, and several businesses, but there is not a saloon in sight, due to the passage of Prohibition. Havre was not by any means dry. Due to the town's proximity to Canada and enterprising individuals seeing a chance to make a profit, Havre was a known hub for bootleg liquor. (Courtesy of Don Greytak.)

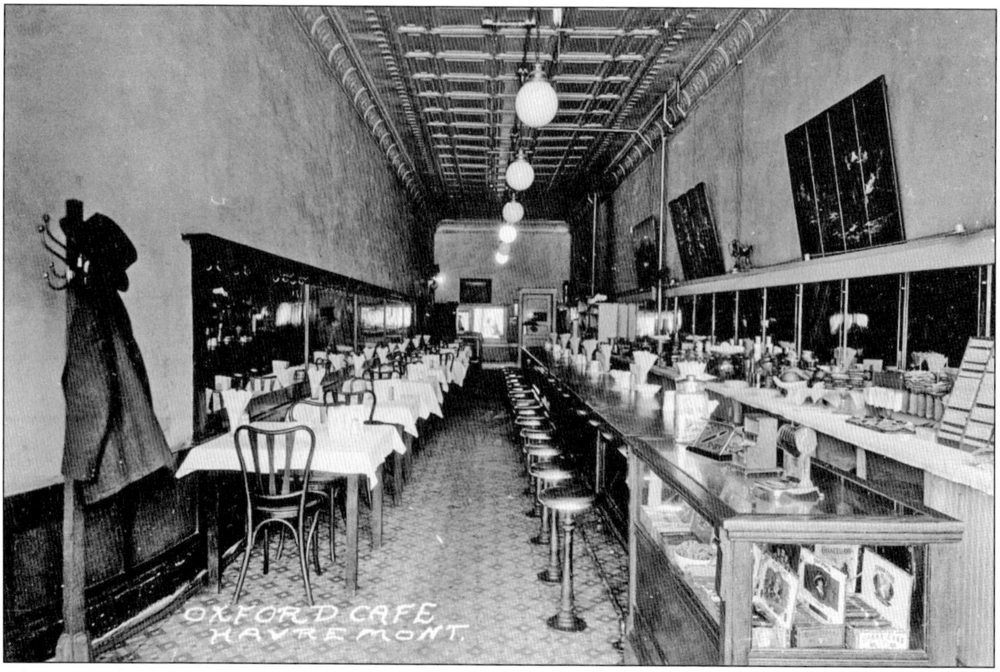

The Oxford Café was a small restaurant and part of the Oxford Hotel and Billiard Room, located at the corner of First Street and Fourth Avenue. It also sold cigars; three of Havre's cigar factories were the Hall and Halvorson, Kaste, and Charles H. Rothrock. Tobacco was brought in from Southern states, or more preferably Cuba, and cigars were made locally. (Courtesy of Don Greytak.)

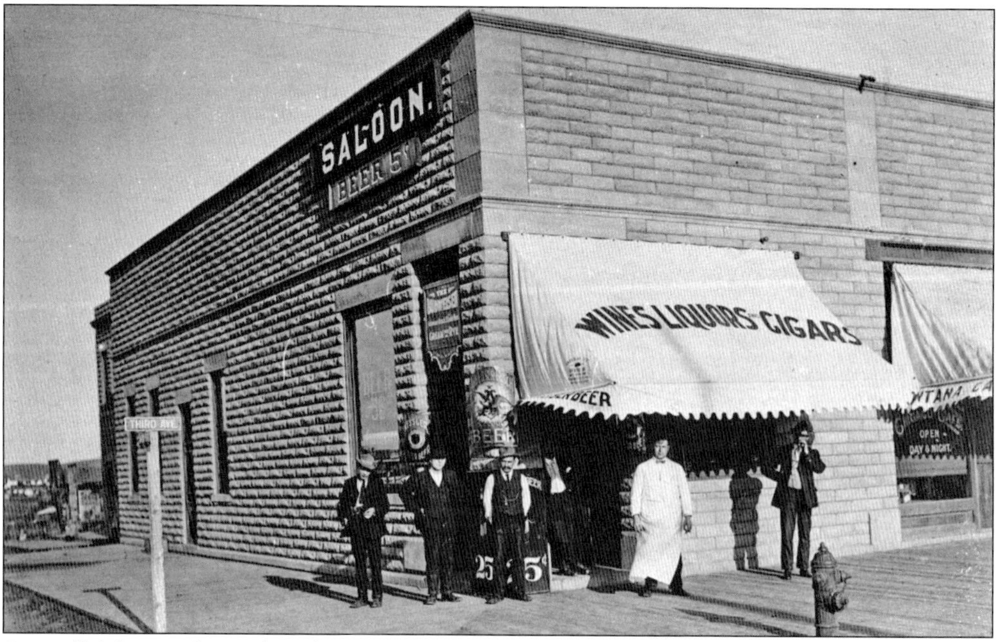

Connelly's Bar was located on the corner of Main Street and Third Avenue. Its convenient location near the Great Northern Railroad Depot made it an easy stop for travelers on the train or railroaders finishing a shift for the day. One could purchase a glass of beer for 5¢. The Chicago Café is to the right of Connelly's Bar and was open both day and night. (Courtesy of Don Greytak.)

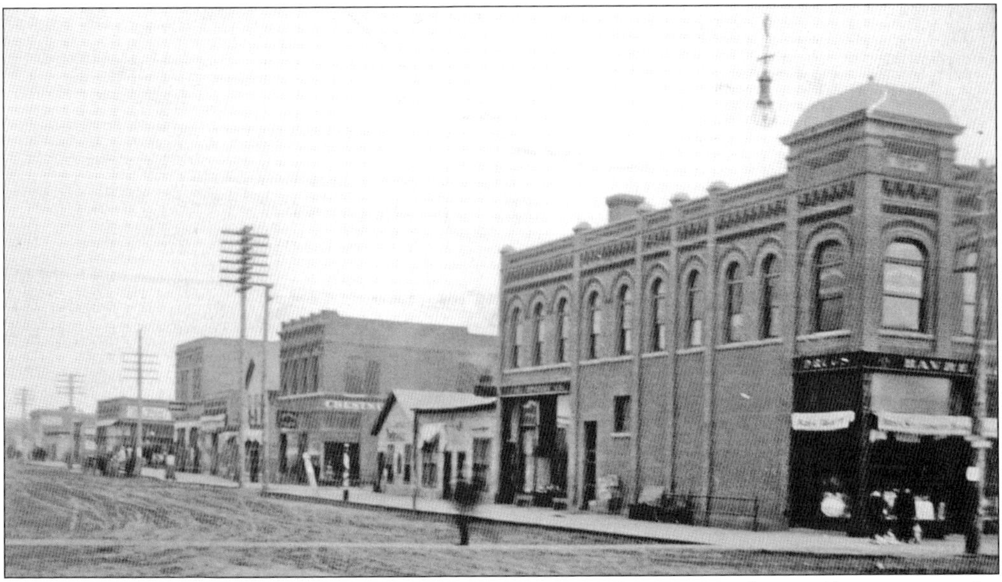

Third Avenue and First Street had the Havre Drug Store on the corner and several businesses to the south, including the 1906 Fair Store toward the left of the photograph. The Havre Drug Store was owned by Daniel Boone, who arrived in Havre in 1897. The store sold prescriptions and a myriad of merchandise, and it also had a soda fountain. (Courtesy of High Line Heritage House.)

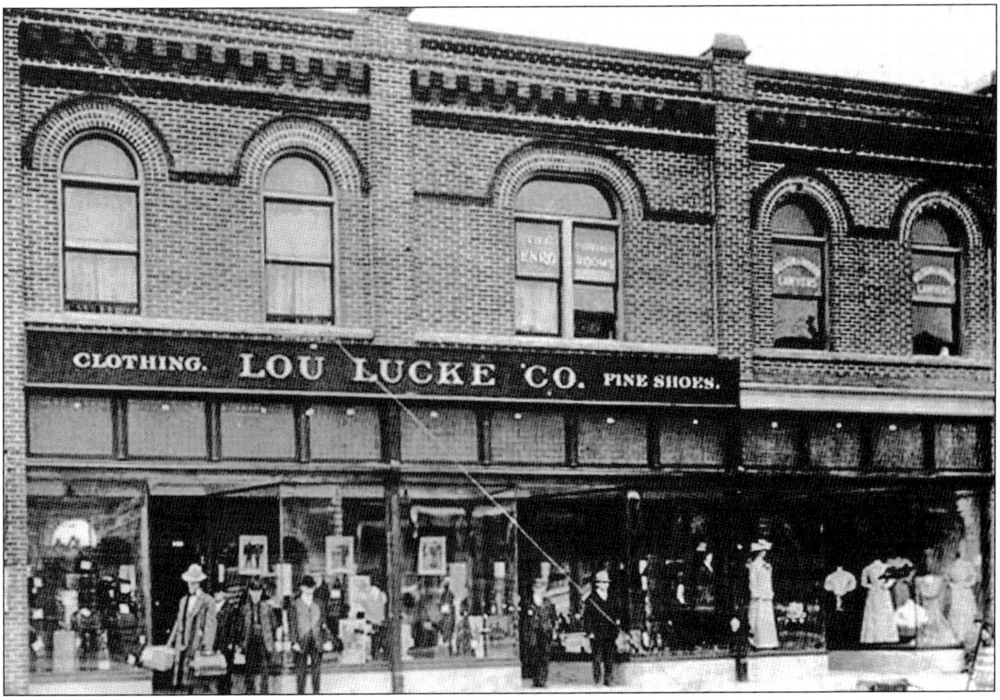

Louis Lucke came to Havre in 1903. He partnered with August Mund and purchased a boot and shoe repair shop from Frank Kaste and Lou Brell. In 1908, the Lou Lucke Company was incorporated, adding clothing to the shoe line. Lucke moved to this location in 1911, and in 1915 the store was enlarged. The Lou Lucke Company was known for its high-quality goods and excellent customer service. (Courtesy of High Line Heritage House.)

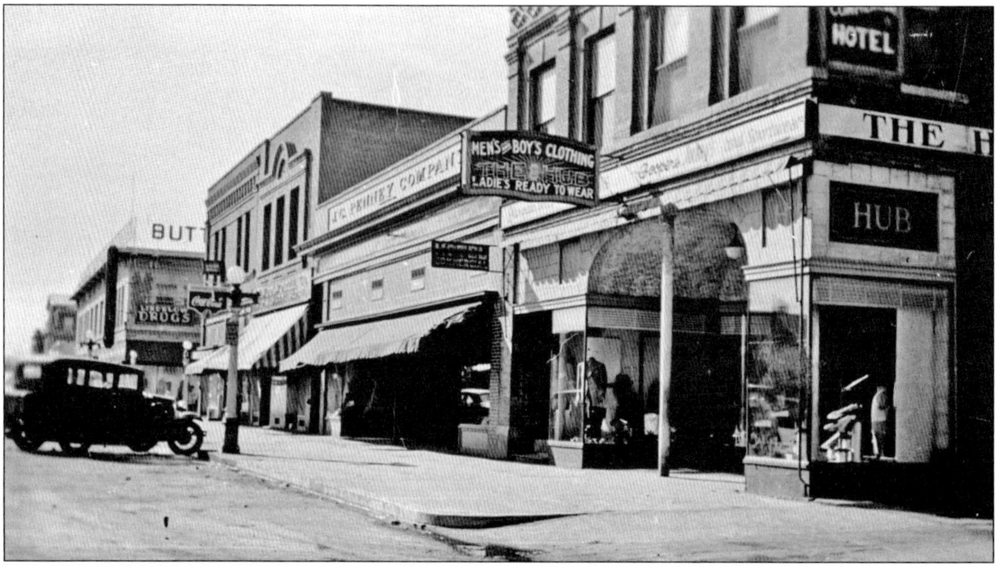

In 1941, Third Avenue had the Hub, owned by Morris Feuer, one of Havre's few Jewish citizens. Originally from Poland, Feuer was very active in Havre civic causes, including the formation of Northern Montana College. Other businesses include the Commercial Hotel above the Hub, J.C. Penney Company, F.W. Woolworth Company, the Lindelow Drug Store with Union Hall above it, Buttrey's, and the post office and federal building. (Courtesy of Don Greytak.)

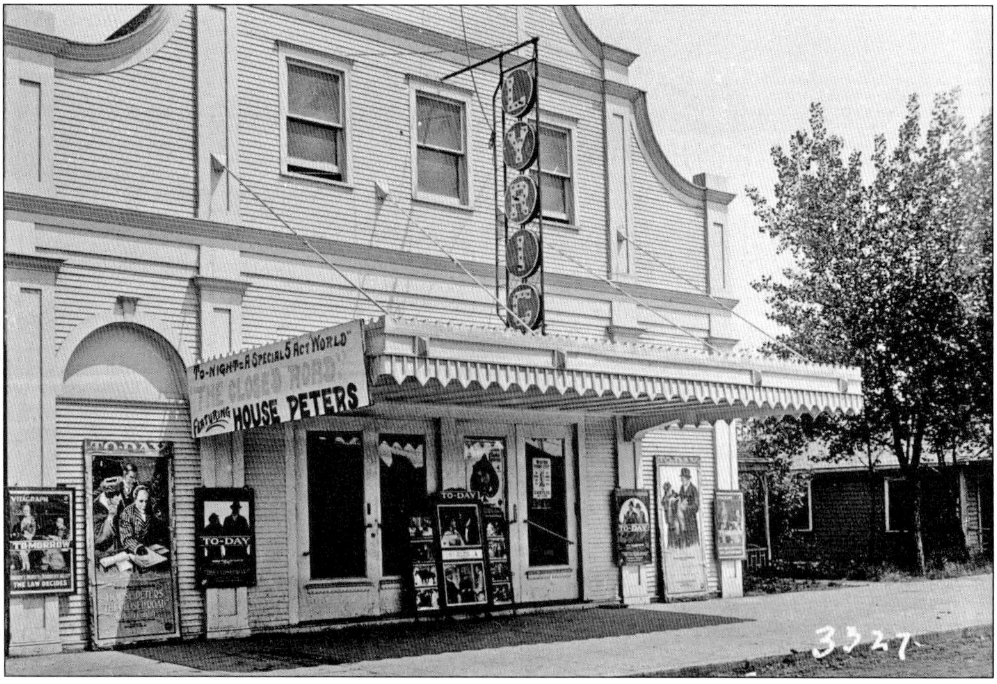

The Lyric Theatre was located on the north side of Second Street between Third and Fourth Avenues. It was formerly the McIntyre Opera House. Both were social centers in Havre's early days, with both live performances and silent moving pictures. In 1922, the theater was moved from this location to the south side of Second Street between First and Second Avenues. (Courtesy of Don Greytak.)

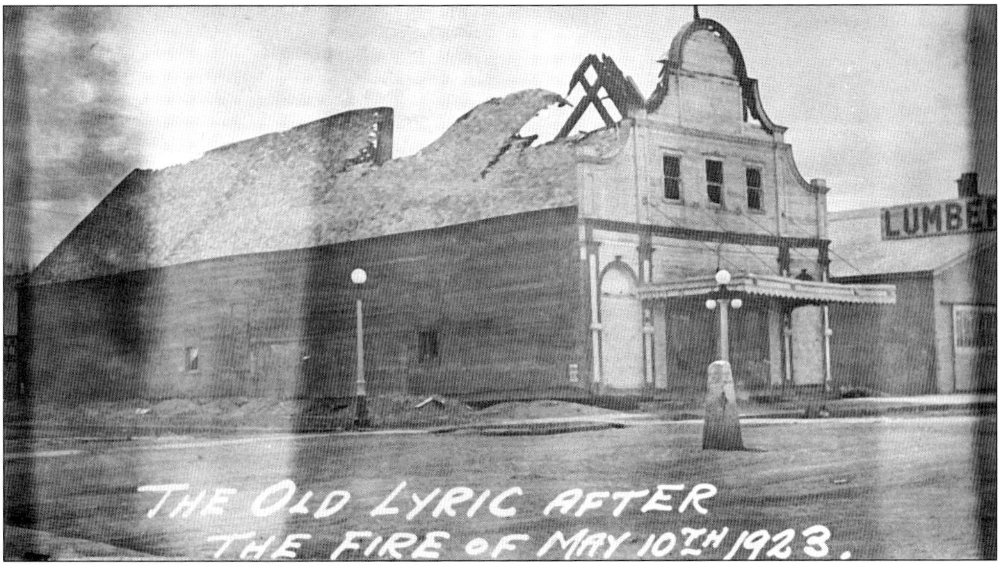

The Lyric Theatre burned May 10, 1923—a sad end to one of Havre's oldest buildings and one of very few wooden buildings allowed to exist after the great fire of 1904. The other businesses, homes, and the first Methodist church located on this block would later be razed to make room for other buildings such as Safeway. Today, the post office, dedicated in 1995, occupies the block. (Courtesy of Don Greytak.)

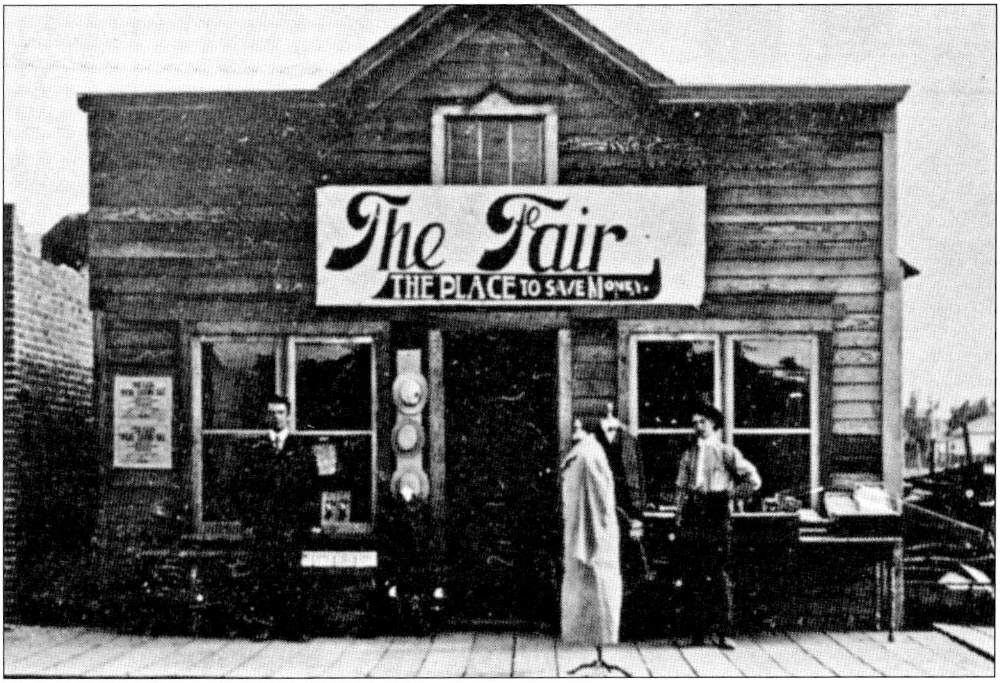

Frank Buttrey came to Montana in 1889, his first stop being in Great Falls. He later went to Livingston before opening a store of his own in Aldridge, Montana. In 1896, he married Jane Boucher at Cinnabar, Montana, and they moved to Havre in 1902, feeling this area would grow and prosper. They opened the Fair on First Street in 1902, but it burned in the great fire of 1904. (Courtesy of Don Greytak.)

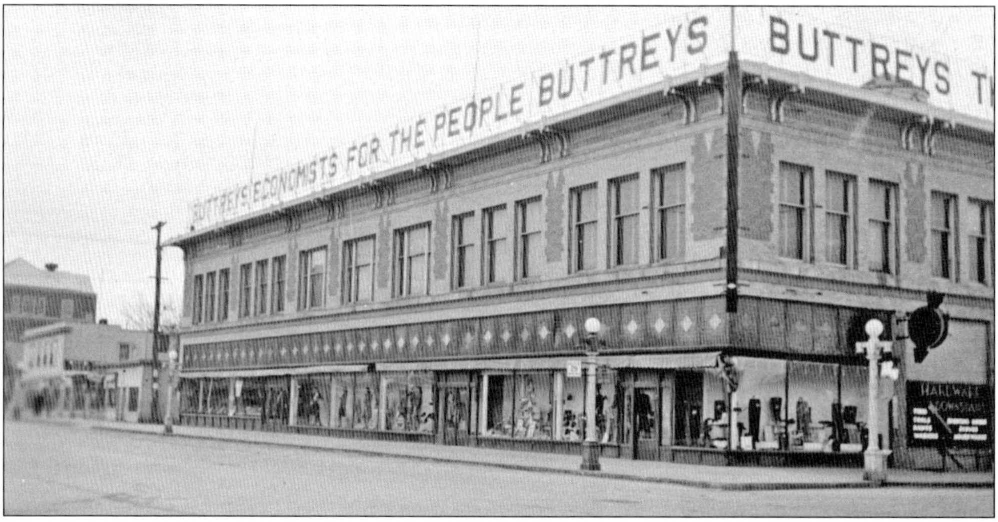

After the 1904 fire, Frank Buttrey moved what stock he saved to the Swanton Building. By 1906, he had constructed a new Fair Store at the southwest corner of Third Avenue and Second Street, and in doing so, he enlarged his business. By 1911, he enlarged it further and renamed it the F.A. Buttrey Company. (Courtesy of Don Greytak.)

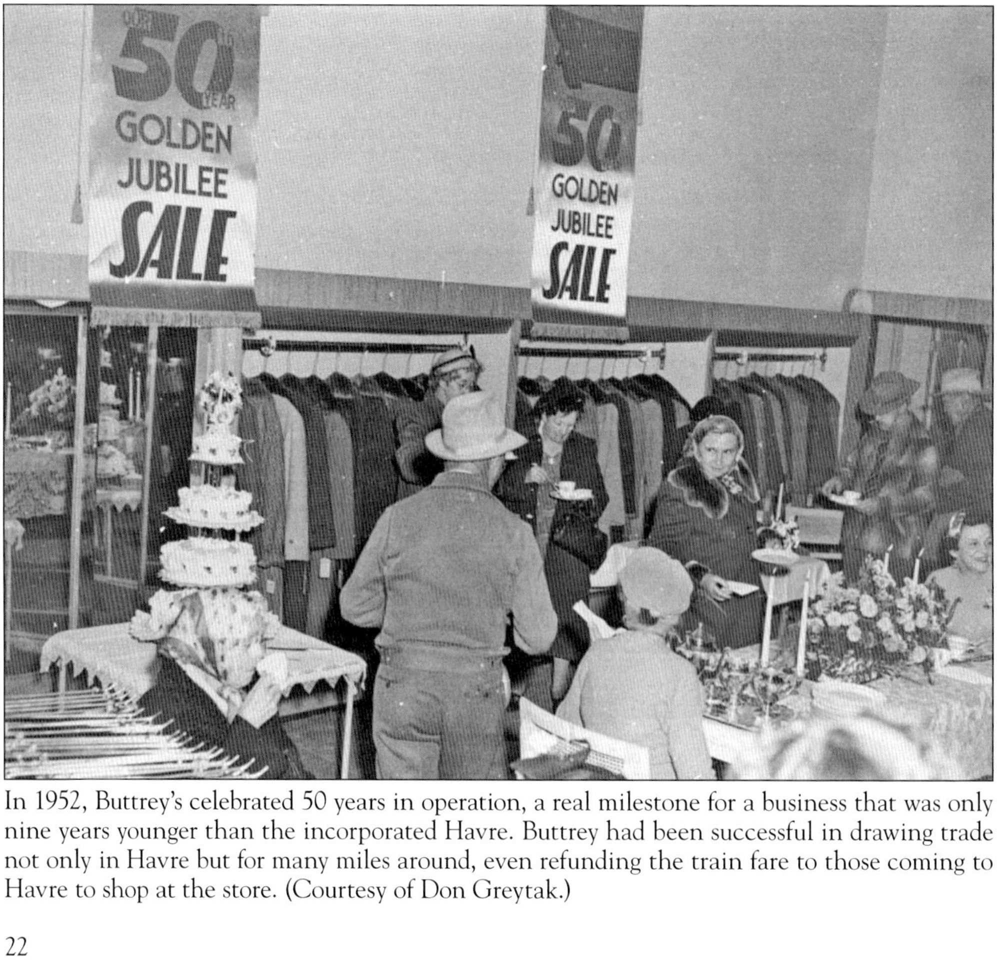

In 1952, Buttrey's celebrated 50 years in operation, a real milestone for a business that was only nine years younger than the incorporated Havre. Buttrey had been successful in drawing trade not only in Havre but for many miles around, even refunding the train fare to those coming to Havre to shop at the store. (Courtesy of Don Greytak.)

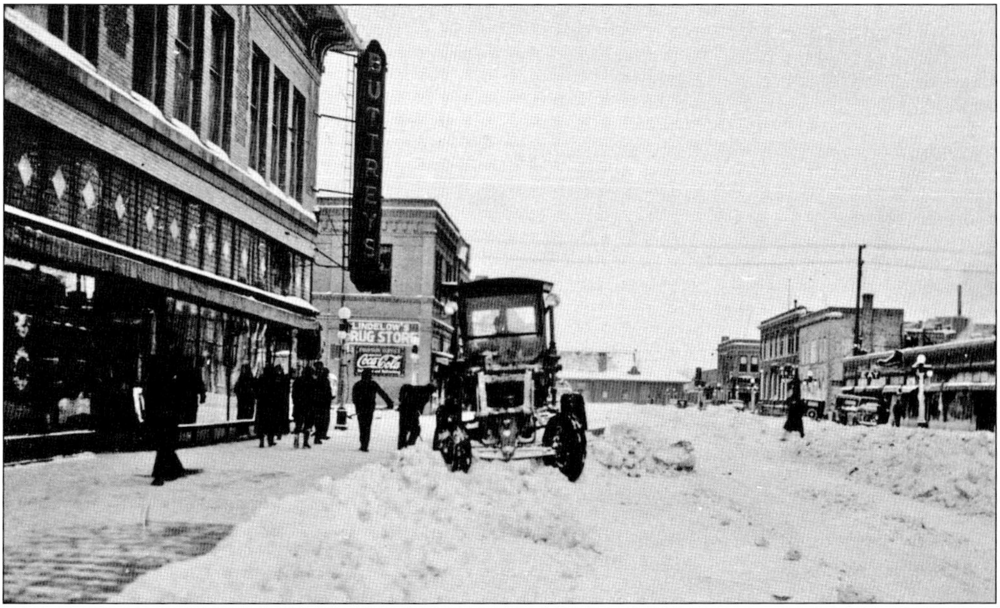

Snow removal has always been an issue in Havre. This plow is busy at work on Third Avenue in front of Buttrey's removing snow. Other businesses are Marra's Grocery, E.C. Carruth's real estate office, the Security State Bank, and the Great Northern Depot. Lindelow's Drug Store is across from Buttrey's. (Courtesy of Don Greytak.)

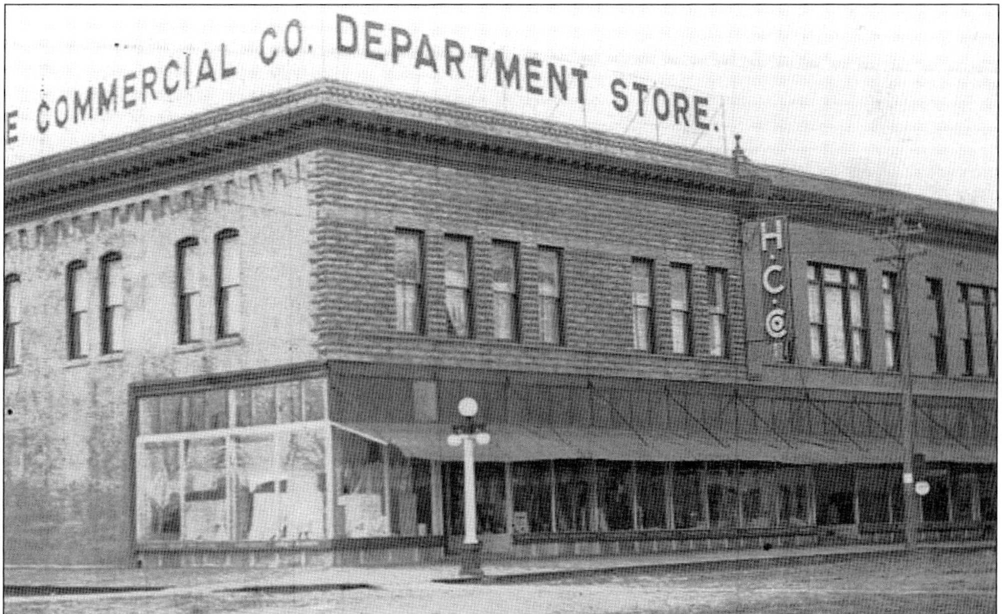

The Havre Commercial Company was started by Henry Stringfellow shortly after the great fire of 1904. In 1918, construction began on a fireproof concrete and brick building adjoining the Commercial to the east for Stringfellow's Havre Motor Company. In 1924, he sold his controlling stock to Bertha Sailor, making her one of Havre's first women CEOs. (Courtesy of High Line Heritage House.)

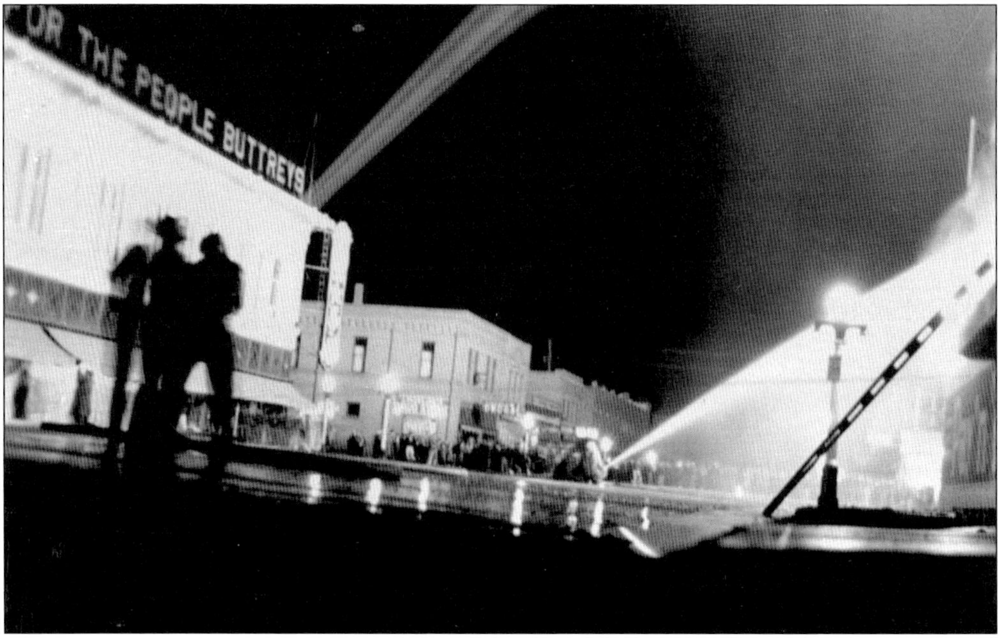

In 1938, the Havre Commercial Company caught fire. The store was completely destroyed, which signaled the end of a long-established business in Havre. Contrast this fire with the great fire of 1904 and how much the Havre Fire Department had advanced over the years. Back in 1904, Havre had a volunteer fire department, using manpower to fight the blaze. By 1938, Havre boasted professional firefighters and modern firefighting equipment. (Courtesy of Don Greytak.)

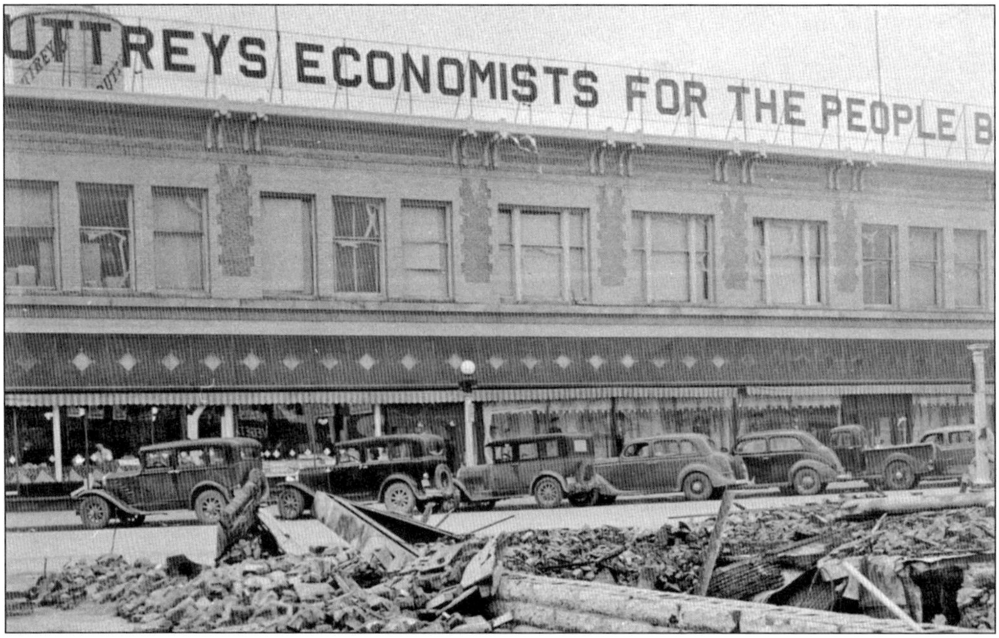

This image taken the morning after fire had consumed the Havre Commercial Company shows the devastation to the building. The Buttrey store also suffered some broken windows during the fire. The Havre Commercial Company and Buttrey's Department Store competed with each other for decades to earn customers' business. (Courtesy of Don Greytak.)

The weather bureau building was found just to the west of the Buttrey store. In May 1892, the weather bureau was moved to Havre from Fort Assinniboine. It moved to 210 Second Street in 1904. Charles Ling, US Army Signal Corps, was in charge of the weather station in Havre from 1879 until his death in 1926. (Courtesy of High Line Heritage House.)

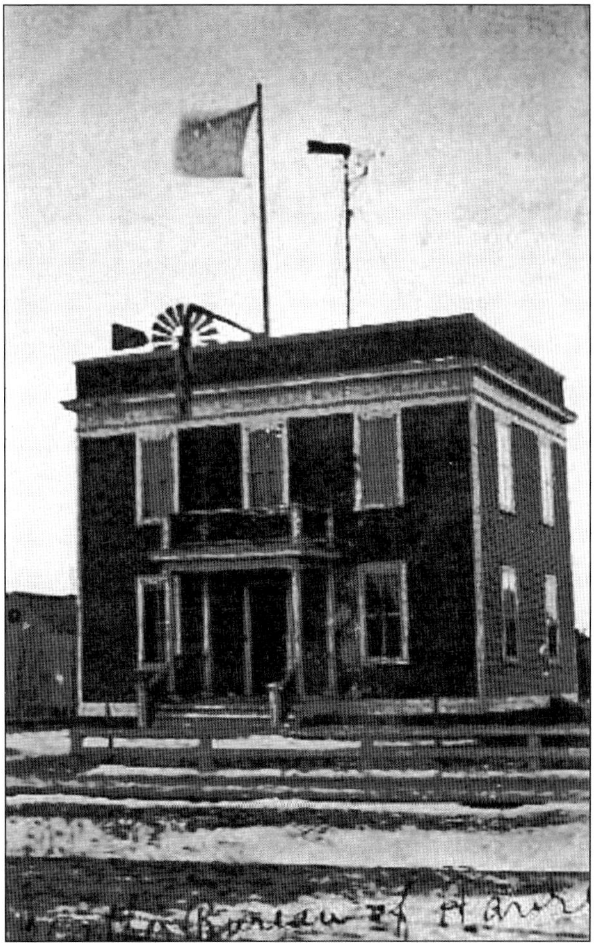

Third Avenue and Third Street businesses are pictured here in May 1929. Larson's Shoe Repair, Atwater Kent Radios, and Herndon's are to the right, along with a grove of cottonwood trees that would later cause controversy when the post office and federal building were constructed. Some Havreites wanted the trees to remain. The Masonic temple and a Texaco gas station are to the left of the photograph. (Courtesy of Don Greytak.)

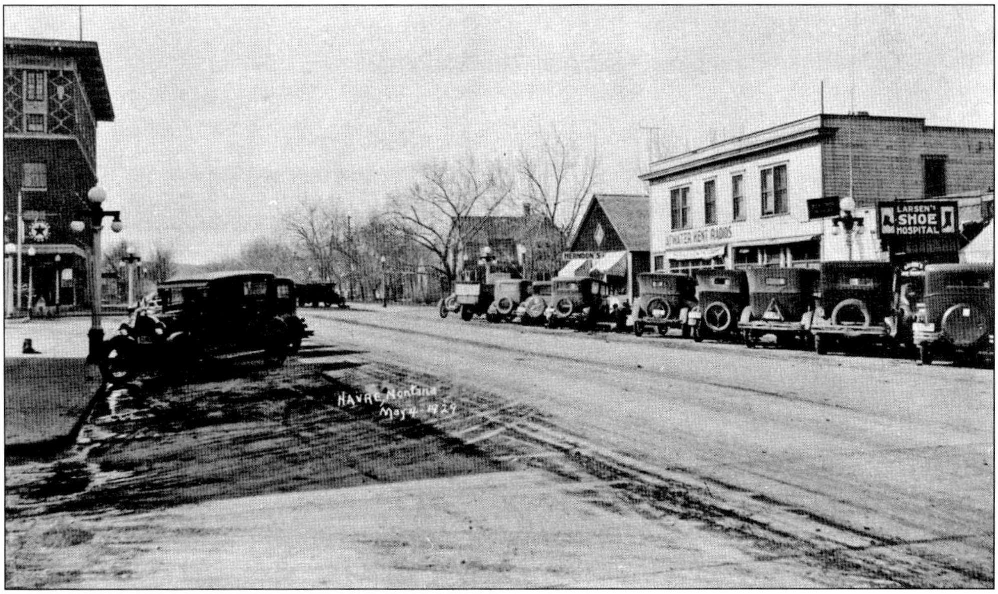

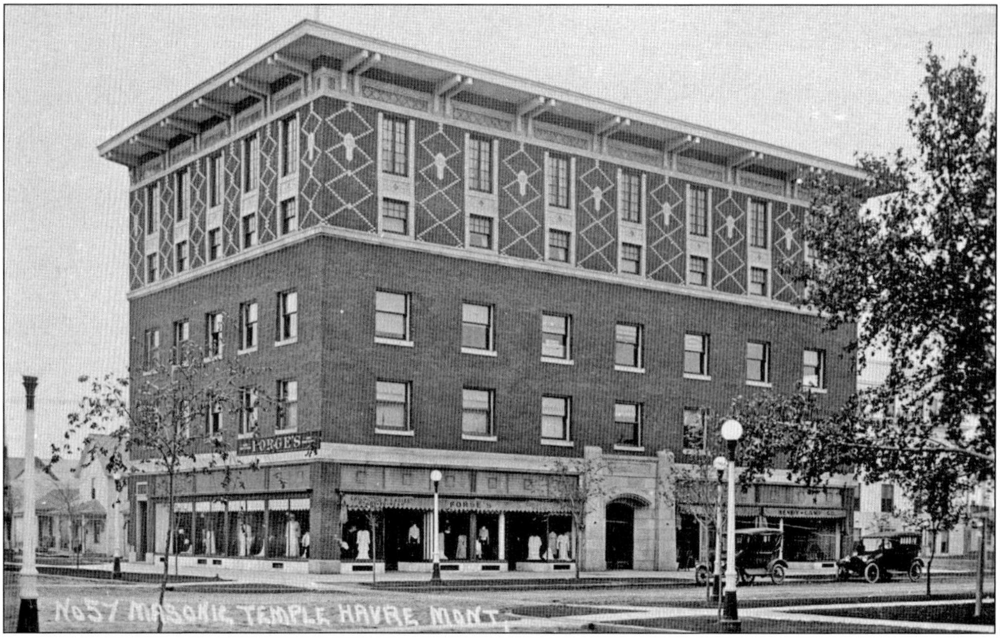

The Masonic temple was constructed in 1915 and designed by local architect Frank Bossout in the Egyptian Revival style. It remains the tallest building downtown and featured shops on the ground floor and offices on the second and third stories, with the fourth and fifth stories reserved for Masons. Forge's women's store was one of the businesses located in the Masonic temple. It later moved next to the Lou Lucke Company. (Courtesy of Don Greytak.)

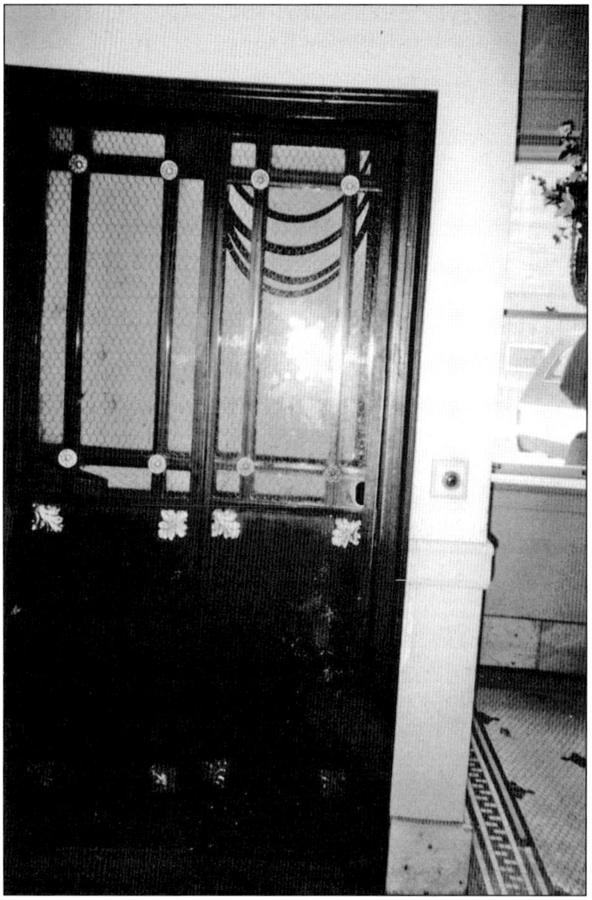

Havre's Masonic Temple boasts the oldest operating elevator in the state of Montana. It has not changed much in the century since the building was constructed. This elevator was made by the Otis Elevator Company and still retains its cage doors. Elisha Otis pioneered the safety elevator in 1853, and today the Otis Elevator Company is the world's largest manufacturer of elevators and escalators. (Photograph by the author, courtesy of High Line Heritage House.)

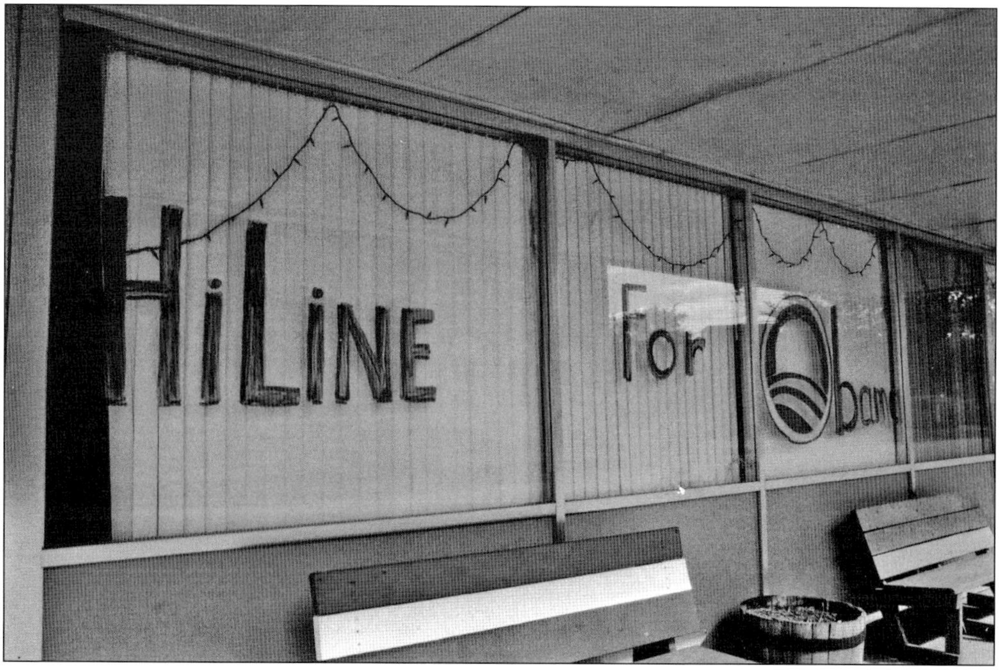

Havre is not normally a town major politicians visit. Havre has seen four visits by three presidents: Franklin Roosevelt in 1934, Harry Truman in 1950 and 1952, and Bill Clinton in 2008. In 2008, the campaign of presidential candidate Barack Obama opened an office in the Masonic temple, the first office dedicated solely to a presidential candidate in Havre. The office later moved to the basement of the Atrium. (Photograph by the author, courtesy of High Line Heritage House.)

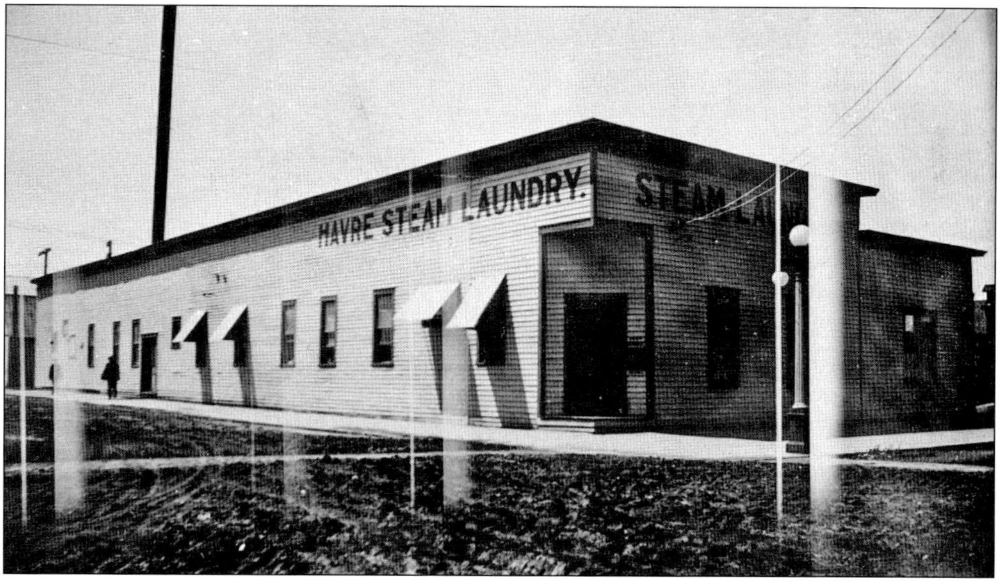

Laundries were among the first businesses in Havre and often included hot baths for those needing one after coming off the hot, dusty trail. In 1904, brothers James and Walter MacKenzie were among those incorporating Havre Steam Laundry. That same year, the building was constructed. It was enlarged in 1916 and in subsequent years added dry cleaning and a linen supply to its offerings. It remains one of Havre's longest-running businesses. (Courtesy of Don Greytak.)

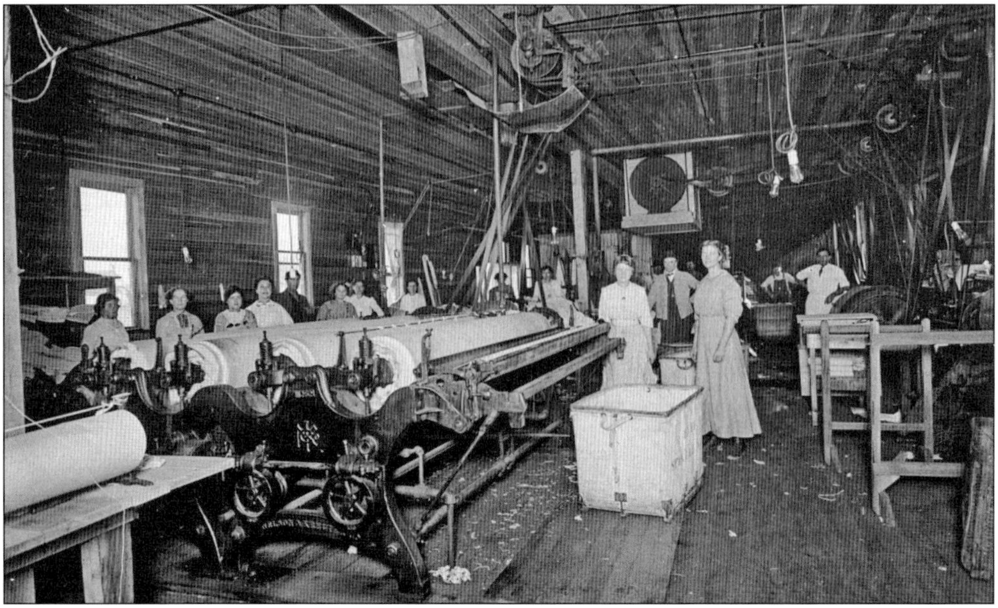

No one said working in a laundry was easy work. It required a person in good physical shape, and conditions could be hot and uncomfortable. It was, however, one of only a few early industries that employed women. The crew of the Havre Steam Laundry is pictured next to a large mangle, or wringer, used to press sheets, tablecloths, and other pieces of laundry. (Courtesy of Don Greytak.)

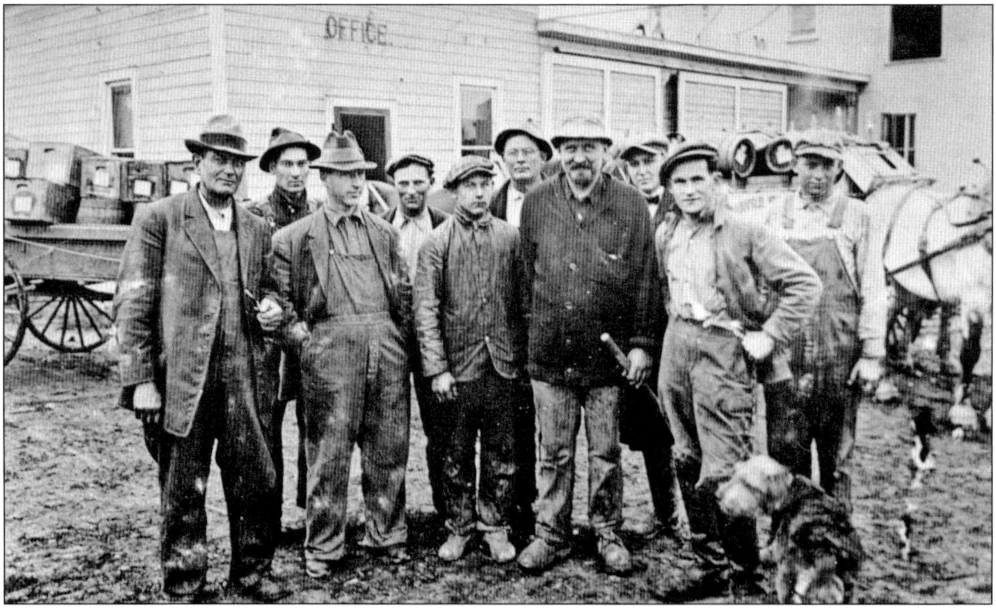

The Havre Brewing and Malting Company was incorporated on November 9, 1910, and began operations in the spring of 1911. George Kuehhorn was president, Aloys Wutz, secretary and treasurer, Henry Schmidt, vice president, and Fred Denninger, brewmaster and stockholder. Kuehhorn, Wutz, and Denninger were born in Germany. After the Havre Brewing and Malting Company closed, the buildings were sold to Rocky Mountain Packing Company and razed in 2007. (Courtesy of Don Greytak.)

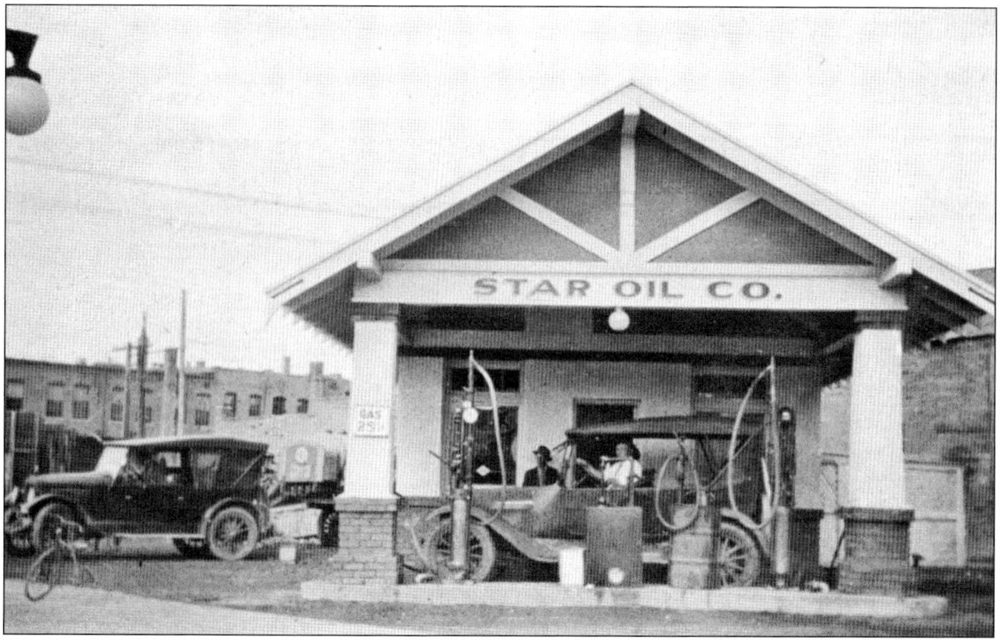

The Star Oil Gas Station is pictured here in 1923. Havre had several neighborhood gas and service stations throughout the town in its early days. Today, gas and service stations are found mostly on main thoroughfares. The Star Oil Gas Station was located at201 Second Street, where Bear Paw Credit Union is today, and gasoline cost 25¢ per gallon in 1923. (Courtesy of Don Greytak.)

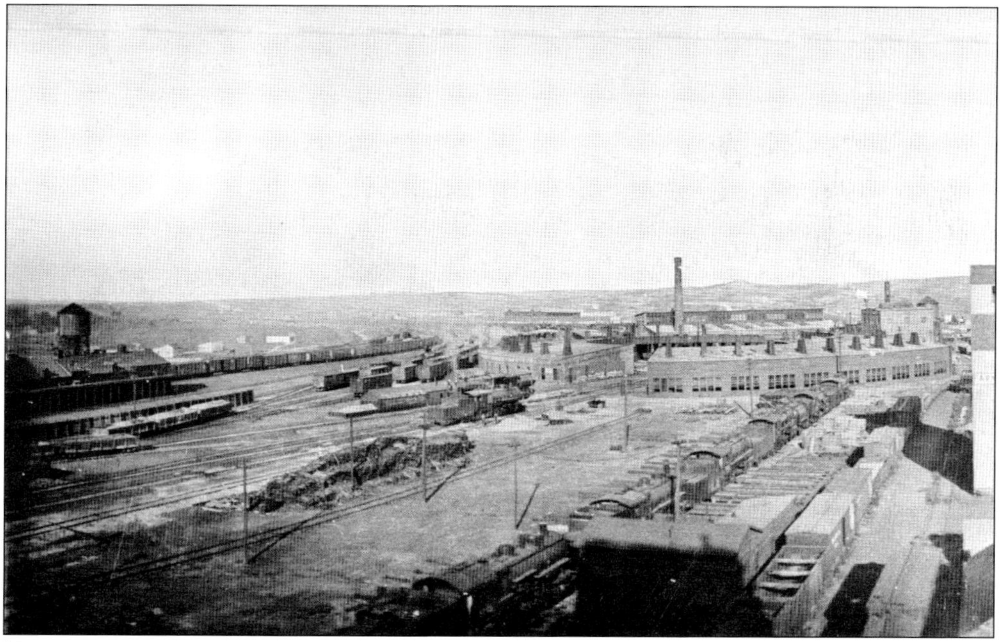

Havre owes its existence to the arrival of the St. Paul, Minneapolis & Manitoba Railroad in September 1887. Havre was chosen as a division point, and the town grew from there. The railroad was later named the Great Northern, then Burlington Northern, then Burlington Northern Santa Fe, and is now BNSF Railway. The rail yards are pictured here, complete with the roundhouse to the right of the photograph and coal chute to the left. (Courtesy of Don Greytak.)

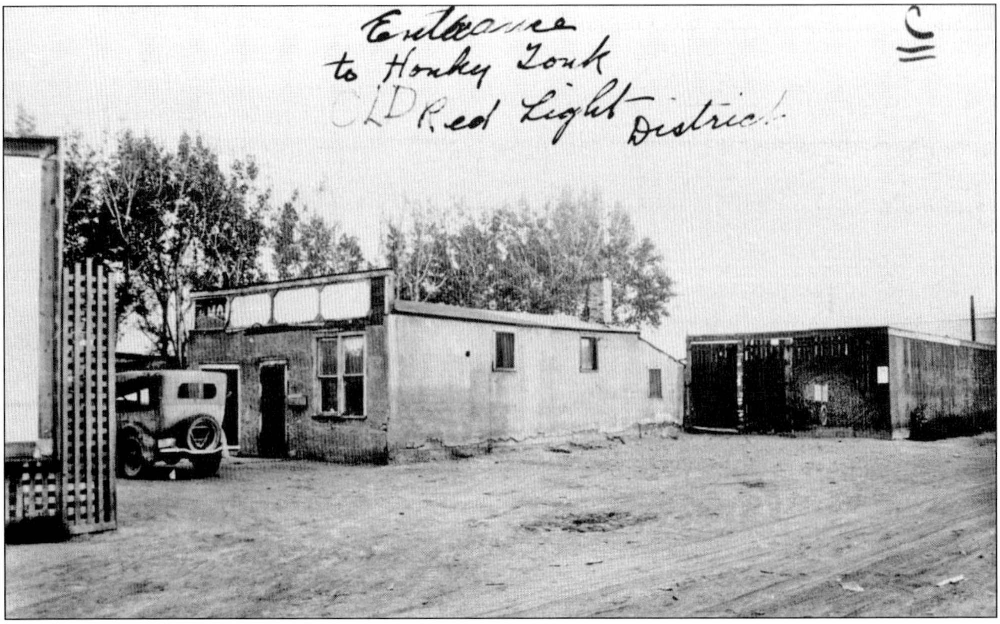

In its early days, Havre was known for its vice elements such as illegal booze, gambling, prostitution, and illicit drugs. Havre's seamier side was panned in the press and often overlooked by residents who knew what was going on but chose to ignore it as much as possible, for as long as possible. Pictured here is Christopher "Shorty" Young's Honky Tonk, one of Havre's most notorious red-light districts. (Courtesy of Don Greytak.)

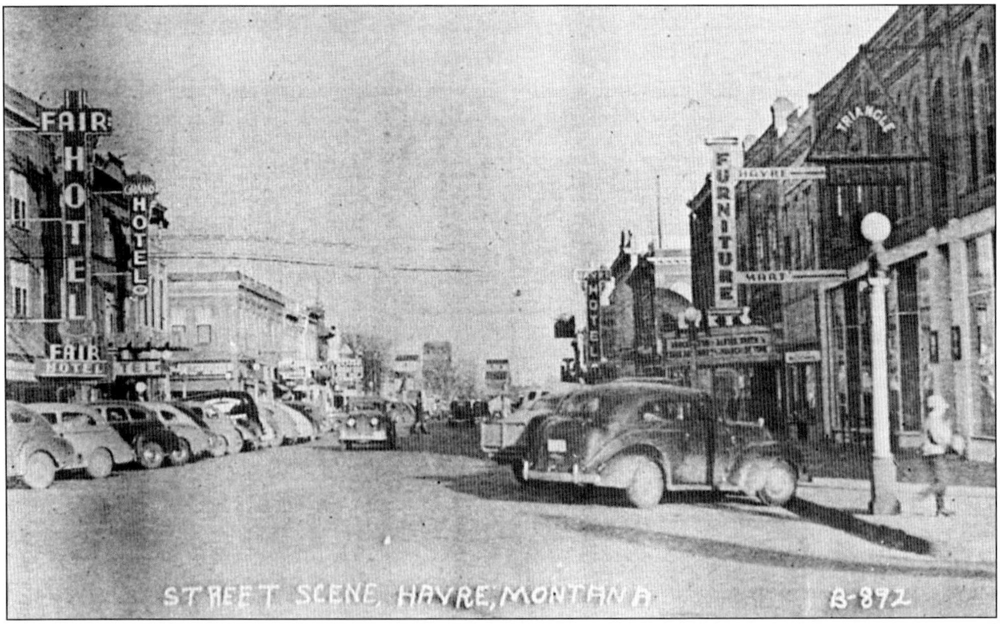

By the 1940s, the cars got bigger and Havre's downtown kept busy. Among the business pictured are the Havre Furniture Mart, Triangle Apartments, the Lyric Theatre, and Havre Hotel to the right, and to the left are the Fair Hotel and the Grand Hotel. First Street is two lanes with angled parking and no traffic lights. Today, there are four lanes, four traffic lights, and parallel parking. (Courtesy of High Line Heritage House.)

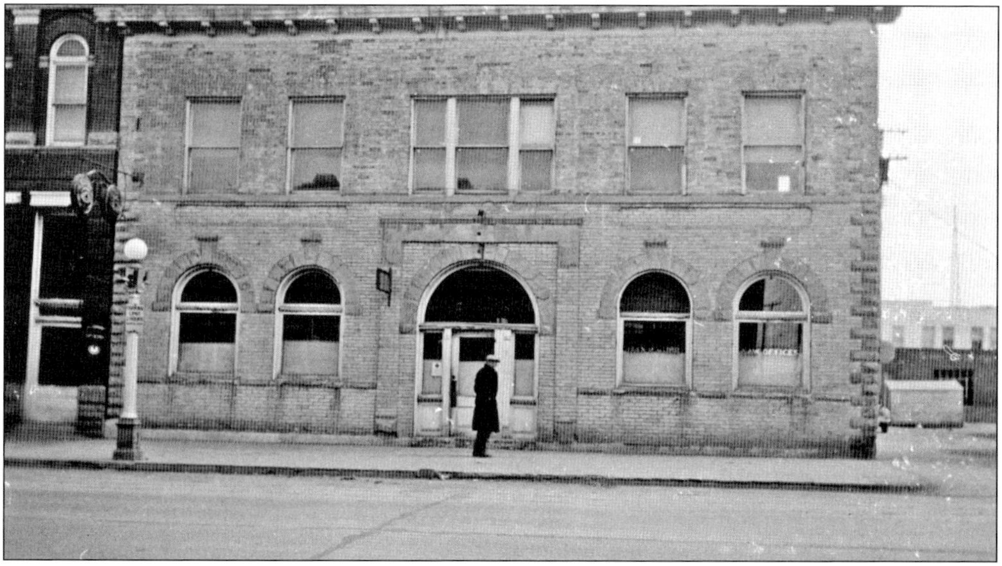

One of Havre's first buildings constructed after the great fire of 1904 was this one, which was home to Edwin Cooley Carruth's real estate and insurance office. Carruth was one of Havre's earliest and strongest boosters, starting as a manager of the first Havre Hotel, which he later owned, and moving into many other interests. His proudest achievement was assisting with the creation of Northern Montana College. (Courtesy of Don Greytak.)

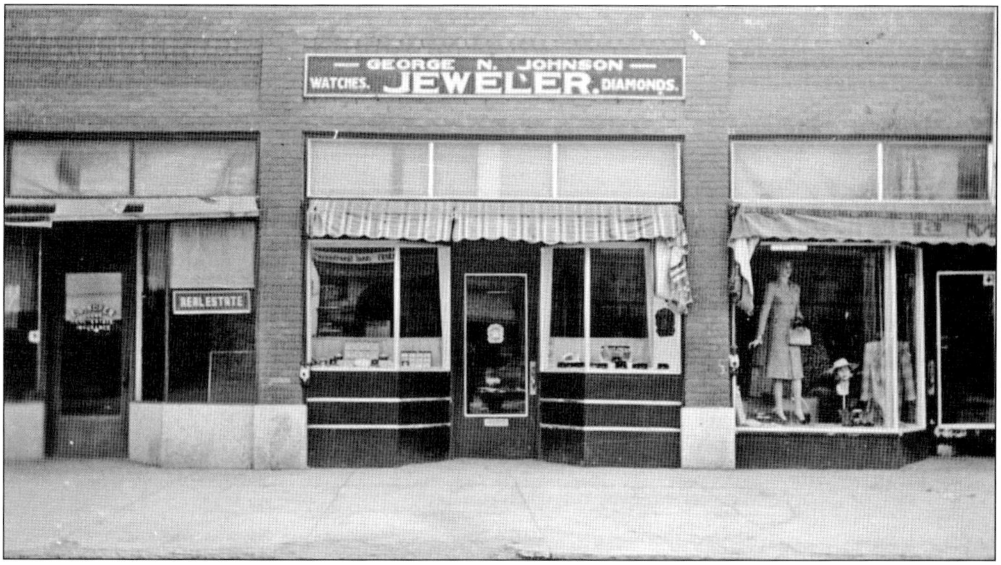

Across the alley to the south of the Carruth Building in 1941 were a series of smaller shops, including Roper's Real Estate and Insurance, George Johnson Jeweler, La Mode women's fashions, Steve's Café, Champion Shoe Shop, Havre Meat Market, and Marra Brothers Cash Grocery. George Johnson was one of Havre's finest jewelers, and his workbench and tools were donated to the Clack Museum, where they are on exhibit today. (Courtesy of Don Greytak.)

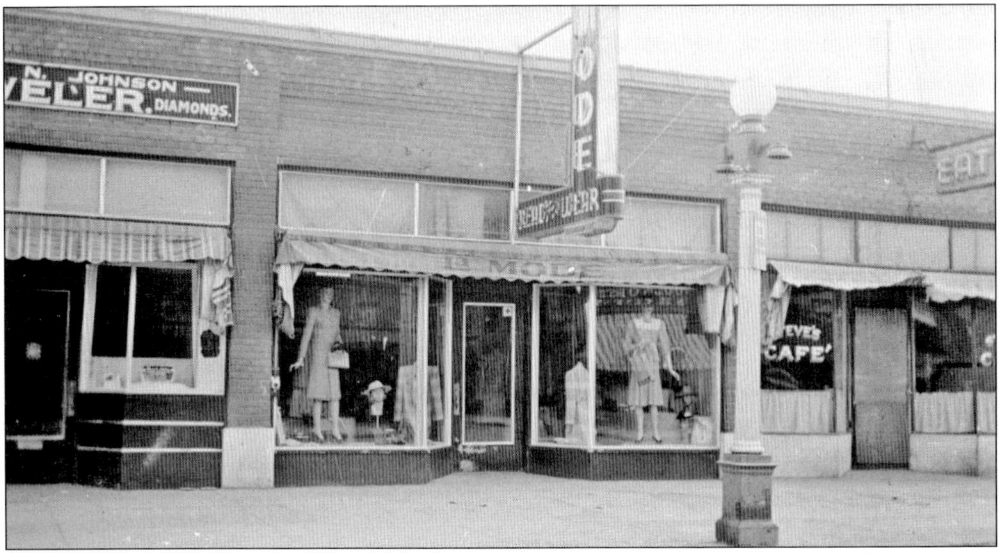

Havre played host to several fine clothing shops for women. Among the most revered is La Mode, where the latest styles could be purchased. It is pictured here in 1941; later that decade, the building La Mode and other businesses were located in was razed to make way for Citizen's Bank. La Mode moved to the 200 block of Third Avenue. (Courtesy of Don Greytak.)

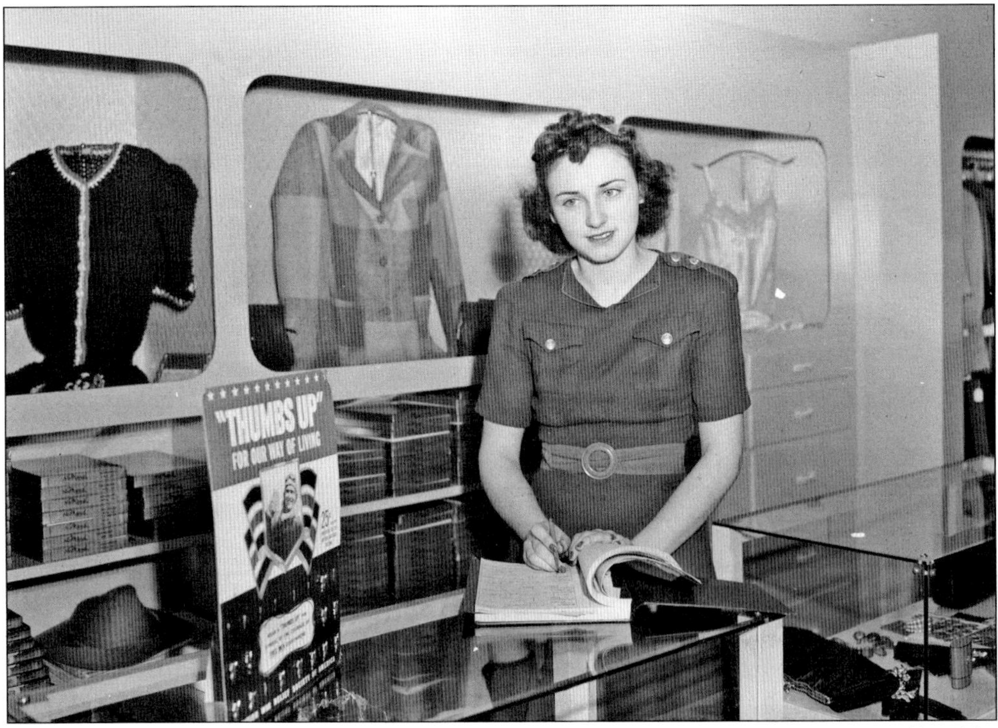

Evelyn Bough works at La Mode in January 1942. Gloves, pocketbooks, and jewelry are offered for sale in the glass cabinet in the right of the photograph, and to the left are "Thumbs Up" pins for sale. The sign reads "Wear a 'Thumbs Up' pin for symbol of the courage of Free Men everywhere." They were 25¢ each, and proceeds went to the British War Relief Society of America. (Photograph by Frances Hulm, courtesy of Don Greytak.)

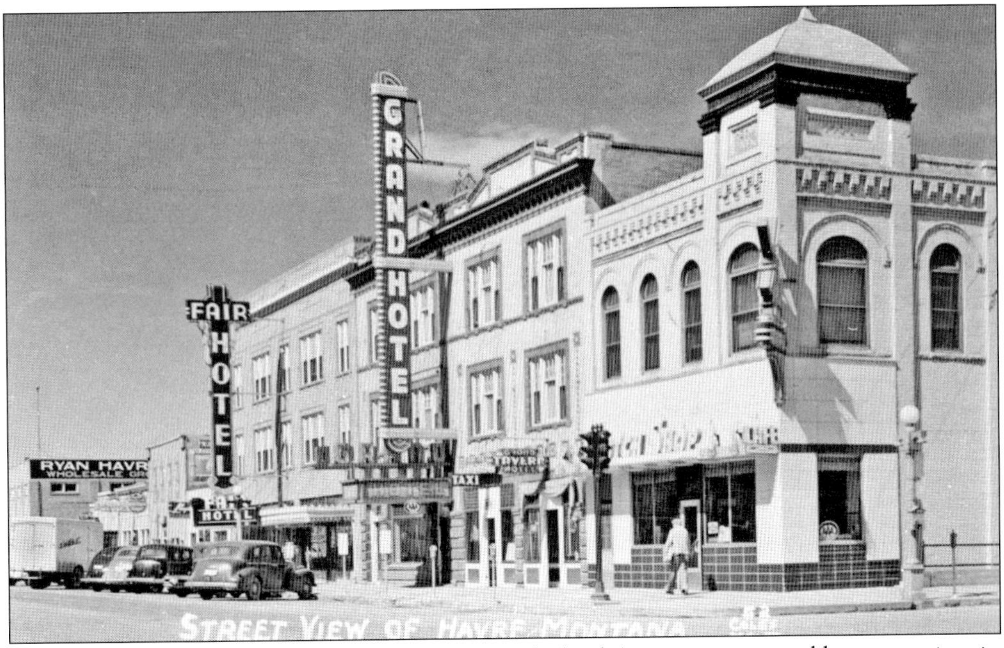

The north side of First Street between Second and Third Avenues is pictured here sometime in the 1940s. The Dutch Shop Café occupied the Pepin Block, constructed in 1904 after the fire, for many years. Also on this block were a tavern and taxi service in the Grand Hotel, the Fair Hotel, smaller businesses, and Ryan Havre Wholesale Groceries. (Courtesy of Don Greytak.)

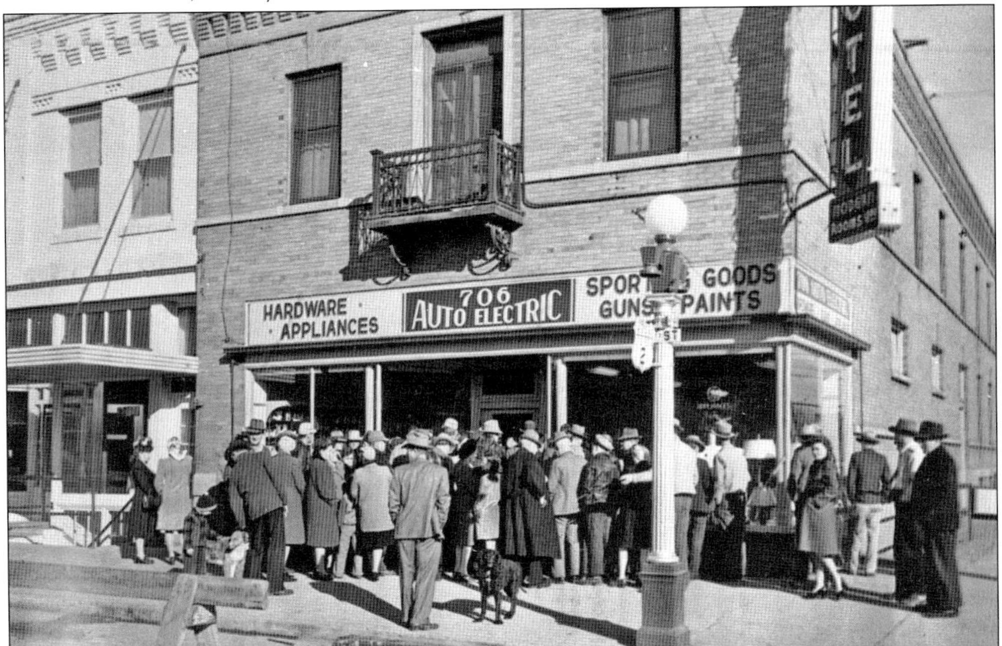

The grand opening of 706 Auto Electric took place in the late 1940s. The shop was started in 1929 and was originally located at 108 First Street. Owner O.P. Johnson expanded to hardware, appliances, sporting goods, guns, and paints. It was relocated to the corner of First Street and Fourth Avenue. The shop got its name from its phone number—706. (Courtesy of Don Greytak.)

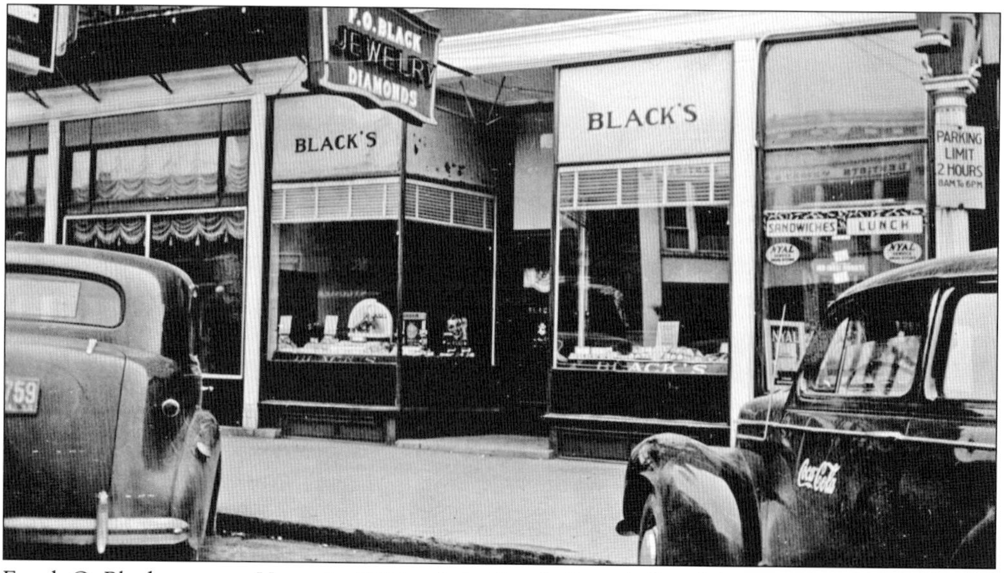

Frank O. Black came to Havre in 1902 to help Frank Churchill in Jake Yound's jewelry store. It was located between Third and Fourth Avenues and burned in the 1904 fire. They opened in the new Havre Hotel and later moved to a space next door. Black passed away in 1933, and his son Francis took over the business. The store moved to 211 Third Avenue in 1941. (Courtesy of Don Greytak.)

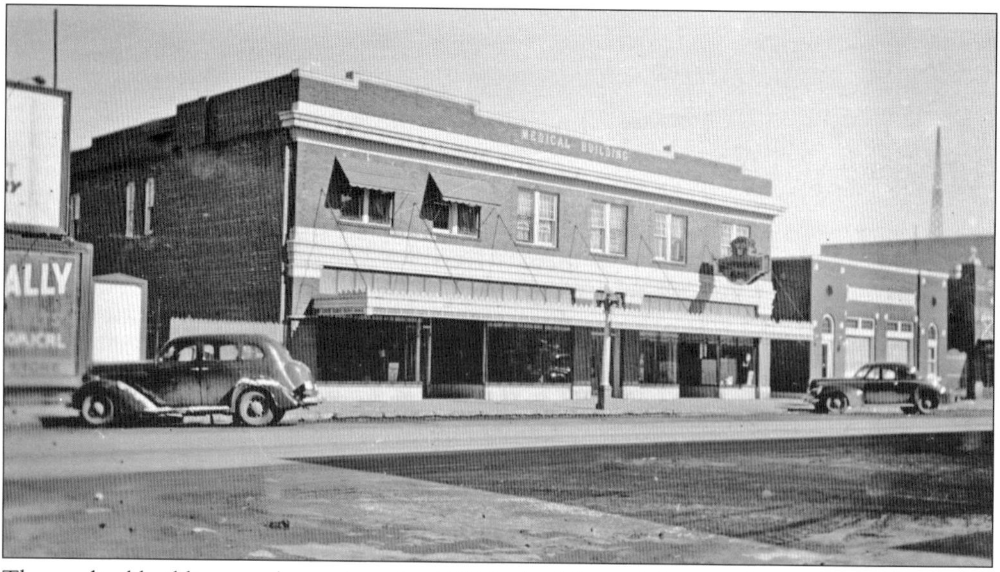

The medical building was located on the 300 block of Second Street, where part of the current Wells Fargo building and the parking lot are today. This was the predecessor to the Havre Clinic. Havre had two hospitals at the time. The Catholic Sacred Heart Hospital was on Havre's east end, while the Presbyterian Deaconess Hospital was at Havre's west end. The two hospitals merged in the mid-1970s. (Courtesy of Don Greytak.)

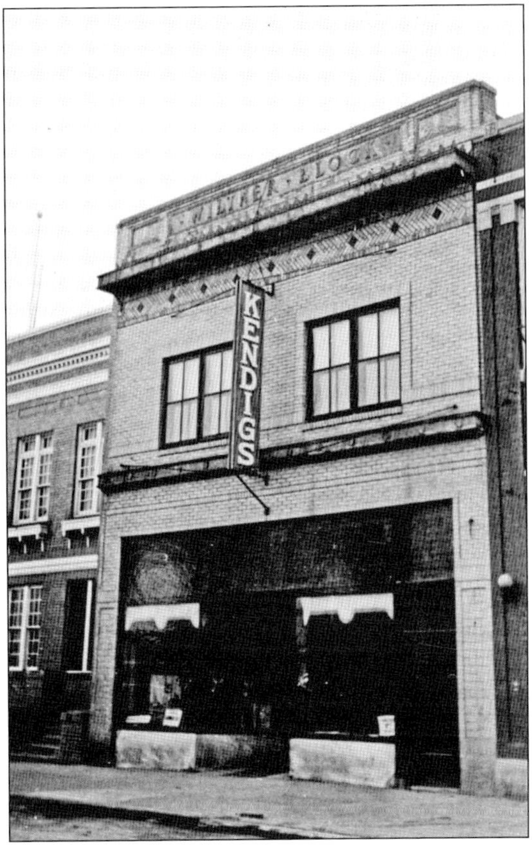

Kendig's was located in the Wiltner Block on the 300 block of Second Street. William Wiltner came to Havre in 1895 and opened a meat business. In 1915, he built the Wiltner Block, which became known as Wiltner's Meat and Grocery Store. In 1927, William Kendig purchased the building and opened a dry goods and clothing store. He also served as the treasurer for the City of Havre. (Courtesy of Don Greytak.)

Super Ice Cream, located on the 100 block of Fourth Avenue, was a fun spot for locals to enjoy ice cream, sodas, candy, and other treats. It was often packed with people, and Havre lost a special place when it finally closed its doors. After a few decades, a new Super Ice Cream was built; however, it closed and now the Cigarette Store occupies the space. (Courtesy of Don Greytak.)

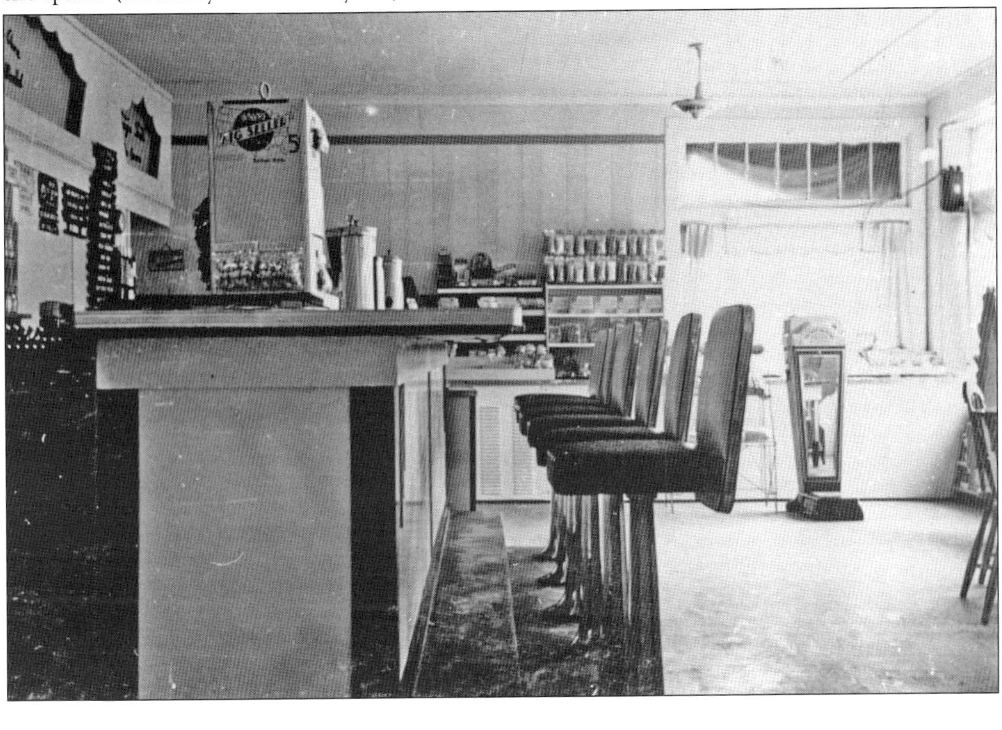

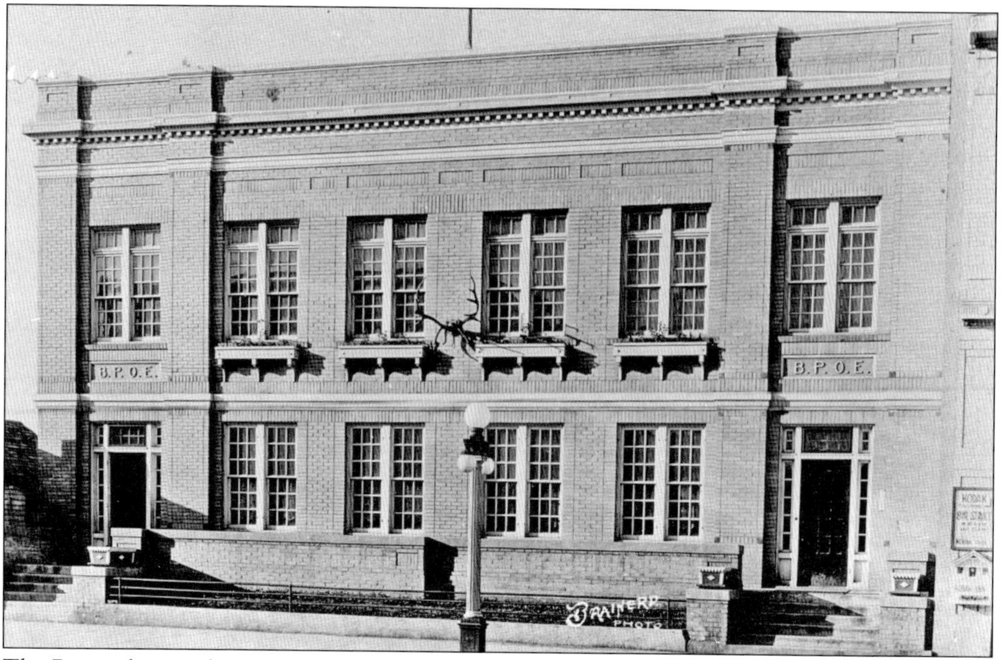

The Benevolent and Protective Order of Elks Havre Lodge 1201 was located on the 300 block of Second Street. Members who had been initiated at other lodges living in Havre had been getting together as early as 1904. After the Elks was chartered in Havre in 1910, the members built their own lodge. It sustained heavy damage in January 1972 after a fire started in the neighboring Crown Jewelers. (Courtesy of Don Greytak.)

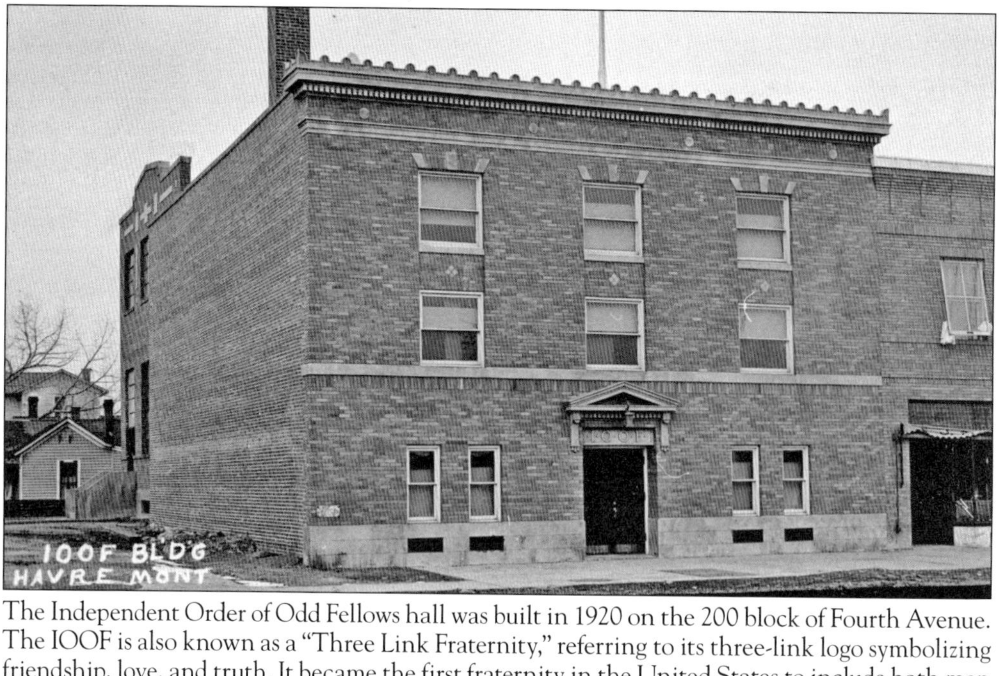

The Independent Order of Odd Fellows hall was built in 1920 on the 200 block of Fourth Avenue. The IOOF is also known as a "Three Link Fraternity," referring to its three-link logo symbolizing friendship, love, and truth. It became the first fraternity in the United States to include both men and women and attempts to help the poor, to rally against vice, and to elevate every member to a nobler plane. (Courtesy of Don Greytak.)

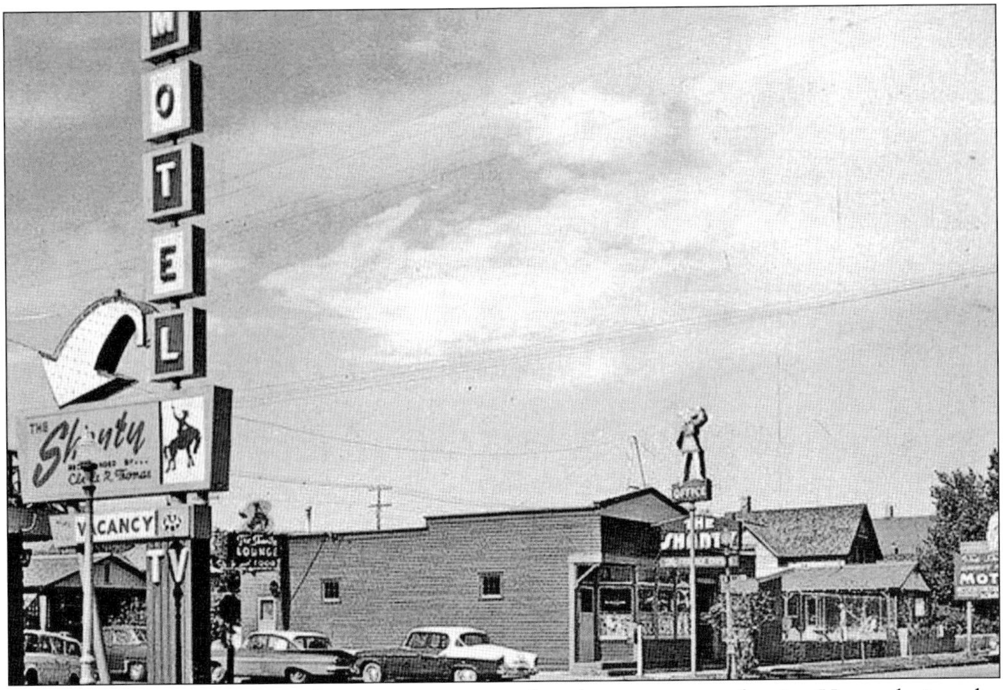

The Shanty Hotel, Café, and Lounge was a popular place to stay and enjoy Havre during the middle part of the 20th century. It boasted one of Havre's best slogans, "Recommended by Clyde R. Thomas." Thomas started the enterprise, which also had its own swimming pool behind the lounge. The establishment featured a Western-style flair, and the café was known to have good food, especially hamburgers. (Courtesy of High Line Heritage House.)

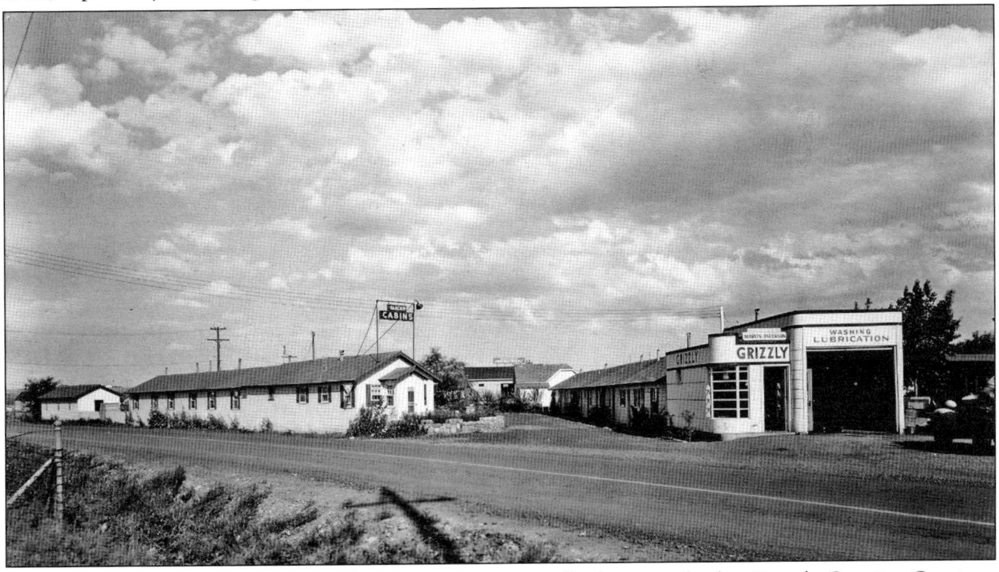

The Glacier Cabins were located on Havre's east end, along with the Grizzly Service Station. Sig and Elsie Nelson bought the Glacier Cabins in 1941, and Dan Heltne was leasing the Grizzly Service Station. In 1948, the Nelsons partnered with F.E. Peterson to build Pete's Oldsmobile Auto and GMC pickup truck agency, later known as Glacier Auto Sales, which burned in 1965. (Courtesy of Elsie K. Nelson.)

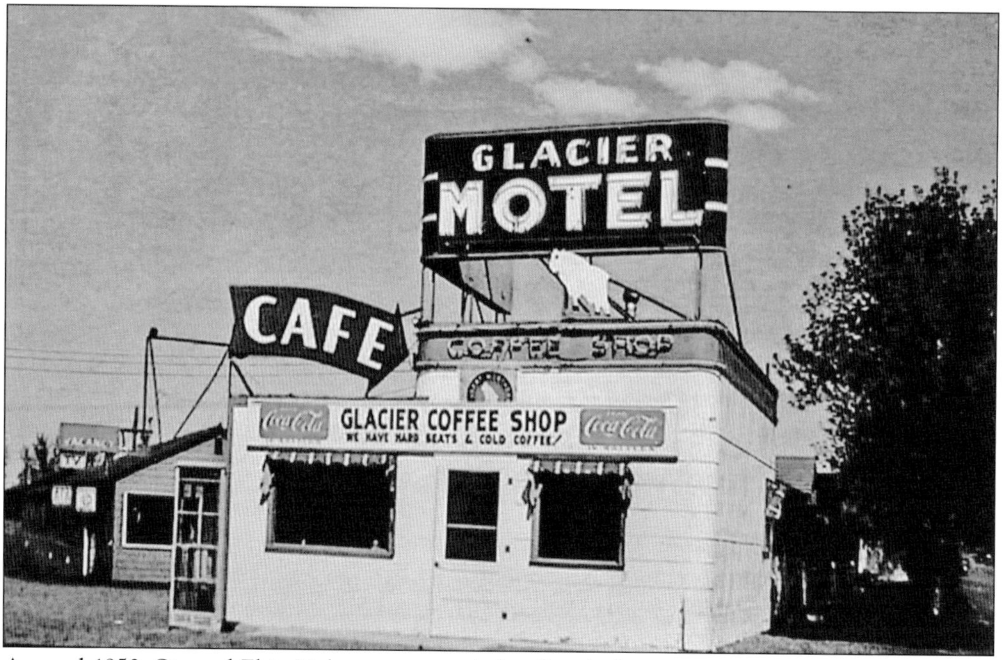

Around 1950, Sig and Elsie Nelson converted the Grizzly Service Station to the Glacier Café, featuring a mountain goat, a symbol of the Great Northern Railroad. "We Have Hard Seats and Cold Coffee" read the sign on the front of the building, but people knew the café offered hot coffee and good diner food in a welcoming atmosphere. The Glacier Café closed in the latter part of the 20th century. (Courtesy of Elsie K. Nelson.)

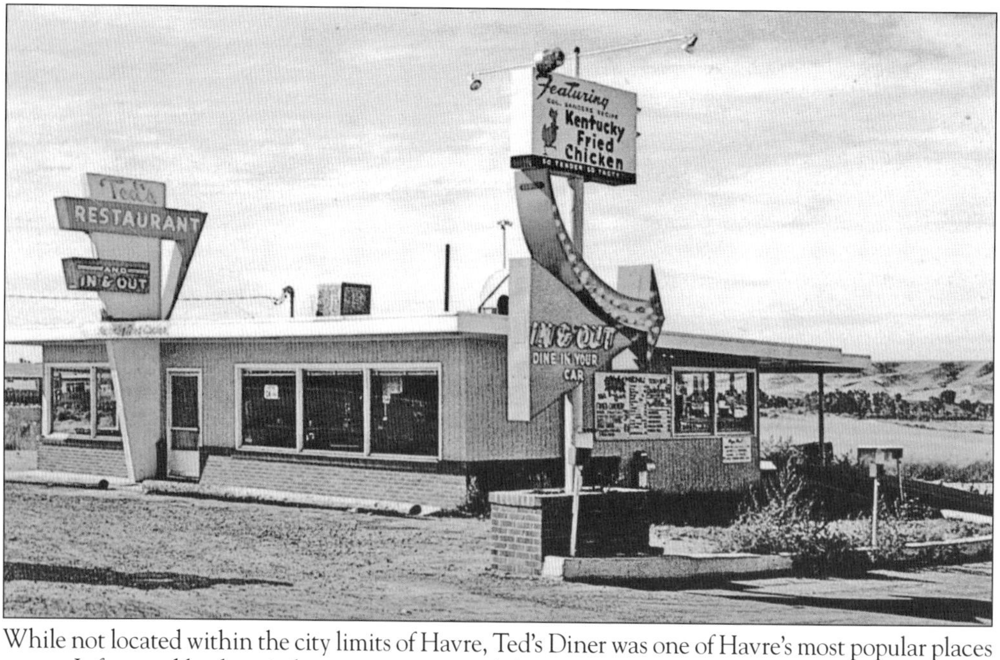

While not located within the city limits of Havre, Ted's Diner was one of Havre's most popular places to eat. It featured both a sit-down restaurant and the "In & Out," where customers could dine in their cars, drive-in style. It also offered the first Kentucky Fried Chicken meals in Havre. Today, the building is home to the East Side Animal Hospital. (Courtesy of High Line Heritage House.)

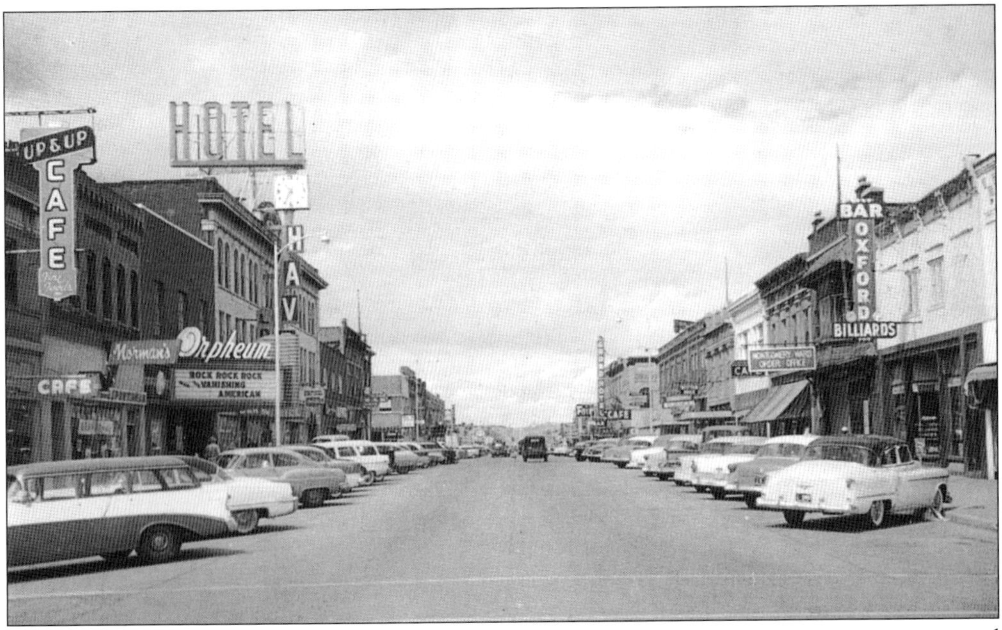

In the 1950s, Havre's downtown had changed little, except for new businesses moving in and updated signage. The Up and Up Café, Norman's, Orpheum Theatre, and the Havre Hotel and Lounge all occupied the south side of First Street between Third and Fourth Avenues, while the Oxford Bar, Montgomery Ward Catalog Office, and Coast to Coast could be found on its north side. The view in this photograph is facing west. (Courtesy of High Line Heritage House.)

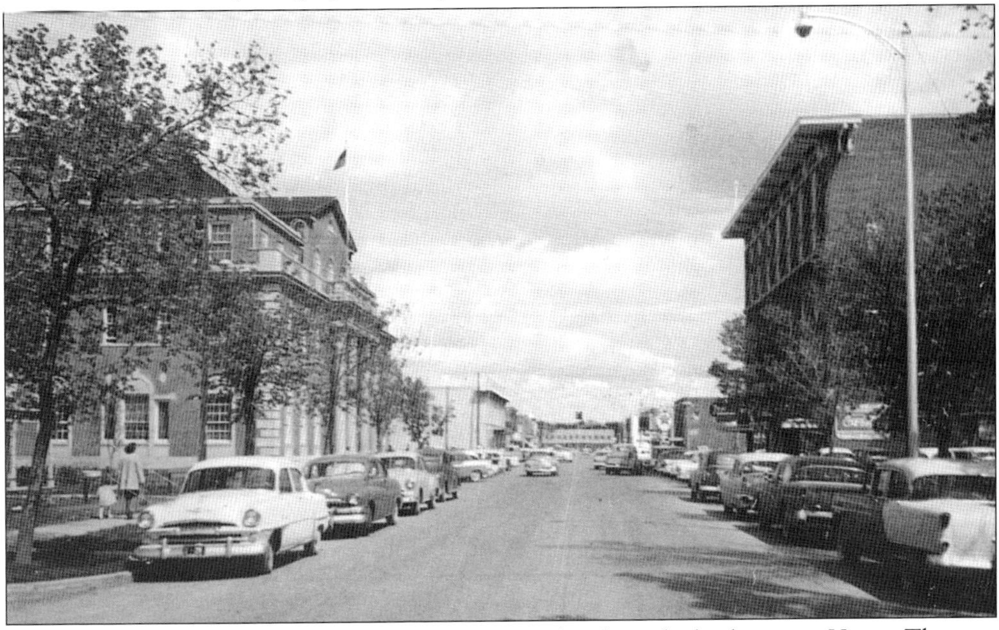

The view farther down Third Avenue in the 1950s also shows little change in Havre. The post office, with the flagpole in its original location, and Buttrey's are to the left, while the Masonic temple is to the right. Third Avenue had one traffic light at this time, which can be seen hanging at the intersection with Second Street. It was later replaced with a four-way stop. (Courtesy of High Line Heritage House.)

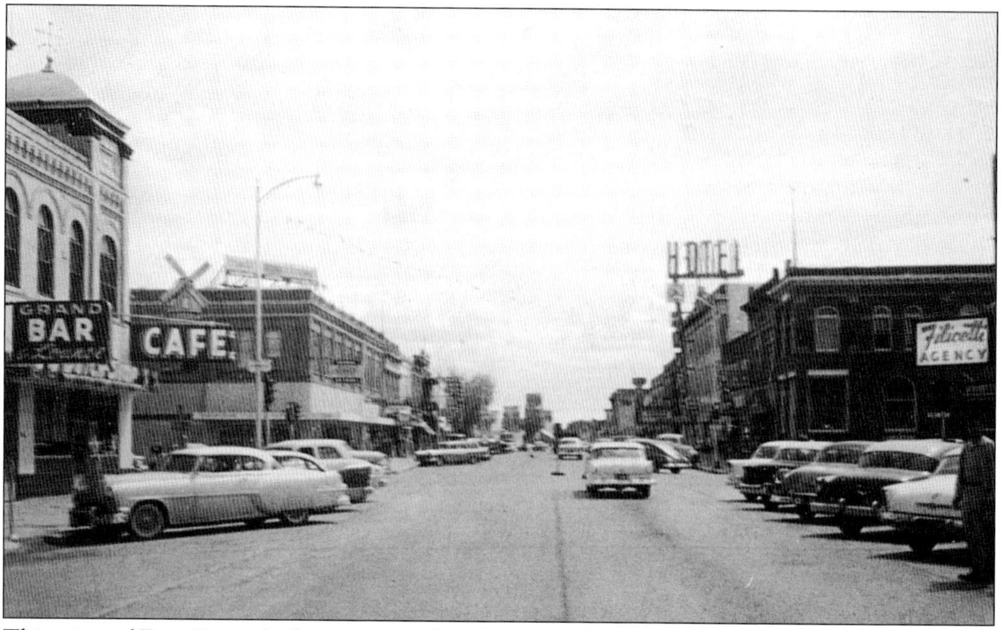

This view of First Street looking east in the 1950s has the Filicetti Agency and Havre Hotel to the right and the Grand Bar and Lounge, Dutch Shop Café, and Coast to Coast Hardware to the left. The entire south side of the 300 block of First Street would either burn down or fall down, with the last remaining building—the old Mansfield Hotel—collapsing September 23, 1994. (Courtesy of High Line Heritage House.)

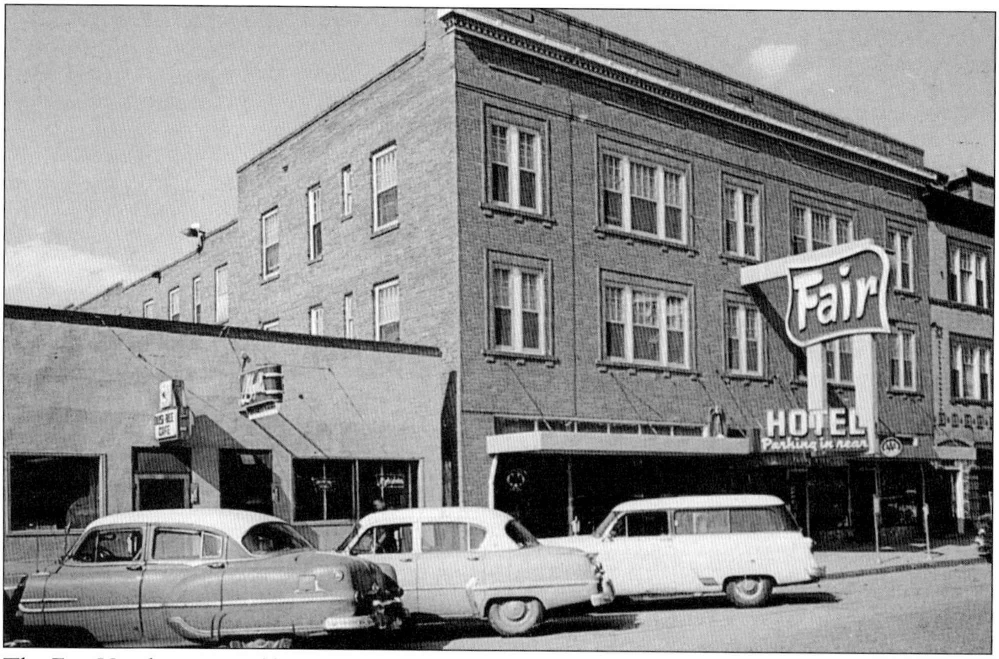

The Fair Hotel is pictured here in the 1940s. It was one of Havre's oldest hotels, and the postcard advertises, "For Comfort and Convenience. 83 rooms equipped with baths, showers and toilets." The Fair, along with the Grand Hotel, Dutch Shop Café, and other businesses, was razed in the late 1970s to make way for a new First Bank Havre. (Courtesy of High Line Heritage House.)

The Grand Hotel is being razed in the late 1970s. The Pepin Block, constructed in 1904 and a host to several businesses, with the Dutch Shop Café being the last, had already been torn down. The Fair and other businesses would be next. However, buildings were not the only objects to meet their demise for the sake of perceived progress. The parking meters would also be removed in later years. (Courtesy of Don Greytak.)

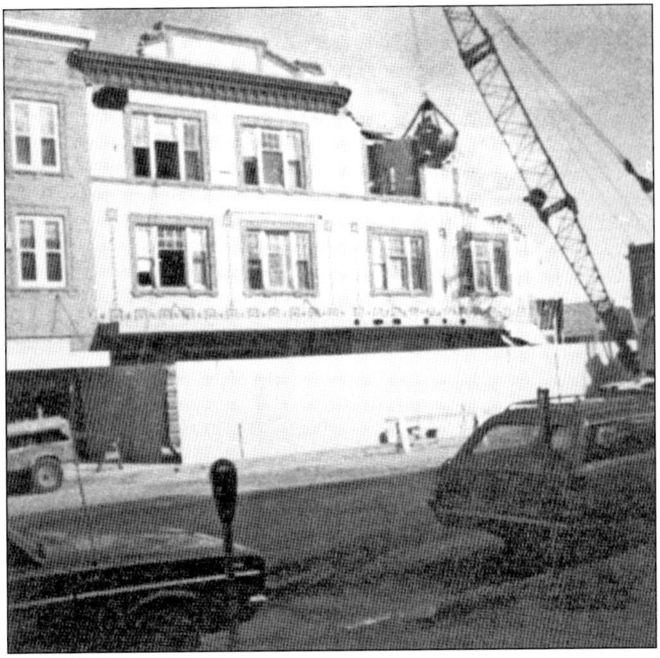

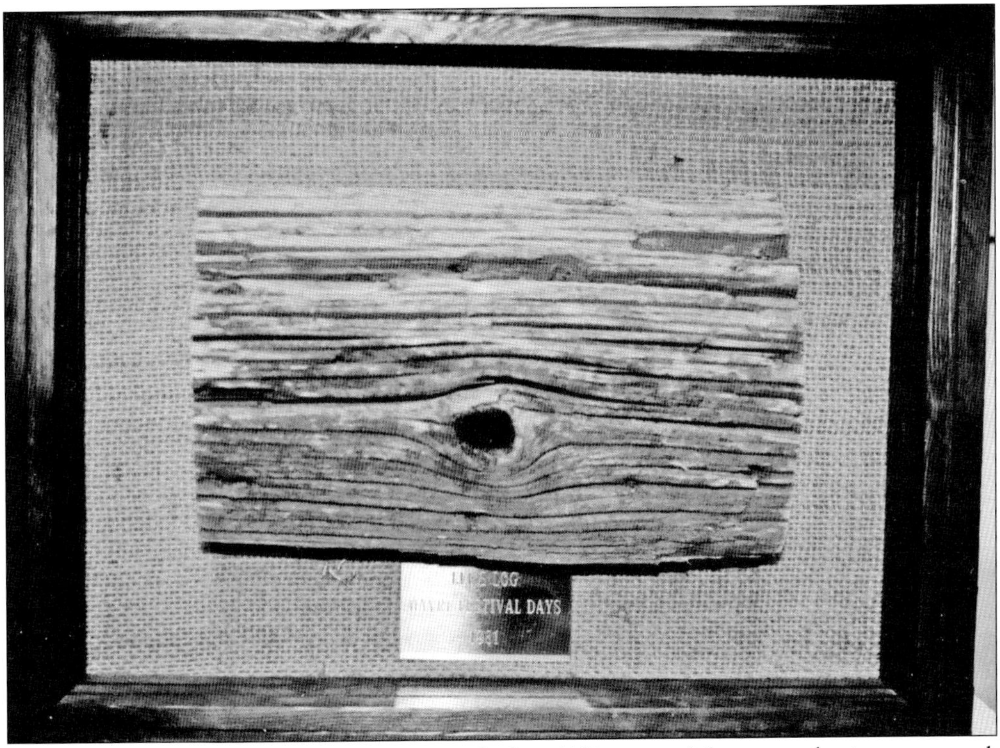

With the arrival of the mall west of Havre in the late 1970s, several downtown businesses moved, leaving empty storefronts. Another eyesore in the downtown area was known as Lee's Log, which sat next to Lee's Tavern on First Street and Fourth Avenue. It was cut into pieces by the city, put into frames, and sold as part of the first Festival Days in 1981, along with a certificate of authenticity. (Photograph by the author, courtesy of High Line Heritage House.)

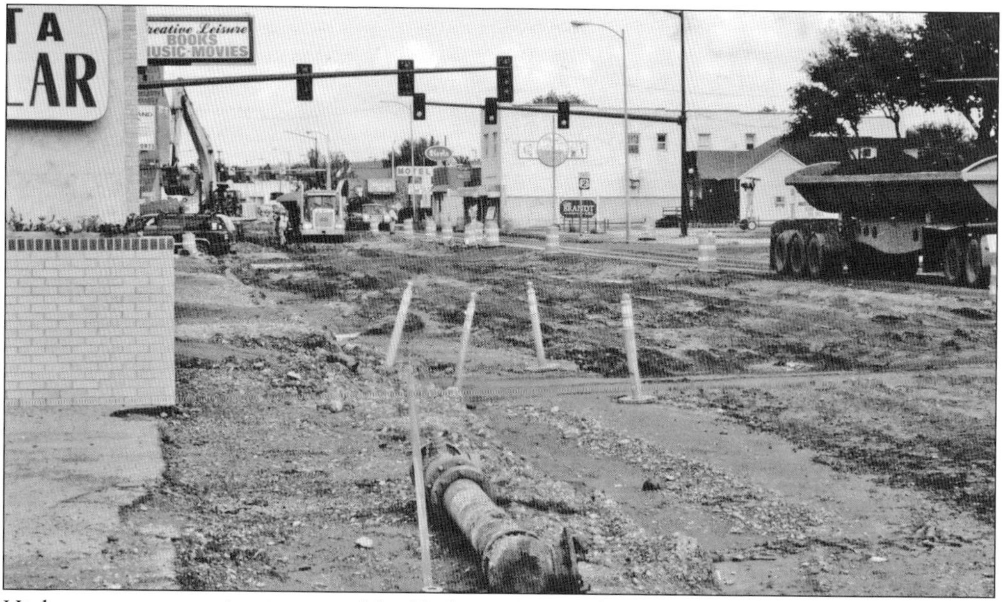

Highway reconstruction is inevitable. Highway 2 runs through downtown and had last been upgraded in the 1970s. From Havre's east end, through the bottom of the hill on the west end, the entire highway was removed, with water and sewer lines and mains replaced. The years 2008 and 2009 in Havre saw one-lane traffic, with some diversions through streets south of the highway. (Photograph by the author, courtesy of High Line Heritage House.)

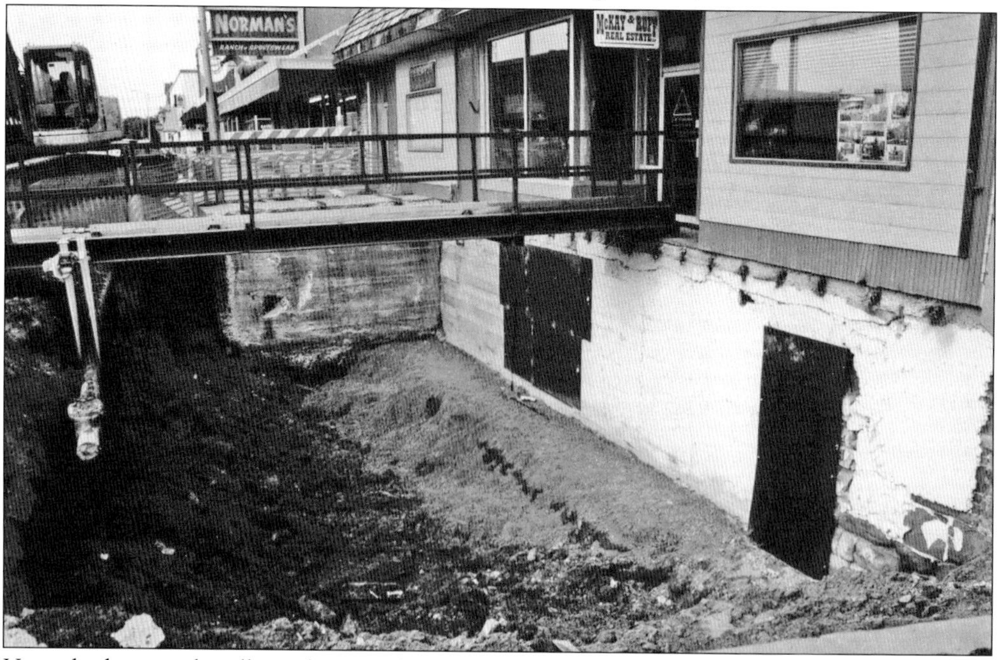

Havre had open sidewalks underground for access to businesses below street level throughout the business district. Over time, these have been filled in, but two can be experienced by the public on tours of Havre Beneath the Streets. These open sidewalks were reconstructed during the Highway 2 reconstruction of 2008–2009, and access to aboveground businesses had to be made using a temporary bridge. (Photograph by the author, courtesy of High Line Heritage House.)

Two

A Place to Call Home

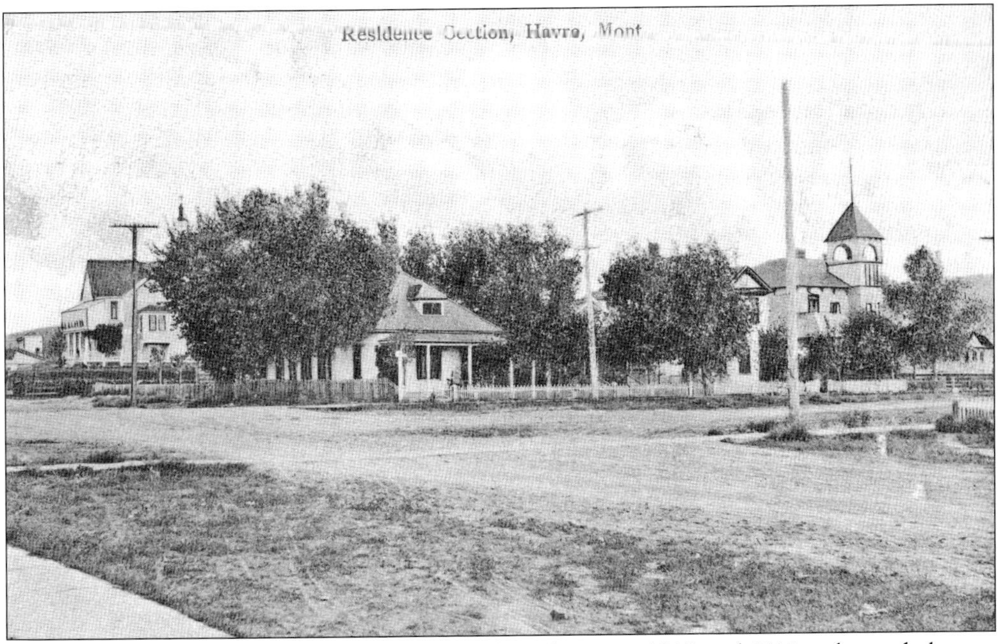

The oldest residential area in Havre, pictured here between 1903 and 1912, is located close to downtown. The Henry Stringfellow home can be seen to the left in the background, while the house on the corner has since been razed. Next door are the Boone and Dalrymple Home and the Mathews Home, which are still standing today. The first permanent school, Washington, is to the right in the photograph. (Courtesy of High Line Heritage House.)

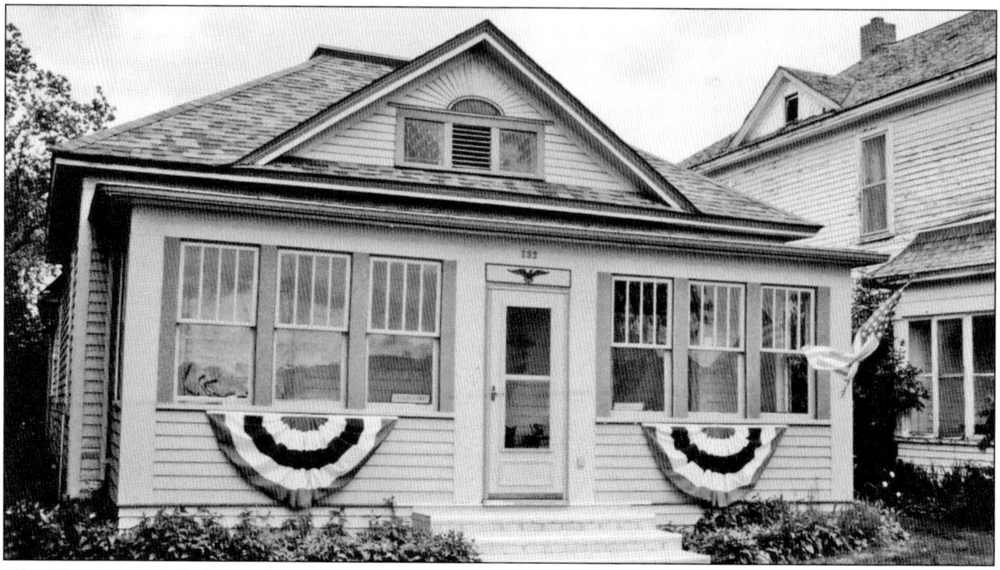

The Boone and Dalrymple Home at 132 Third Street is believed to be the oldest single-family home in the historic district. Daniel and Elizabeth Boone were the first residents; his great-great-grandfather Jacob was a first cousin of famous American pioneer Daniel Boone. In 1926, they sold the home to Dr. Sidney and Alma Dalrymple. It now serves as the High Line Heritage House, showcasing its history and that of Havre and Hill County. (Photograph by the author, courtesy of High Line Heritage House.)

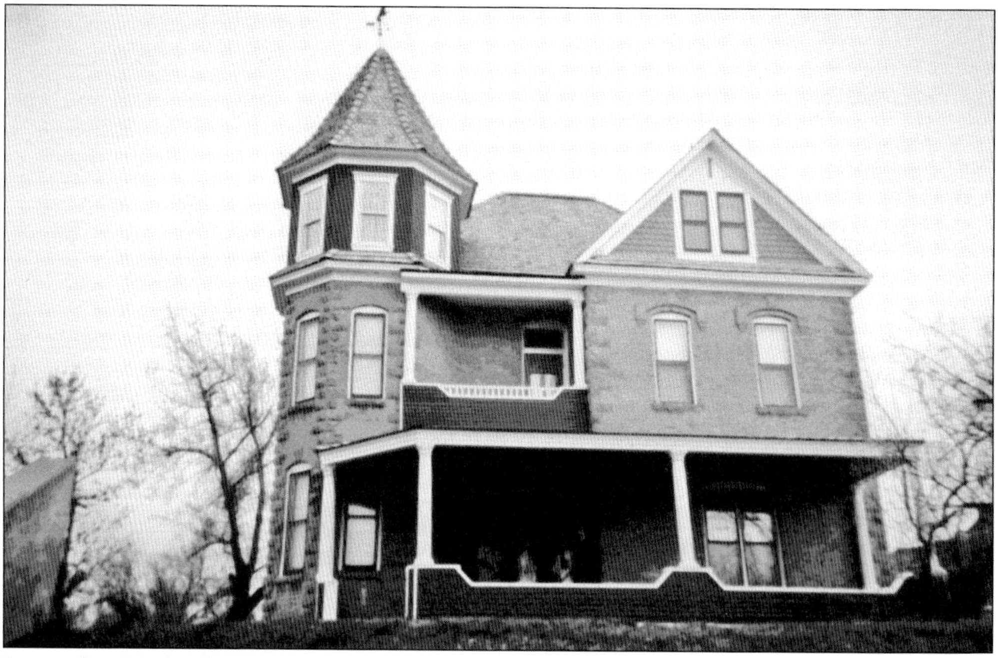

Located at 26 Third Street and also known as the Castle, this home was built in 1903 by Joseph Gussenhoven. He owned a brickyard and lumberyard, so use of these materials can be found both outside and inside the home. It was originally a single-family residence but converted to apartments. Efforts by the Pasma, Swanson, and Coleman families have brought it back to its former glory. (Photograph by the author, courtesy of High Line Heritage House.)

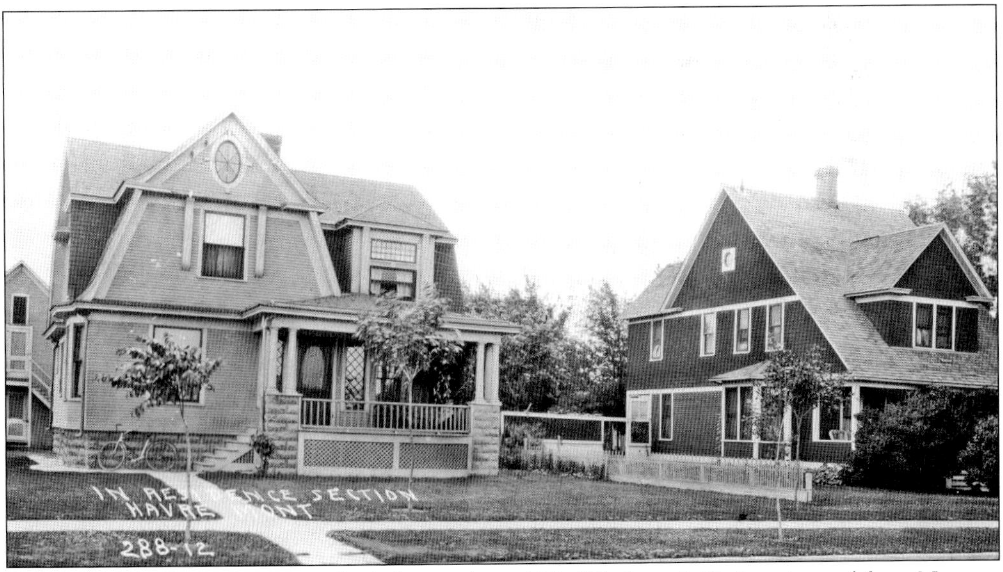

On Third Street, the home on the left was that of Olaf Skylstead. He immigrated from Norway and became a prominent business owner. According to his family, he was scheduled to board the *Titanic*, but due to Hill County splitting from Chouteau County, was called back early from his visit to Norway. The home on the right was owned by Alexander "Nosey" Smith, Havre's first parks director. (Courtesy of High Line Heritage House.)

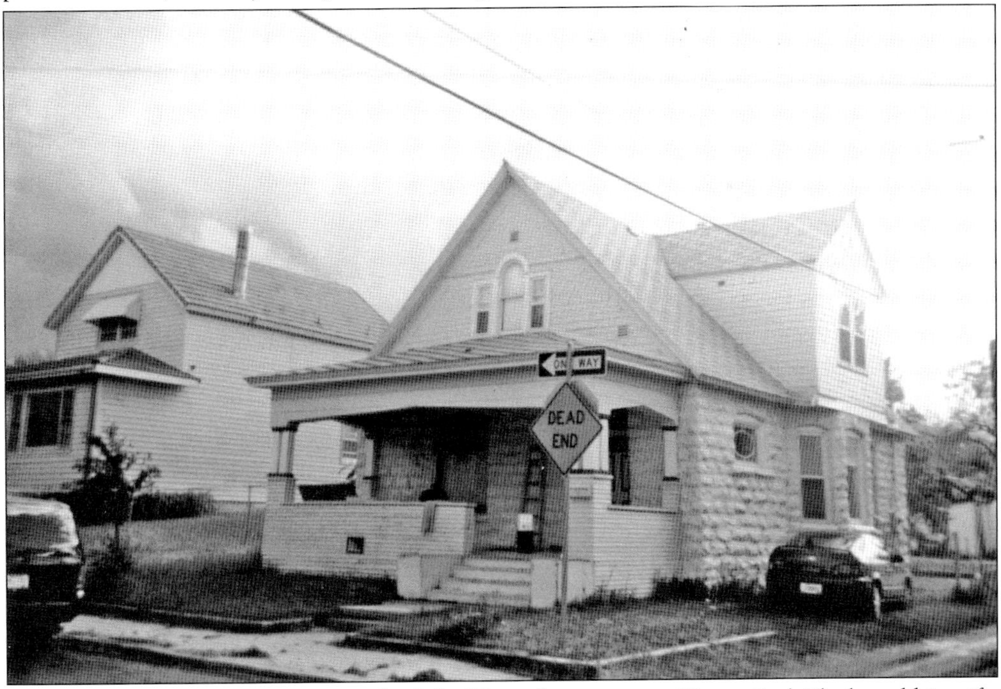

This home at 320 First Avenue was built by Havre businessman Henry Earl Clack and his wife, Margaret. Clack got his start as a hod carrier at Fort Assinniboine and eventually owned a hardware store, grain elevators, and gas and oil interests. He was very successful and widely known throughout the region. The stone was left in its natural state until the late 1990s, when it was painted white. (Photograph by the author, courtesy of High Line Heritage House.)

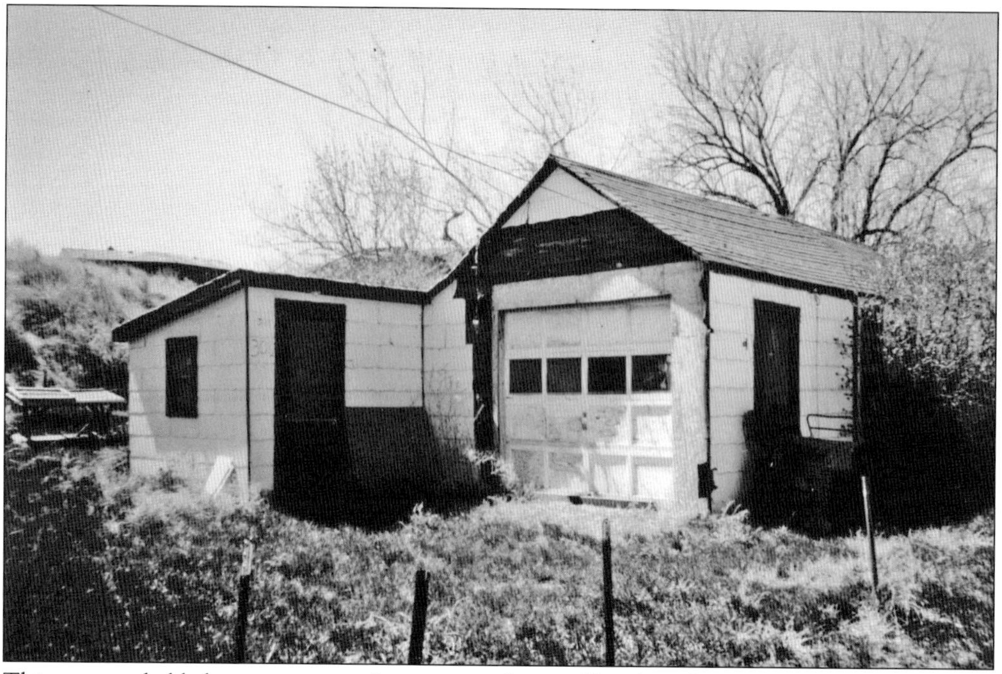

This unremarkable home was once the town residence of local cowboy and convicted horse thief "Long" George Francis. This and another nearby home, both razed in 2014, were constructed in Havre's earliest days. The children of Earl and Margaret Clack would look out their window in awe of the tall and handsome cowboy. Francis committed suicide in 1920. (Photograph by the author, courtesy of High Line Heritage House.)

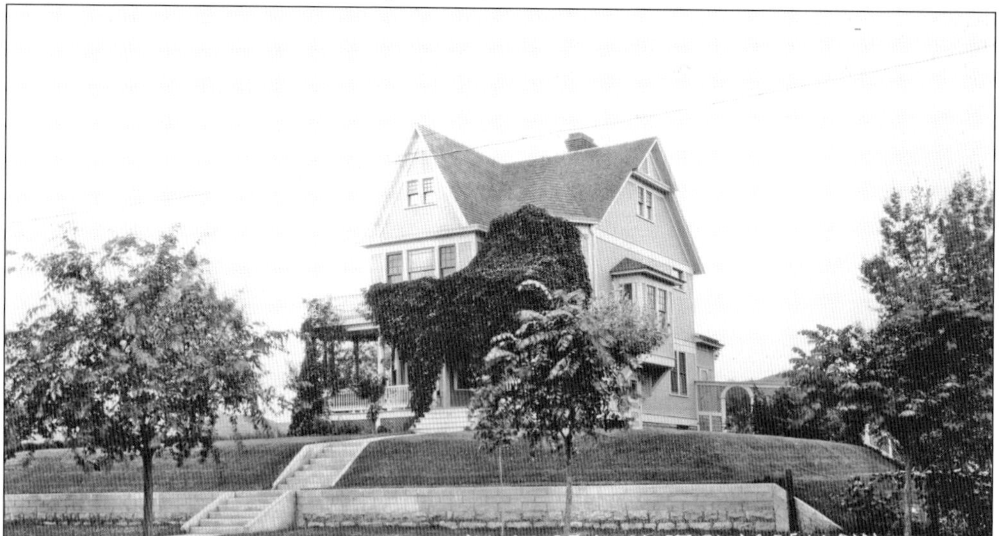

The Stringfellow Home, located at 324 Second Avenue, was constructed around 1903 in the Queen Anne style. It once had a small tower on the north side of the building, which was later removed. Henry Stringfellow was one of Havre's first businessmen, owning a drugstore and later the Havre Commercial Company. He also established Havre's first Ford dealership and served on the school board and the Havre City Council. (Courtesy of High Line Heritage House.)

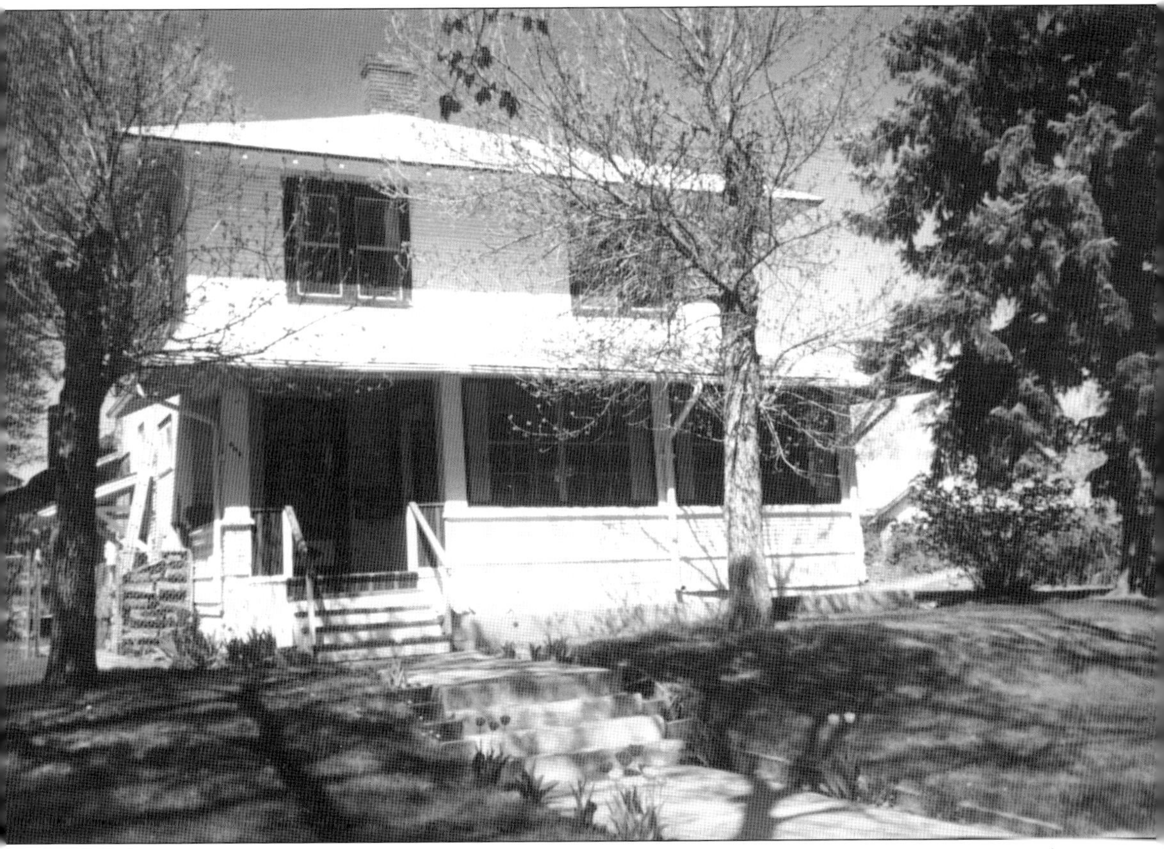

The William Pyper Home, located at 402 Second Avenue, is an American Foursquare–style home with Prairie-style elements. Pyper was originally from Ontario, Canada, and arrived in Havre in 1899 to work in the Stringfellow Drug Store. In November 1904, he was elected justice of the peace as well as police magistrate, and he held both positions until his resignation in 1929. (Photograph by the author, courtesy of High Line Heritage House.)

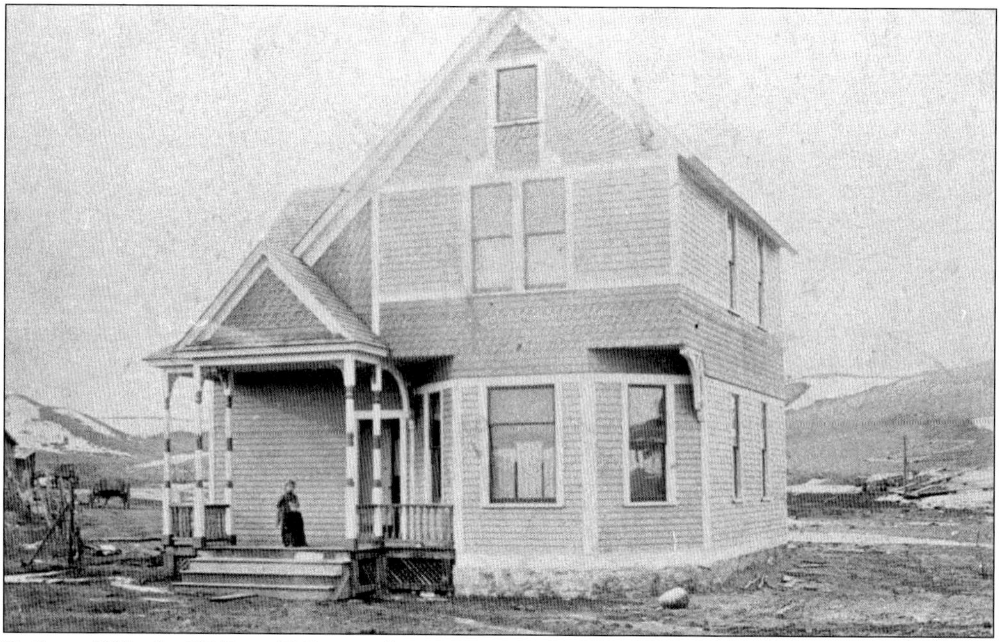

Built in 1903, the William T. Barrett home at 412 Second Avenue is one of the best examples of Queen Anne architecture in Havre. Barrett was an insurance salesman, and his job took him all over Montana and into other states. However, documentation indicates the house was built by Lillian Griffin. In this image, her daughters Melba and Helen are on the front porch. (Courtesy of Don Greytak.)

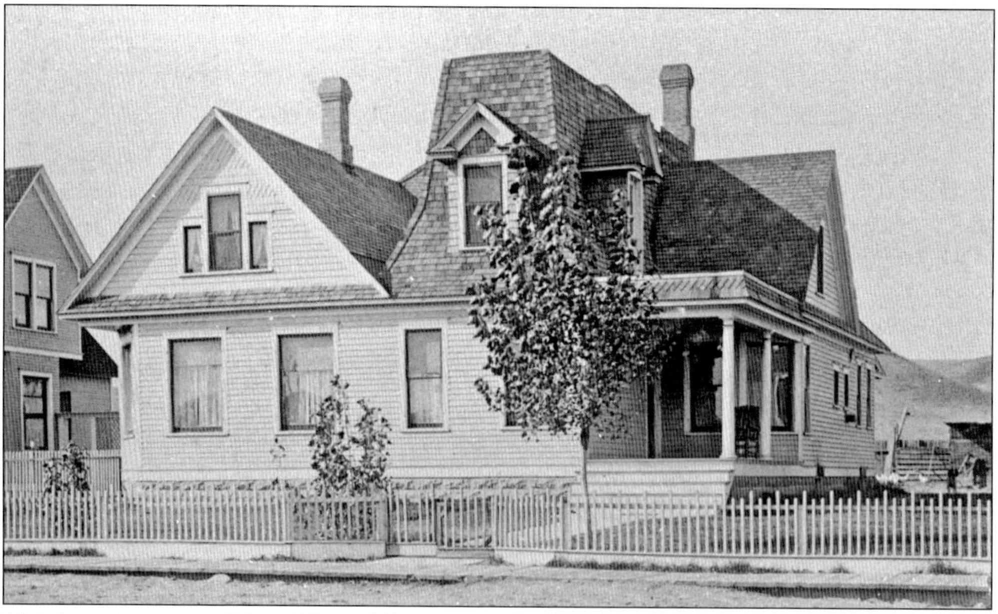

This is perhaps one of the oddest edifices ever to be found in Havre. It was located on the west side of the 400 block of Second Avenue. It appears that the initially simple frame house with chamfered corners and side porch had an addition put on the roof in the mansard style sometime later. Shaped shingles around the roof of the porch and the front gable add period charm. (Courtesy of Don Greytak.)

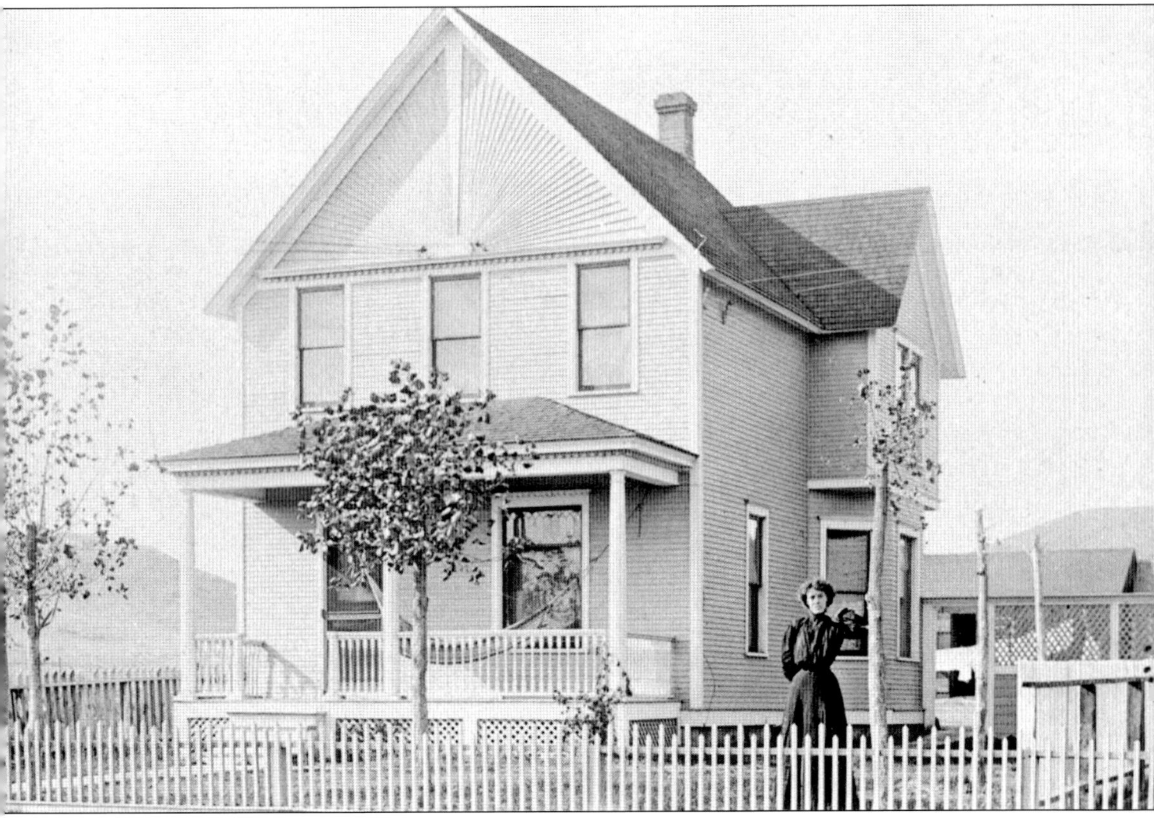

This Queen Anne/Colonial Revival home was built by Gus DeCelles, one of Havre's first residents, in 1906. However, it is likely that he did not live here and instead resided in a cabin just to the north of this home. The following year, DeCelles sold the home to Irish immigrant and rancher Michael J. Healy. After Healy's death, his widow remained in the home and rented out rooms to boarders. (Courtesy of Don Greytak.)

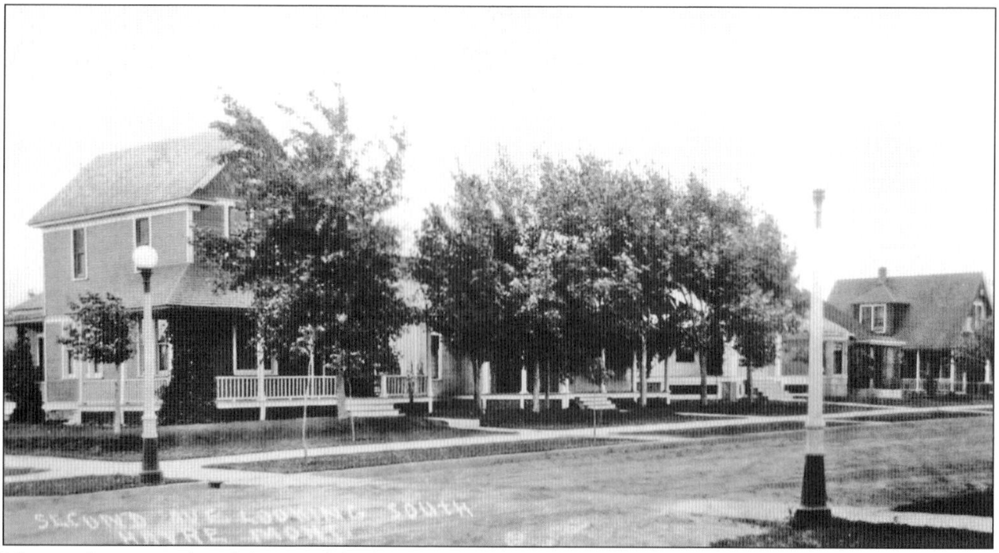

This is the east side of the 500 block of Second Avenue, around 1915. The home on the corner was constructed in 1903, and its first occupant was William Cance. The 1910 census lists Cance, his wife, Della, Bee B. Hall, and Herbert Clifford as residents of this address. This underlines the fact that several homeowners rented rooms to others to bring in extra income for the household. (Courtesy of High Line Heritage House.)

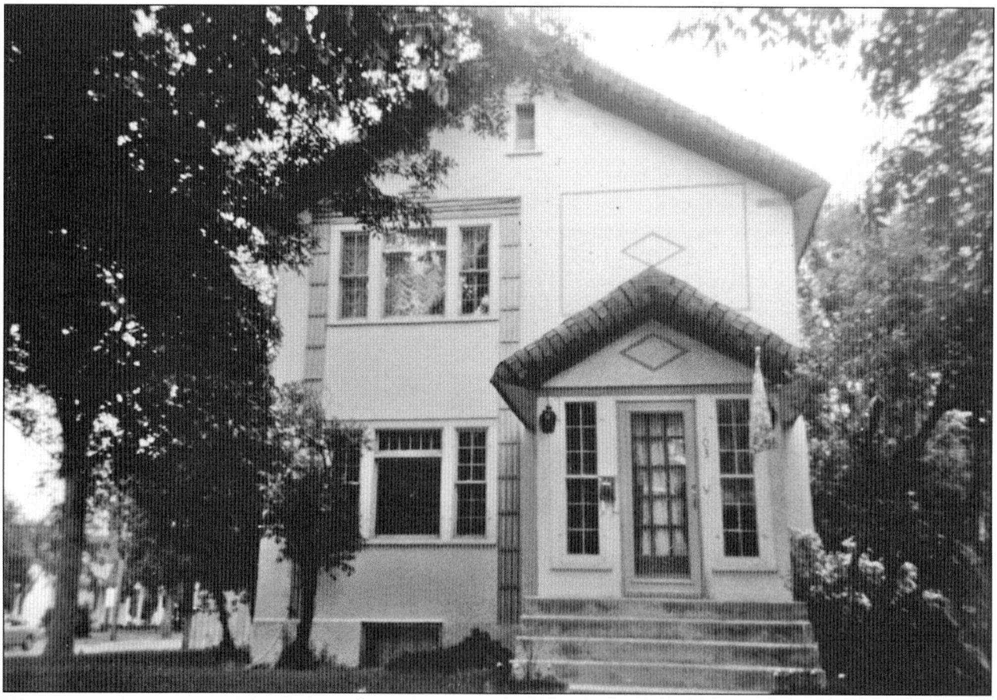

The Cance house was sold to Gerald Casman in 1915. He and his wife, Pearl, were from England, and in 1928 they set about changing the home from a typical wood-frame home of the Victorian era to a residence that reflected ones in their beloved English countryside. Francis and Laened Black, proprietors of Black's Jewelry, bought the home in 1946. (Photograph by the author, courtesy of High Line Heritage House.)

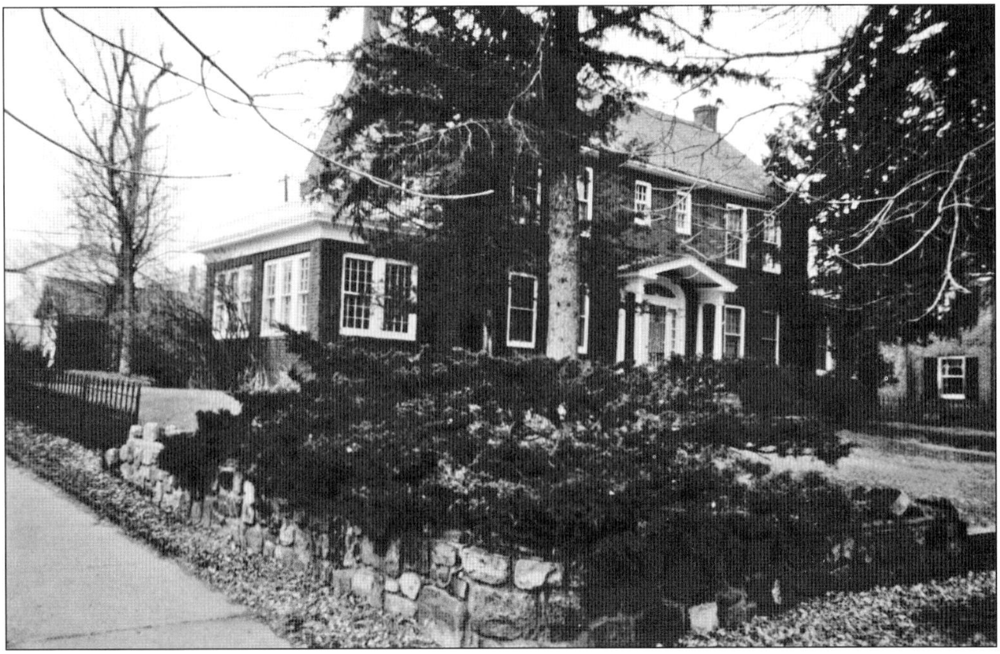

The second Clack Home, located at 532 Second Avenue, was Margaret Turner Clack's dream house. She worked with local architect Frank F. Bossout to design a residence the way she wanted it. Later, an addition was built to the north of the home as a bedroom for her husband, Earl, who was ill and could no longer use the staircase. (Photograph by the author, courtesy of High Line Heritage House.)

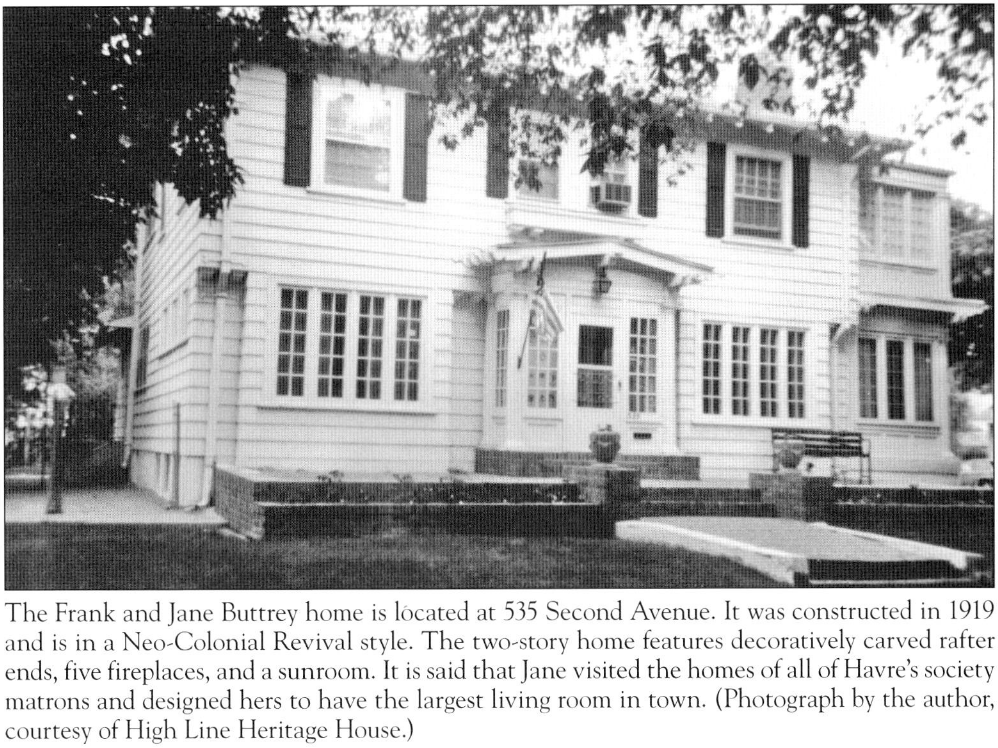

The Frank and Jane Buttrey home is located at 535 Second Avenue. It was constructed in 1919 and is in a Neo-Colonial Revival style. The two-story home features decoratively carved rafter ends, five fireplaces, and a sunroom. It is said that Jane visited the homes of all of Havre's society matrons and designed hers to have the largest living room in town. (Photograph by the author, courtesy of High Line Heritage House.)

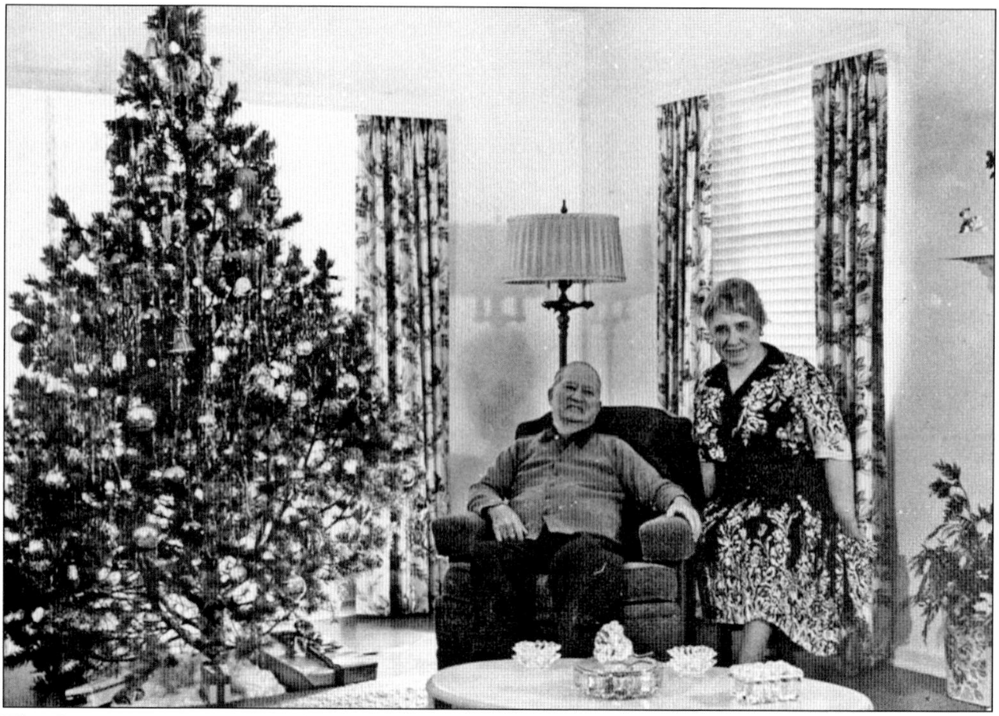

The Buttreys are enjoying their beautiful front room during Christmastime. One of Frank's business ventures was KFBB radio station, using his initials for the call signal. Others claim it meant "Keep Frank Buttrey Broke," as the venture did not pan out well for him, despite being the first commercial radio station in Montana. It was later sold to a new owner in Great Falls and is now a television station. (Courtesy of Don Greytak.)

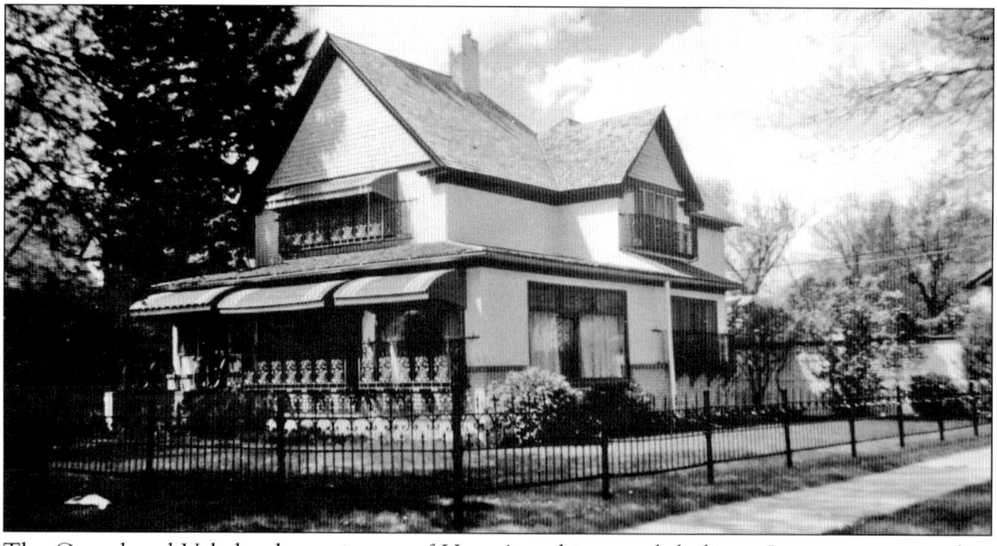

The Carnal and Valadon home is one of Havre's architectural darlings. It was constructed in 1905 for Charles Griffin, a trainmaster for the Great Northern. In 1906, lawyer Florian Carnal owned the home, and Joseph Valadon purchased the house at a sheriff's sale in 1919. He and his wife, Policeena, made changes to suit their tastes, and the home is still currently owned by the Valadon family. (Photograph by the author, courtesy of High Line Heritage House.)

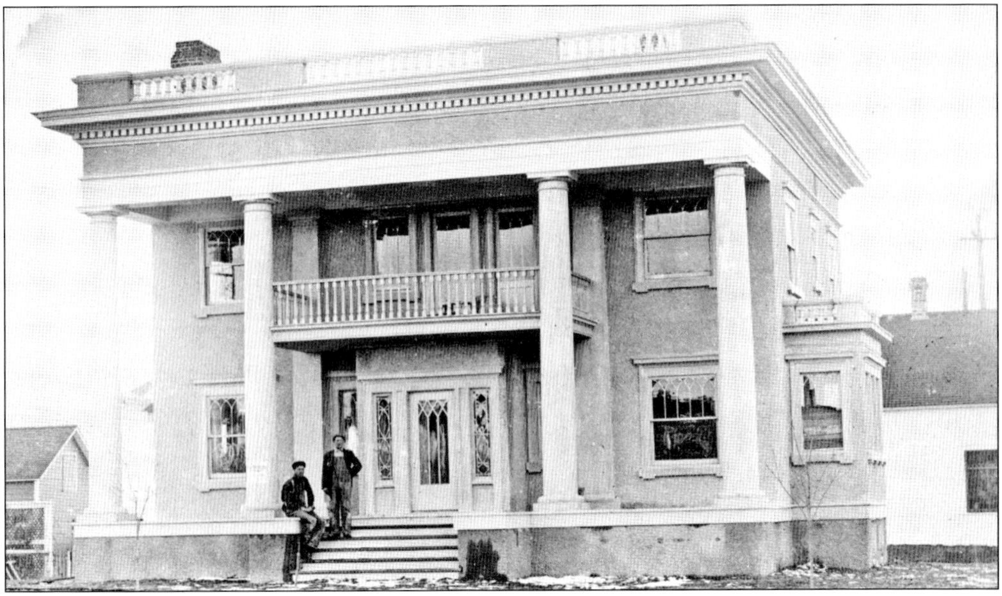

The Exelia Pepin home is located at 606 Third Avenue. It was constructed in 1914 for Pepin, who was the Havre postmaster and nephew of Simon Pepin, who many revere as the "Father of Havre." By 1929, the house had been converted to apartments. The home is a Neoclassical structure featuring columns in the Doric order. The millwork balustrade is said to come from France. (Courtesy of Don Greytak.)

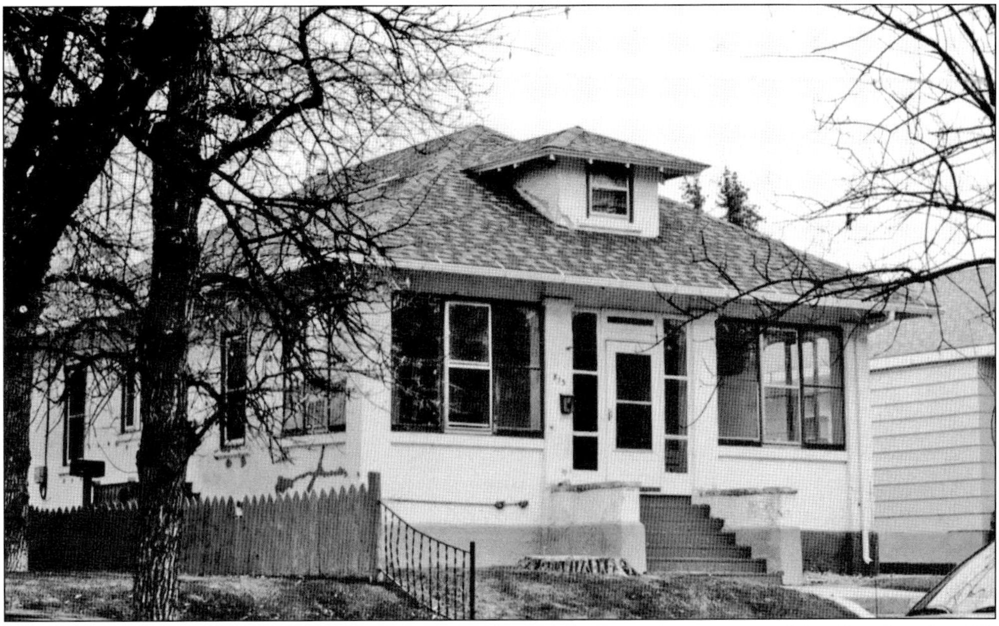

This home at 813 Third Avenue was the site of one of Havre's biggest scandals. On October 27, 1922, Rev. Leonard Christler and his lover Margaret Carleton were found dead, both of gunshot wounds. The only other occupant of the home was Anna, Christler's wife. The popular Havre conclusion was that a crazed Margaret shot the reverend and then committed suicide; however, research indicates she was a victim of murder, not the perpetrator. (Photograph by the author, courtesy of High Line Heritage House.)

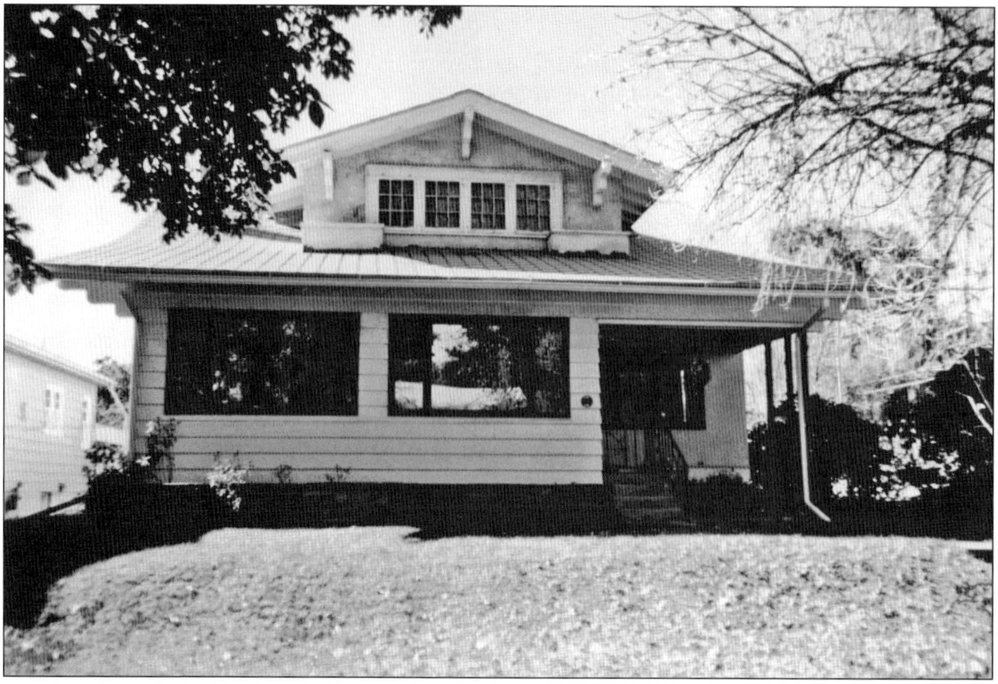

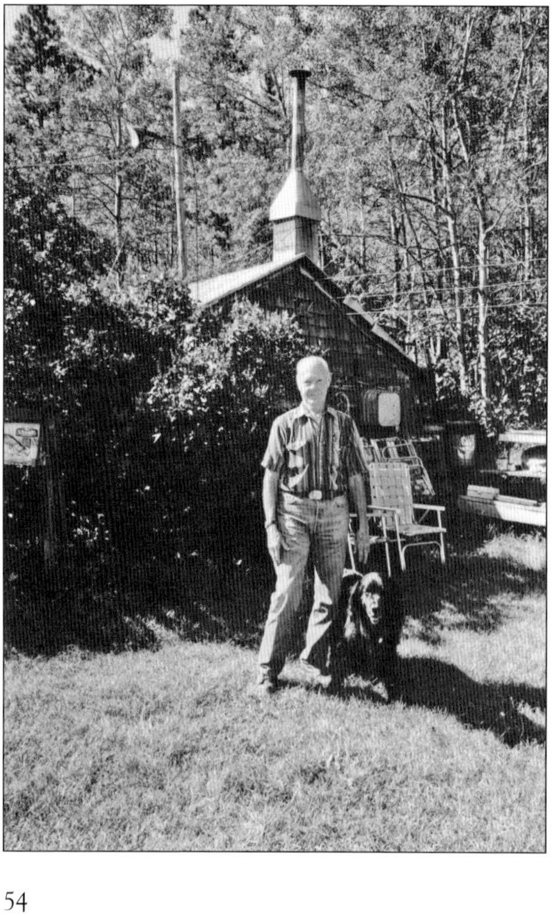

The Lou and Harriet (Thackeray) Lucke Home is located at 900 Third Avenue. Built in the Craftsman style in 1914, the home originally had an open-air porch running the entire length of the home. It was later enclosed to allow for a music room. Frank Bossout was the architect, and the home retains many of its original Craftsman elements. The Thackerays were an early Havre pioneer family. (Photograph by the author, courtesy of High Line Heritage House.)

Allan Louis "Lou" Lucke was the first grandchild of Lou and Harriet Lucke. He held bachelor's degrees in geology and physics and worked on computer systems for the Mercury, Gemini, and Apollo missions, including Apollo 11, which sent man to the moon. He was also a noted local historian. He purchased the Lucke home from his grandmother and lived there until he passed away on May 16, 2009. (Photograph by the author, courtesy of High Line Heritage House.)

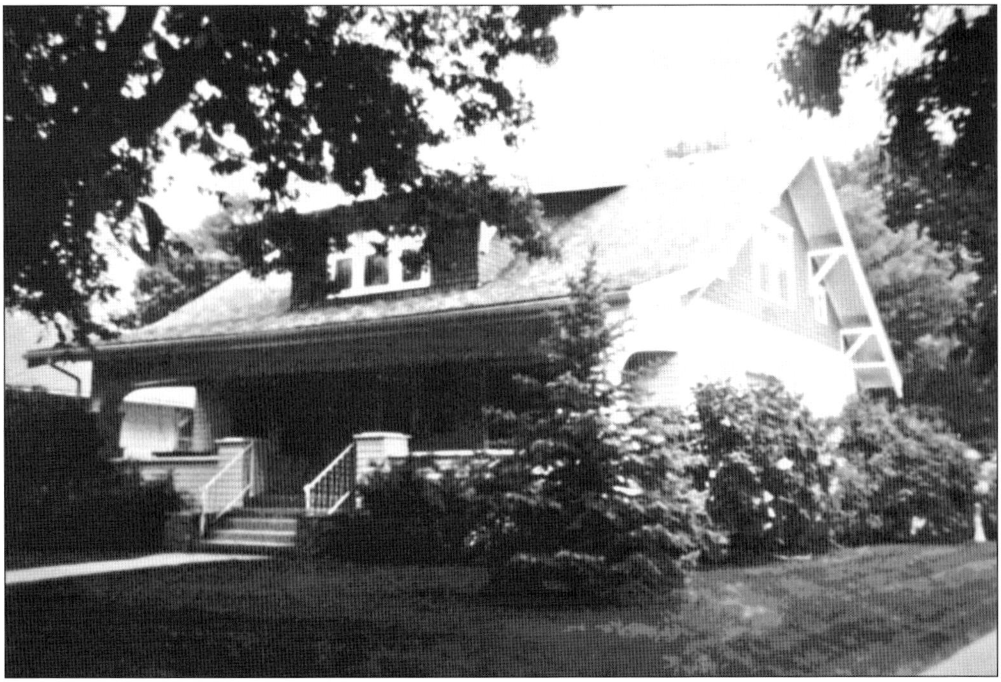

Dr. L.D. Williams built this Craftsman-style home in 1916 and owned a private hospital above the Security State Bank building. The 10-bed facility was equipped with the most modern equipment then available. The home features a lovely front porch, which is still open-air. Homeowners enclosed many of their front porches, allowing extra room for paying students attending Northern Montana College. (Photograph by the author, courtesy of High Line Heritage House.)

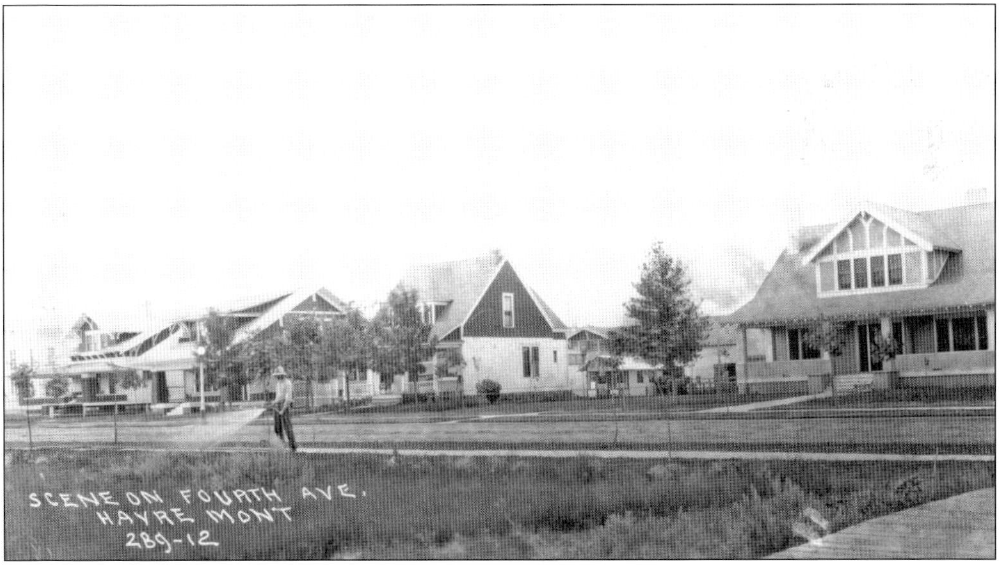

The 600 block of Fourth Avenue is pictured here sometime between 1911 and 1917. The second house from the right is the home of Havre architect Frank Bossout and his wife, Harriett. Bossout designed many buildings in Havre, such as the Hill County Courthouse, Masonic temple, Buttrey Building, Donaldson Hall, and private residences. The first Havre High School can be seen in the background to the left. (Courtesy of High Line Heritage House.)

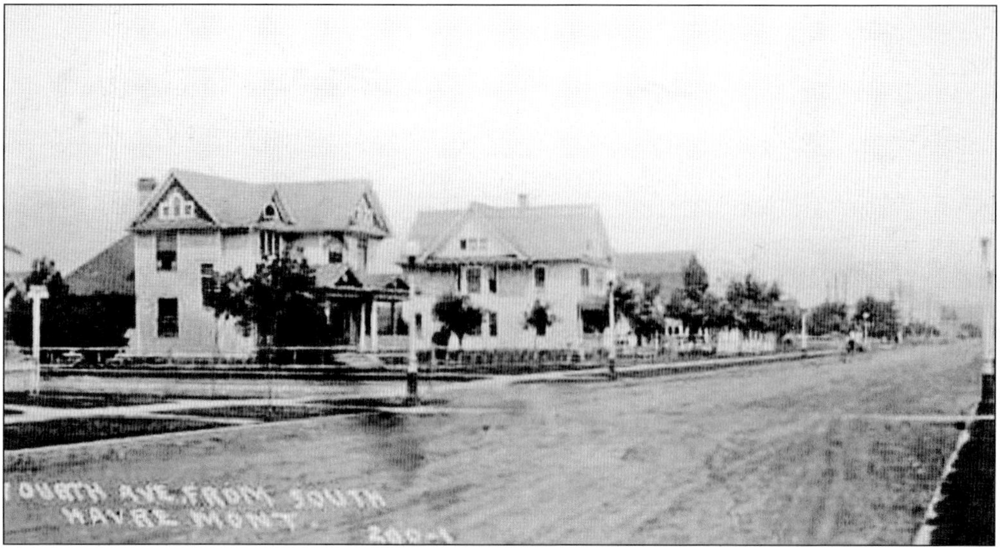

The 400 block of Fourth Avenue's corner home is that of Frank Buttrey and later A.K. Gilboe and is in a Queen Anne/Colonial Revival style. The neighboring house is that of Rudolph Bentzin, built in 1905. Bentzin was a master carpenter for the Great Northern Railroad and also owned a quarry with Lawrence K. Devlin, supplying ballast for the Great Northern tracks. By 1915, the home was a rental. (Courtesy of High Line Heritage House.)

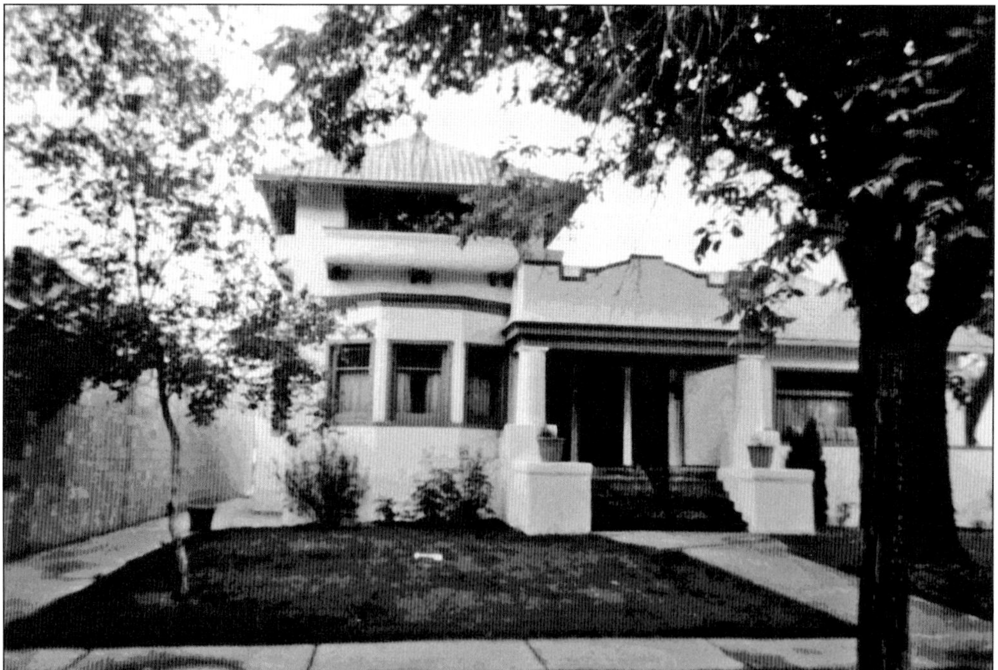

Havre's vice king, Christopher "Shorty" Young, built this Spanish Mission–style home at 419 Fourth Avenue in 1914. Shorty was infamous for his bootlegging escapades and houses of prostitution in Havre. He died 1944, and his will stipulated that his properties be sold and the money put into a trust, with the interest going to the local Elks, Masons, and Eagles for the needy and the children of Havre. (Photograph by the author, courtesy of High Line Heritage House.)

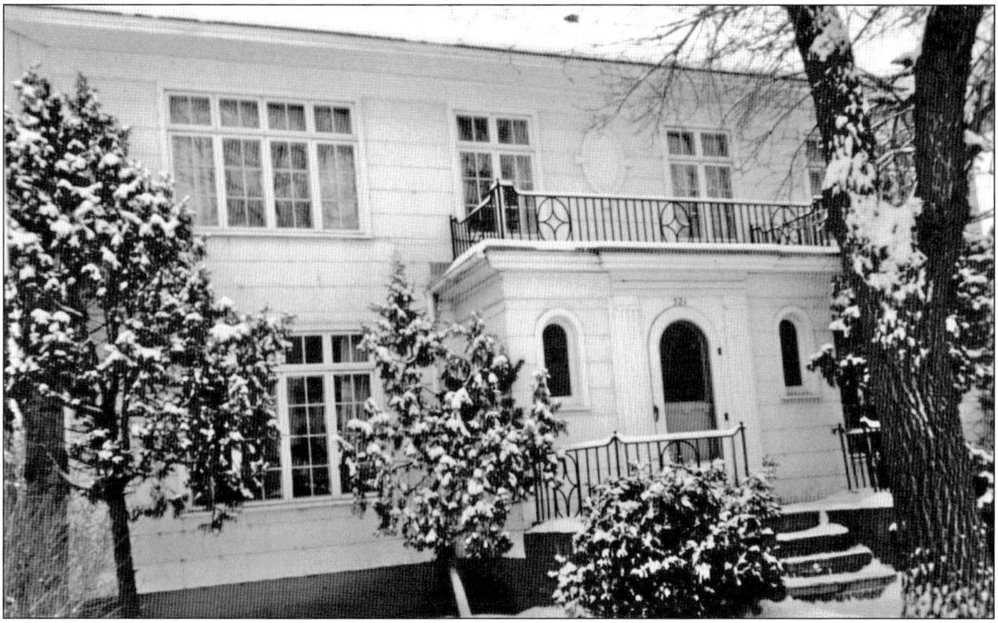

In 1940, Edwin Carruth built this Colonial Revival home for his only child, Cooley. She worked as a clerk for the Great Northern Railroad. Cooley lived in the bottom portion of this home and rented out two apartments on the second story for additional income. After her death, the home was eventually the home of Witt and Loranger Realty. After the partnership dissolved, Don and Margaret Loranger turned the house into four nice apartments. (Photograph by the author, courtesy of High Line Heritage House.)

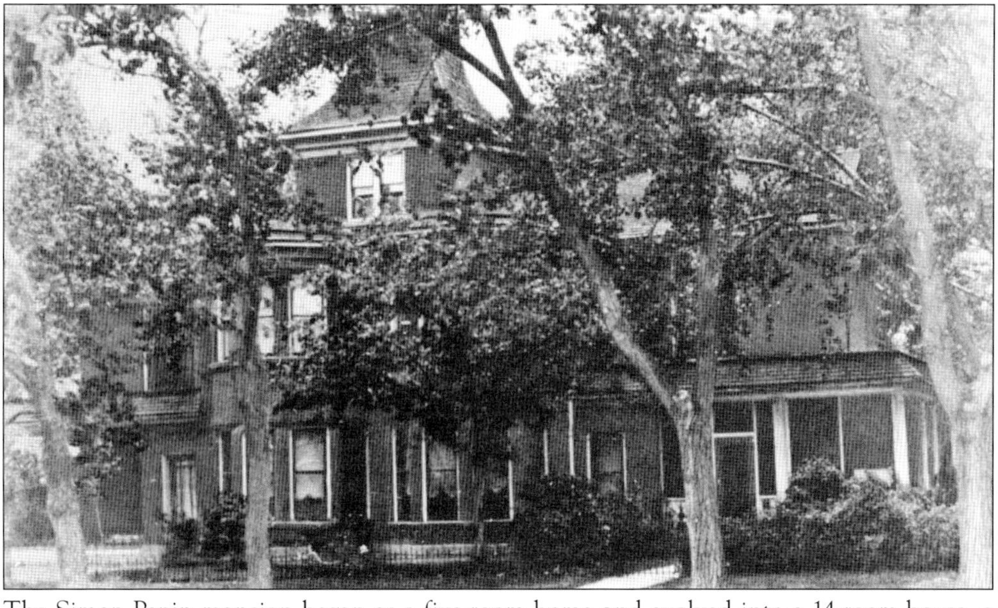

The Simon Pepin mansion began as a five-room home and evolved into a 14-room house, a mansion by Havre standards. Pepin was one of Havre's greatest entrepreneurs and is considered by many to be the "Father of Havre." After his death in 1914, the home went to his daughter, who then sold the house, which was razed in June 1951 to make way for the Havre Clinic. (Courtesy of Don Greytak.)

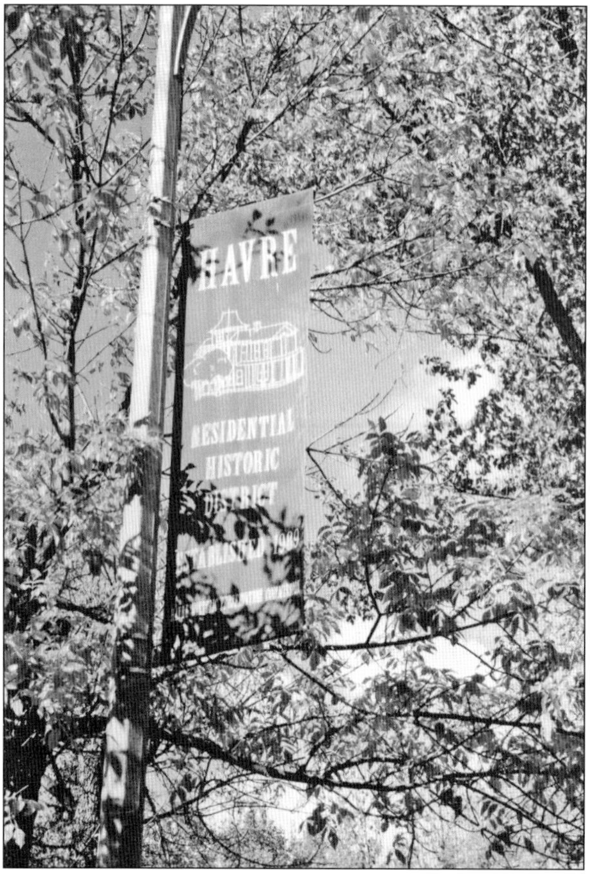

The Pepin Mansion was honored by the Havre Historic Preservation Commission, under the leadership of Emily Mayer, on banners that grace the 36-block Havre Residential Historic District, added to the National Register of Historic Places in 1989. The depiction of the mansion was drawn by Lyle Lossing, and the banners were designed by Mayer. The design reminds Havreites to preserve history—for once it is gone, it is gone forever. (Photograph by the author, courtesy of High Line Heritage House.)

Not all old homes and buildings meet the fate of the wrecking ball. The Assinniboine Apartments, located on the 100 block of Third Avenue, was moved to its current location on Havre's east end, to make room for a new Safeway store, which was located at the northwest corner of Second Avenue and Second Street at the time this photograph was taken, in the 1950s. (Courtesy of Don Greytak.)

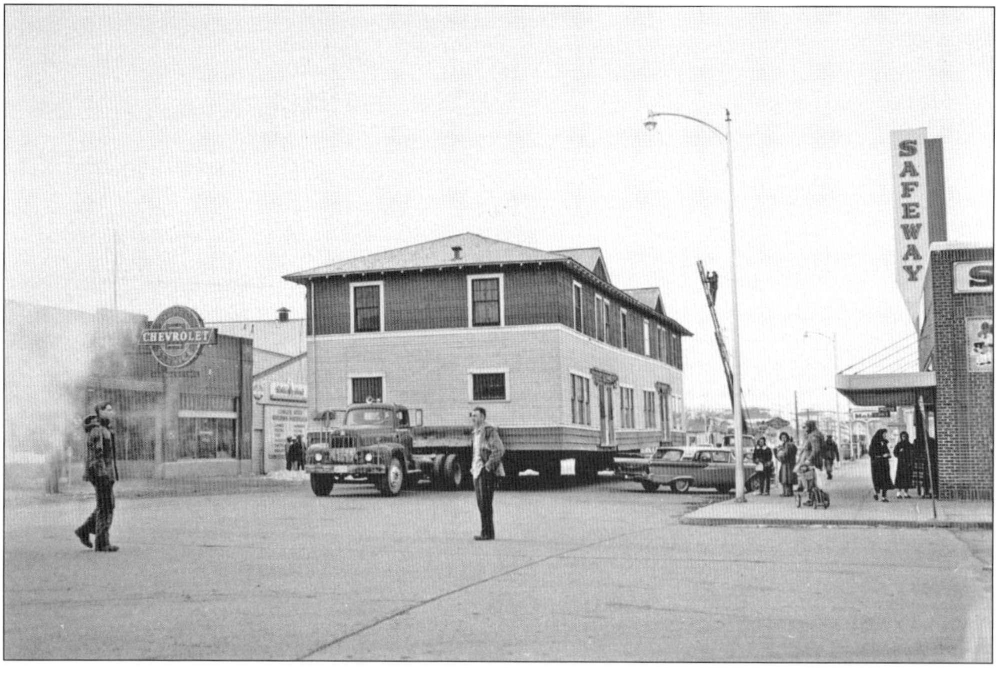

Three

Churches, Schools, and Government Buildings

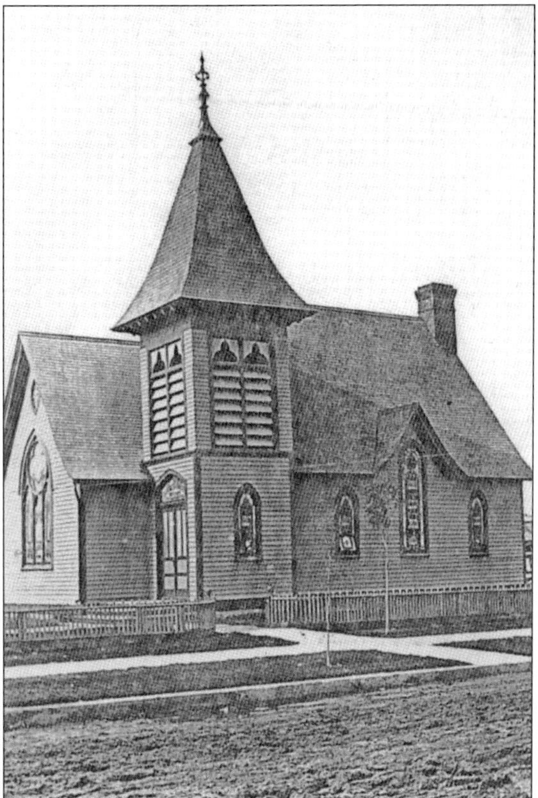

The First Presbyterian Church was located on the northwest corner of Third Street and Fourth Avenue. Construction of this church began in July 1901, but it was not dedicated until November 1902. Prior to 1901, services had been conducted at the first Washington School, then located on the south side of the 100 block of Third Street, and next to a tiny chapel on First Street near Third Avenue. (Courtesy of High Line Heritage House.)

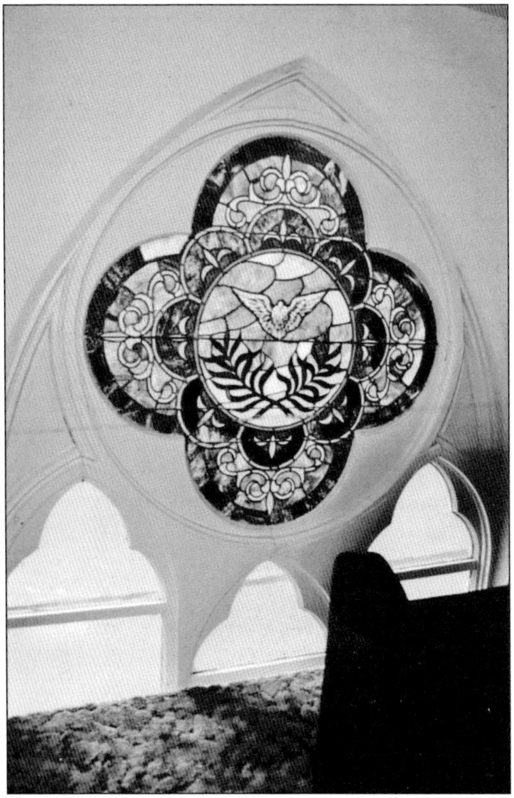

One of the dominant features of the First Presbyterian Church was the stained glass in every window on the building. Over time, many of them have been removed, but this one of the Dove of Peace can still be found on the building. The structure was sold to the First Baptist Church, which moved it to its current location at 625 Fourth Avenue in July 1920. (Photograph by the author, courtesy of High Line Heritage House.)

By 1916, the trustees of the First Presbyterian Church decided a new church and manse were needed. The cornerstone of the new Presbyterian church was laid on November 18, 1917, by the Masonic Grand Lodge of Montana. This church building was finished in 1922, but it would take several years for the interior to be completed. It was finally dedicated on February 15, 1942. (Courtesy of Don Greytak.)

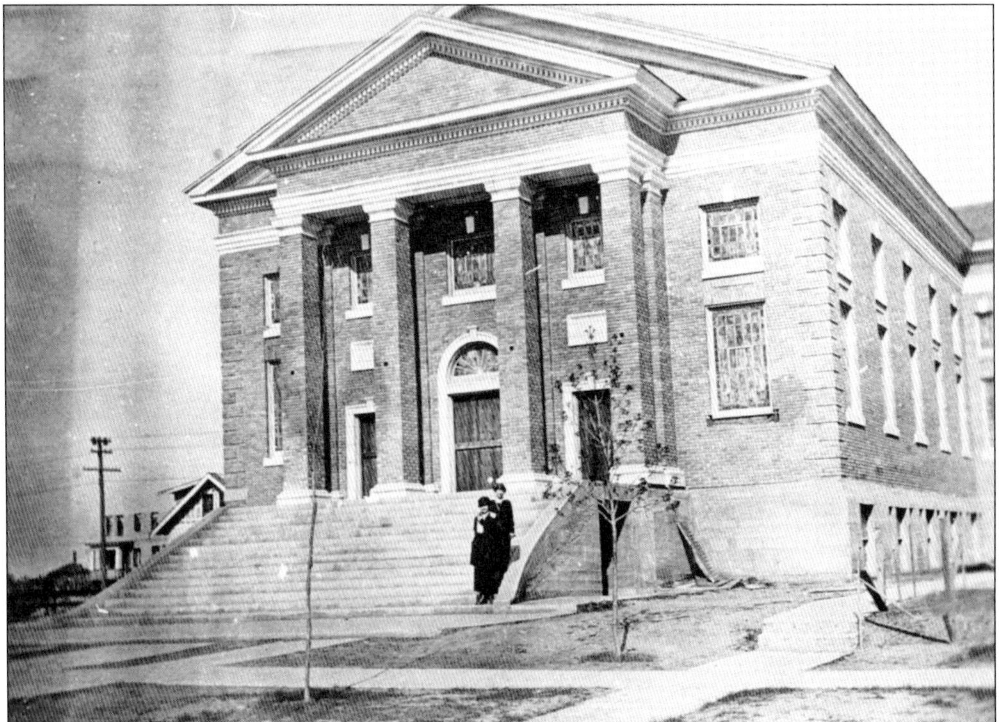

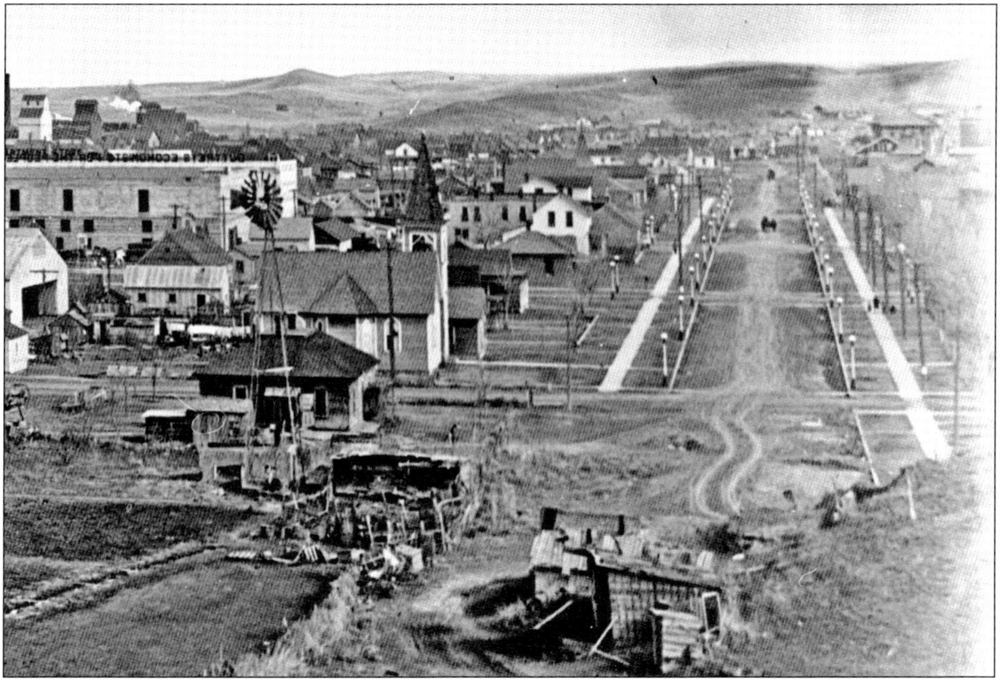

The first Methodist church was located on the northeast corner of First Avenue and Third Street. Rev. William Wesley "Brother Van" Van Orsdel was instrumental in getting the church organized and built. He is fondly referred to as "the minister for all Montana." The church was built in 1893 and would serve at this location until 1915. (Courtesy of Don Greytak.)

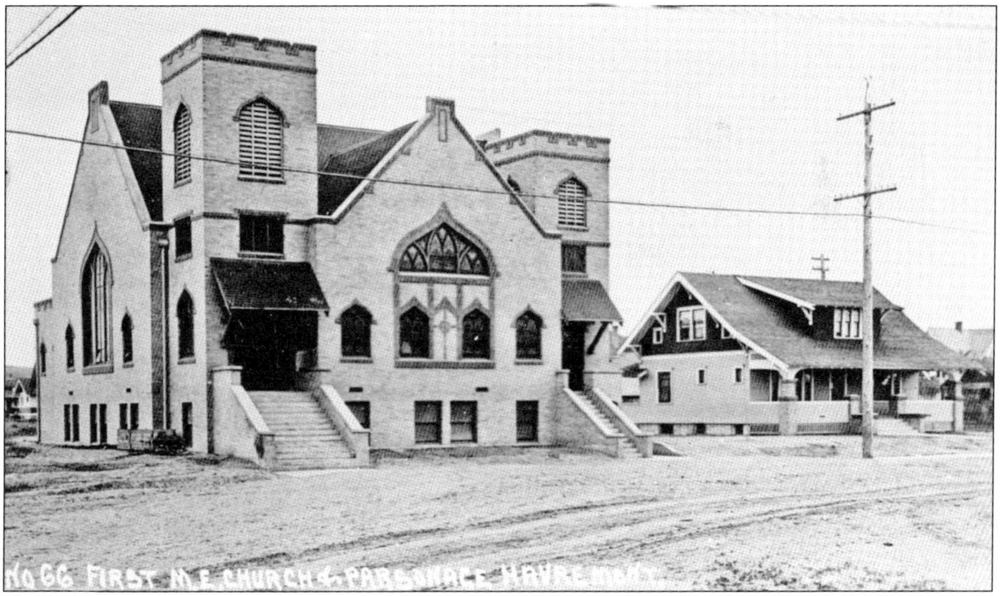

By 1914, Rev. Edgar Huston reported that attendance was low at the Methodist church, and lots on Fourth Street and Fifth Avenue were purchased for a new church and parsonage. It was dedicated on May 13, 1917. At this time, the church was officially named Van Orsdel Methodist Church. This church burned December 6, 1957. Another church was built at that location and dedicated in 1959, and it remains to this day. (Courtesy of Don Greytak.)

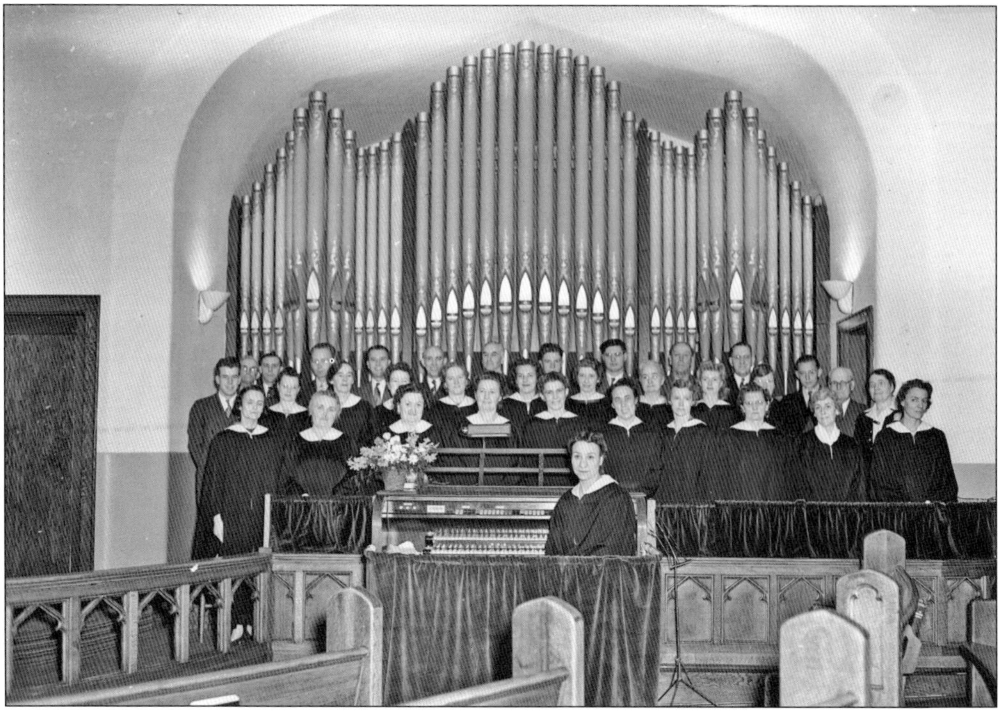

The Methodists were very proud of their Kimball pipe organ, the dream of Dr. A. Elton Williams. He underwrote the purchase of the organ and personally saw to its installation, so it could be dedicated along with the church in 1917. The Methodist choir is pictured here with the organ in 1942. (Photograph by Frances Hulm, courtesy of Don Greytak.)

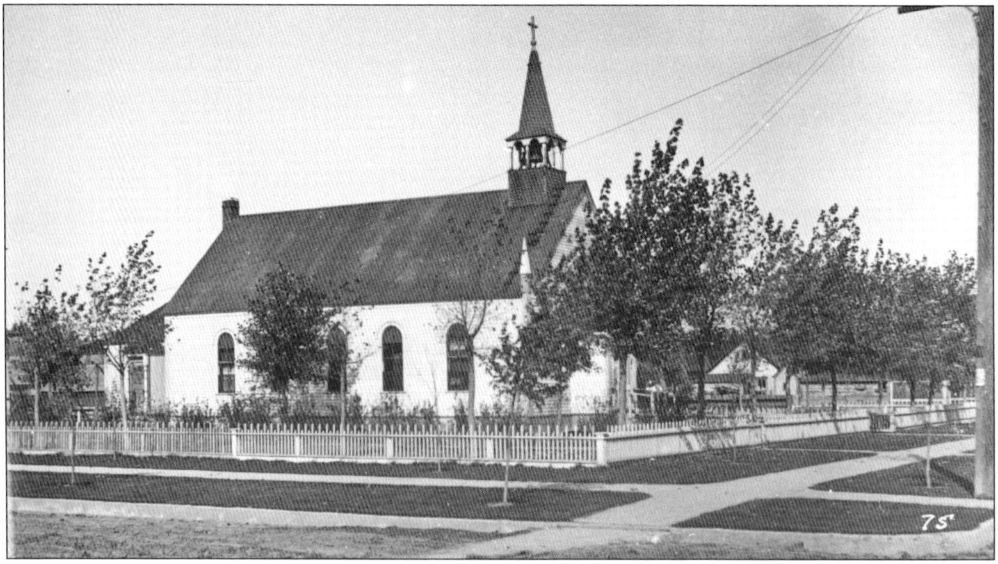

The first Catholic church was a brick structure constructed in 1894 but destroyed in a storm. Mass took place in the Gussenhoven home, at the first Washington School, or in the deLorimer home. This wood-frame church was blessed on September 17, 1905, and mass took place here until 1915, when the land and buildings were sold to Hill County for construction of a courthouse. (Courtesy of Don Greytak.)

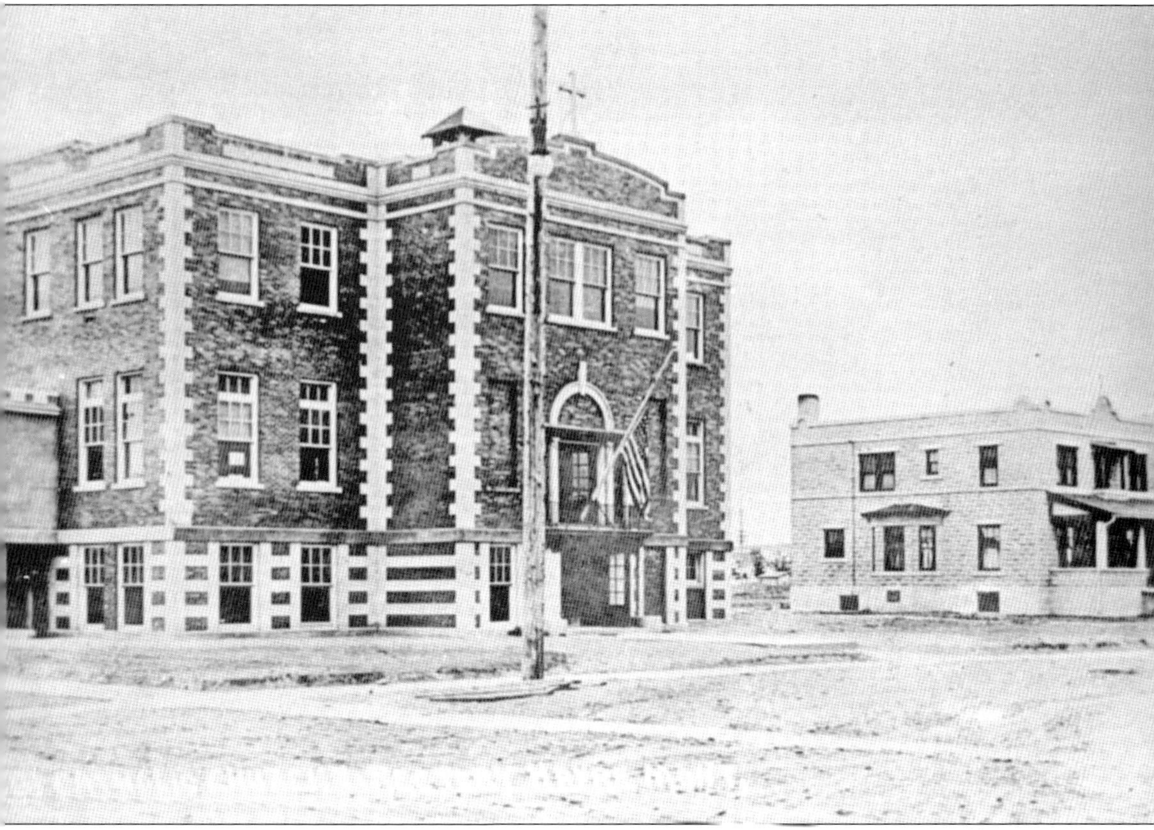

From June 1915 to the summer of 1916, there was no permanent Catholic church building in Havre. Elizabeth Pepin Meyer, daughter of Simon Pepin, offered a building for mass and allowed the priests to live in the Pepin Mansion in the absence of the Meyer family. Construction of a combination church and school started in 1915 and was completed in 1916. The rectory was built from 1916 to 1917 and razed in 2012. (Courtesy of Don Greytak.)

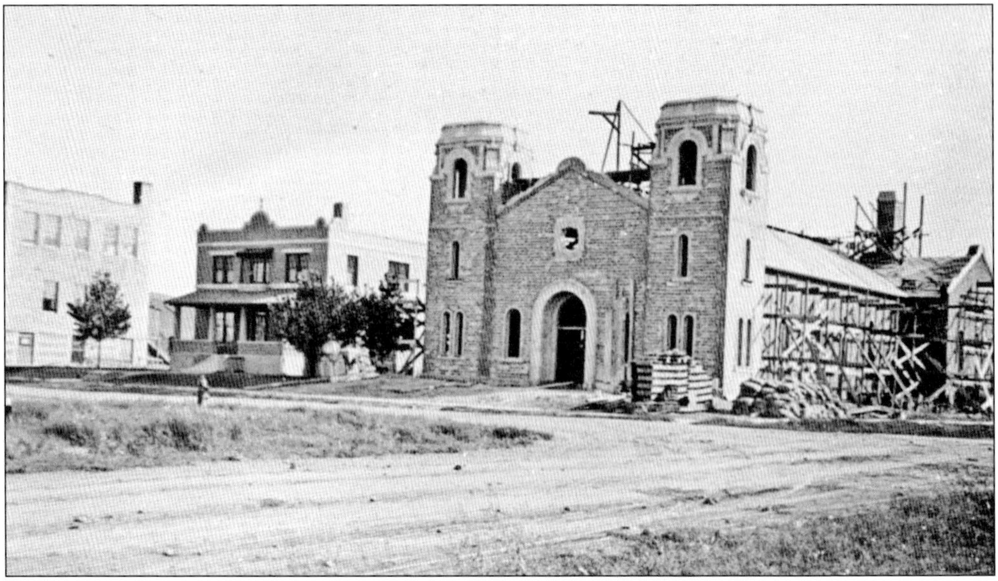

By 1924, there was need for a new Catholic church. The current church, constructed in a Spanish Mission style, was completed in 1925. The church was dedicated to St. Jude Thaddeus back in 1905, the patron saint of desperate cases. While the exterior has changed little, the interior has seen the removal of many old relics due to changes in church organizational structure. (Courtesy of Don Greytak.)

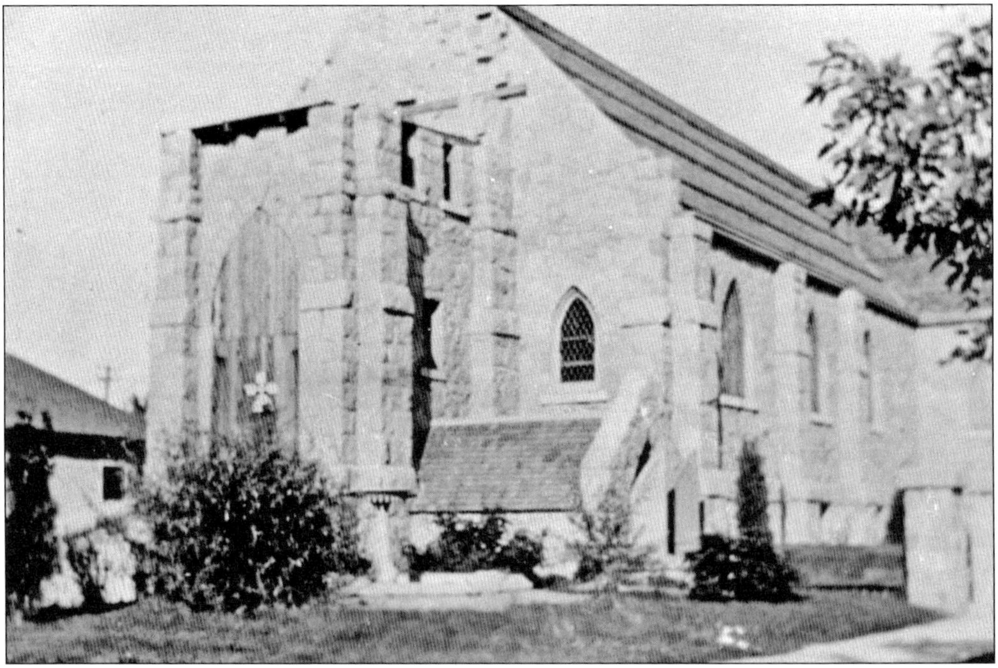

The first recorded Episcopal service in the Havre area took place in 1894 at Fort Assinniboine. In 1907, Rev. Leonard Christler was hired, and the following year work began on the church. Christler worked hard to get the church completed, even getting the stone donated from a quarry near Helena, Montana. Jim Hill had the stone hauled to Havre free of charge, and the church was finally completed in 1918. (Courtesy of Don Greytak.)

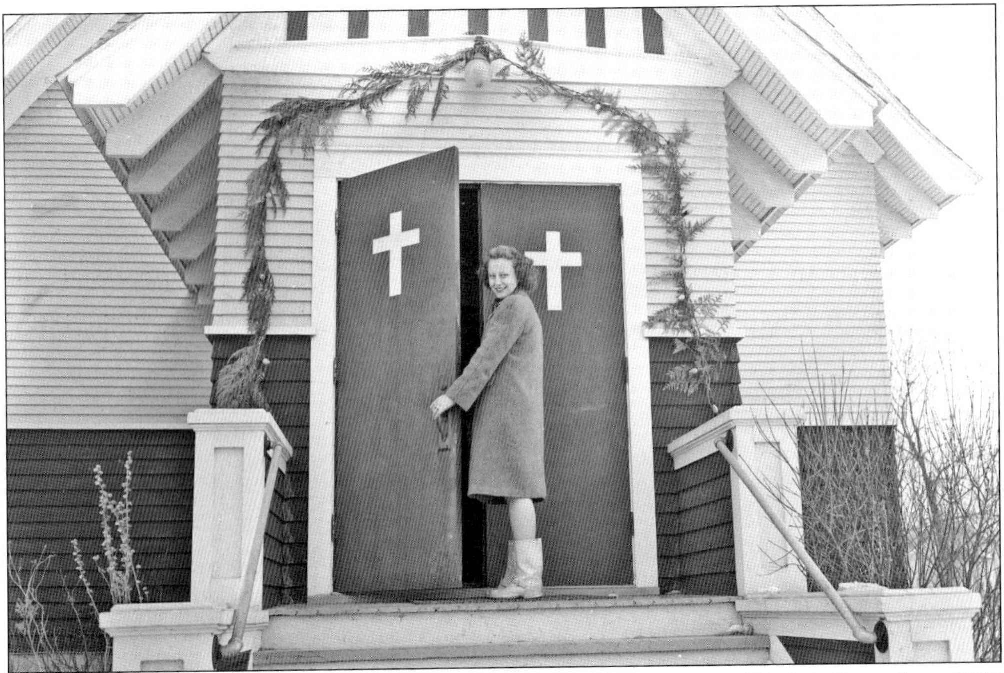

St. Paul Lutheran Church was located at the corner of Fifth Avenue and Eighth Street from 1926 to 1952. The church was started in 1912, known as the German Lutheran Church, and congregants often worshiped in the McKinley School. In 1952, they were offered the First Lutheran Church property a short distance from McKinley School and stayed until 1963, when a new church was built. (Photograph by Frances Hulm, courtesy of Don Greytak.)

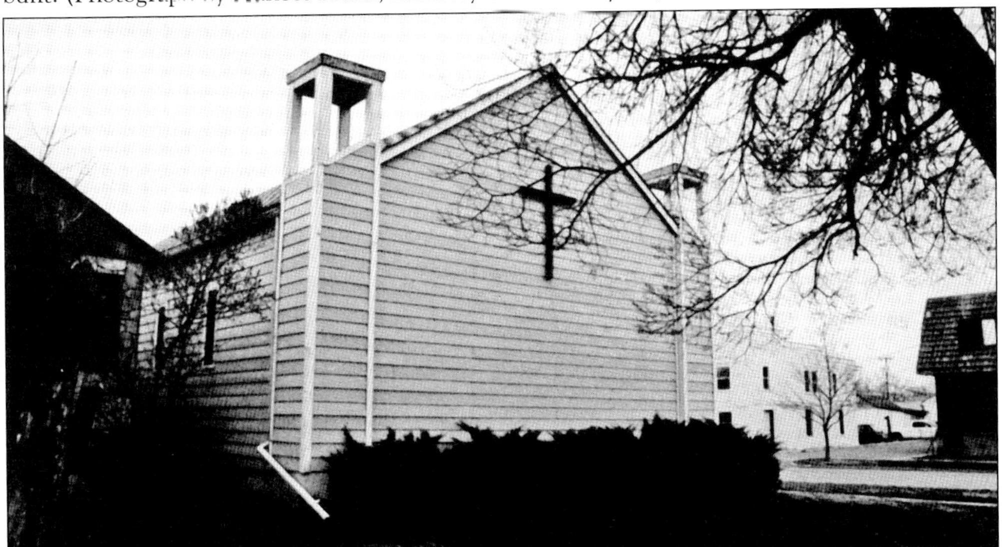

Havre's past included an active African American community. In November 1903, a group of members gathered to form the St. Stephen's African Methodist Episcopal Church. In 1916, they purchased land at the corner of Sixth Avenue and Third Street and built a church. It served the spiritual needs of the African American community until sometime in the 1940s. In 1947, it was sold to the Mormons, and it became a Pentecostal church in 1969. (Photograph by the author, courtesy of High Line Heritage House.)

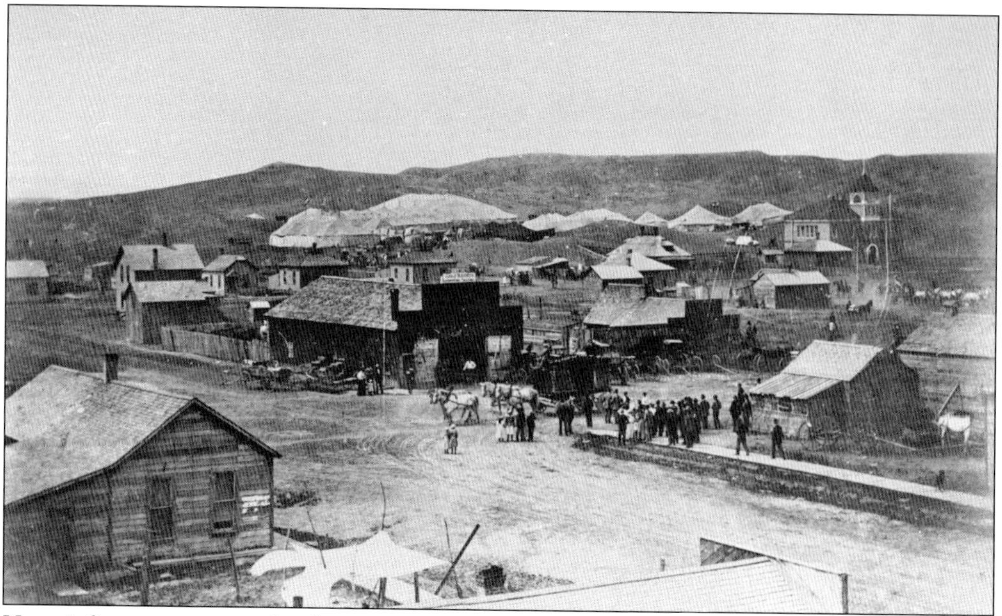

Havre's first permanent school was Washington School, built at the corner of First Avenue and Third Street in 1894. It was a four-room school with a tall bell tower and caused controversy as many thought it was too large and a bigger school would not be needed for many years. By 1900, complaints of overcrowding were already being made. This Washington School burned in 1912, due to an overheated furnace. (Courtesy of Don Greytak.)

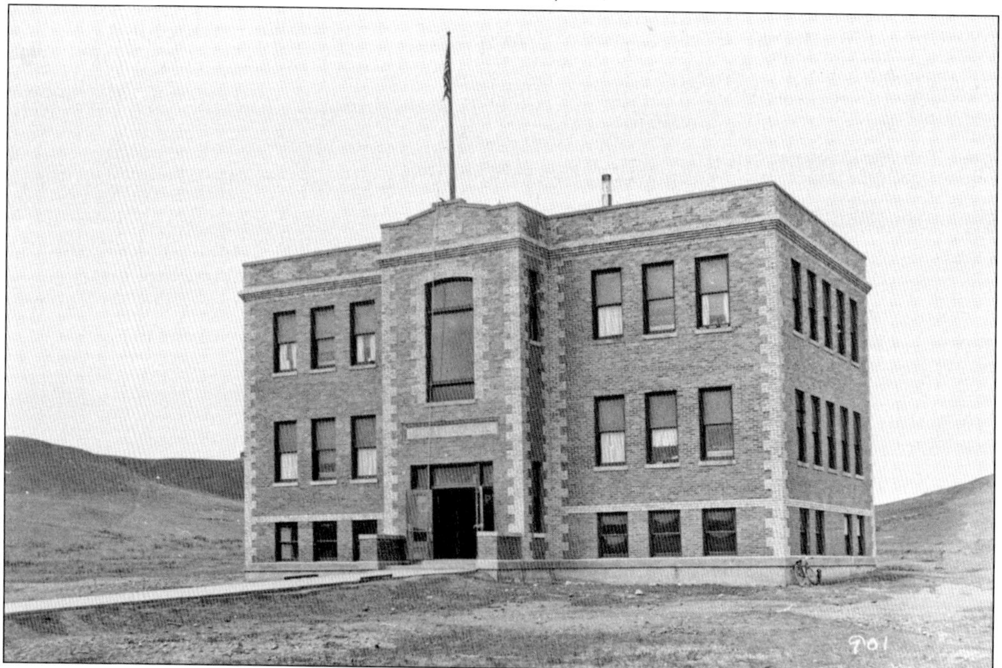

In 1912, after the first Washington School burned, it was decided to build a new school at a different site, rather than rebuild where the Washington School was located. The new school would later be named Devlin School, in honor of Lawrence K. Devlin, who was a strong advocate of education and chairman of the school board at the time. (Courtesy of Don Greytak.)

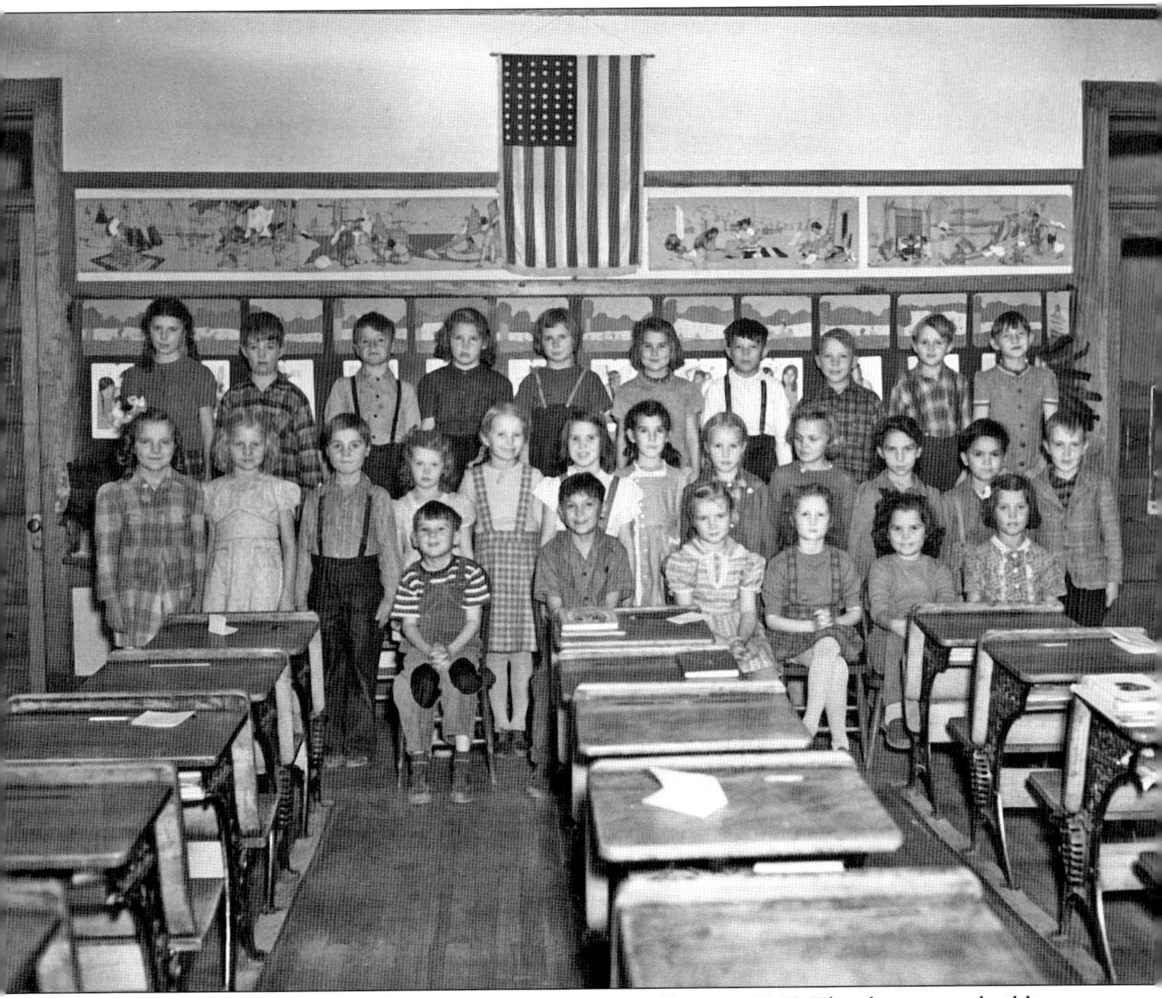

One of the first-grade classes at Devlin School is pictured here in 1945. The three-story building was designed by Havre architect Frank Bossout and built by Lease and Richards of Great Falls. It was not long for overcrowding to become an issue after Devlin was constructed in 1912. Bonds were sold in 1952 for an addition, completed in 1954. (Photograph by Frances Hulm, courtesy of Don Greytak.)

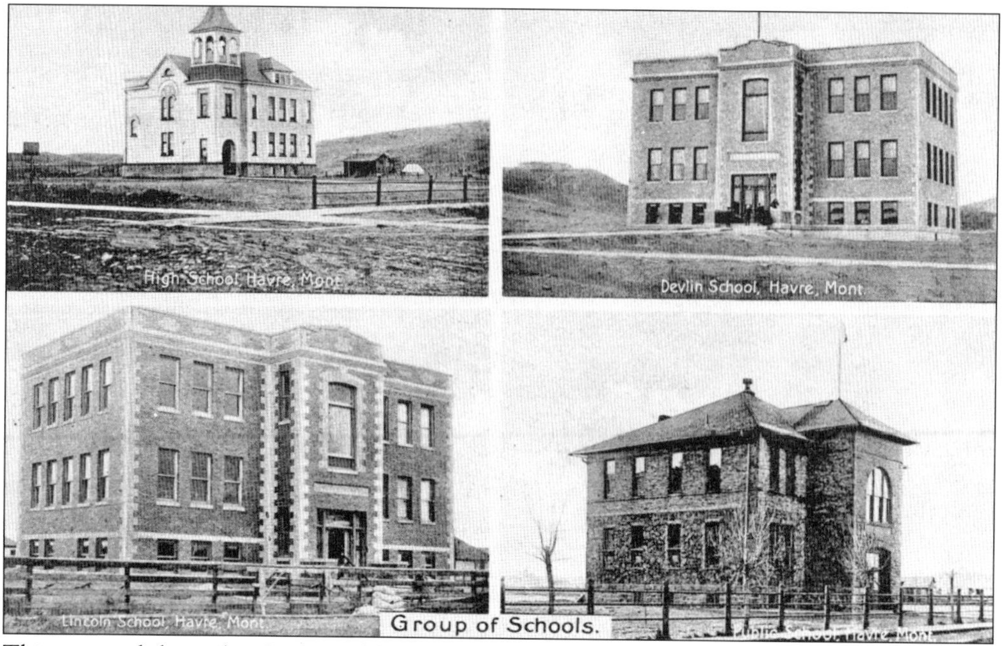

This postcard shows four Havre public schools. Going clockwise from top left, they are the first Havre High School (1909–1917); Devlin School (1912–1995); the neighboring McKinley School (also known as Public or East End school), built in 1902; and Lincoln School, also built in 1912 with Frank Bossout as the architect. Both Lincoln and McKinley were razed in 1953 to build the combined Lincoln-McKinley School, which opened in 1954. (Courtesy of Don Greytak.)

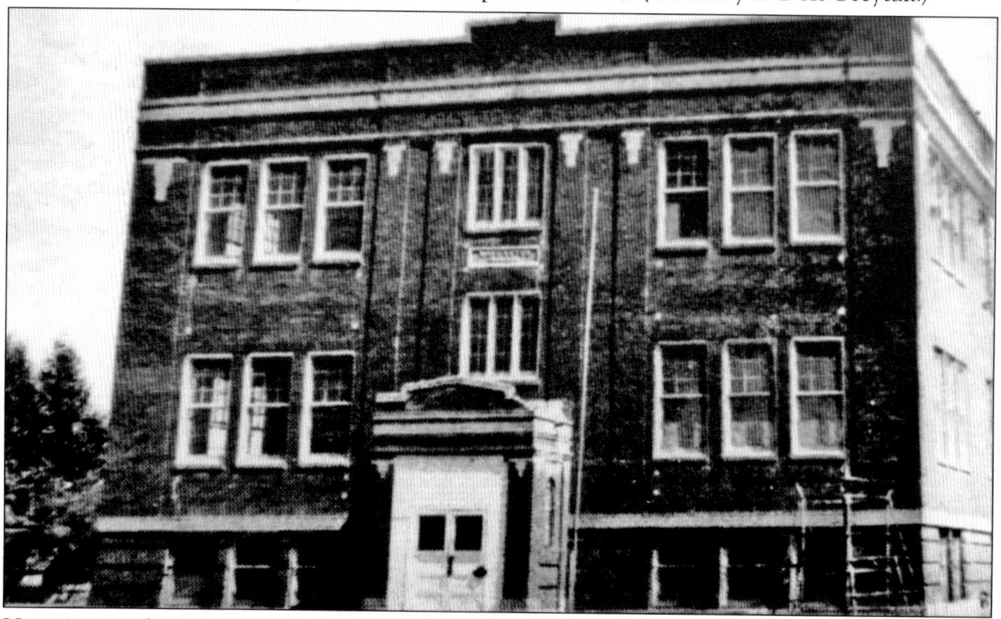

Havre's second Washington School was built in 1920 and served the educational needs of students on Havre's east end. It was located on the south side of Second Street and Fifteenth Avenue. Principals included Jessie Morris, Volborg Buckenberg, Inez Anderson, Gladys Dunham, Vendla Strum, and Joyce Kessinger. This Washington School was closed in 1974 and the structure was razed later that year. (Courtesy of High Line Heritage House.)

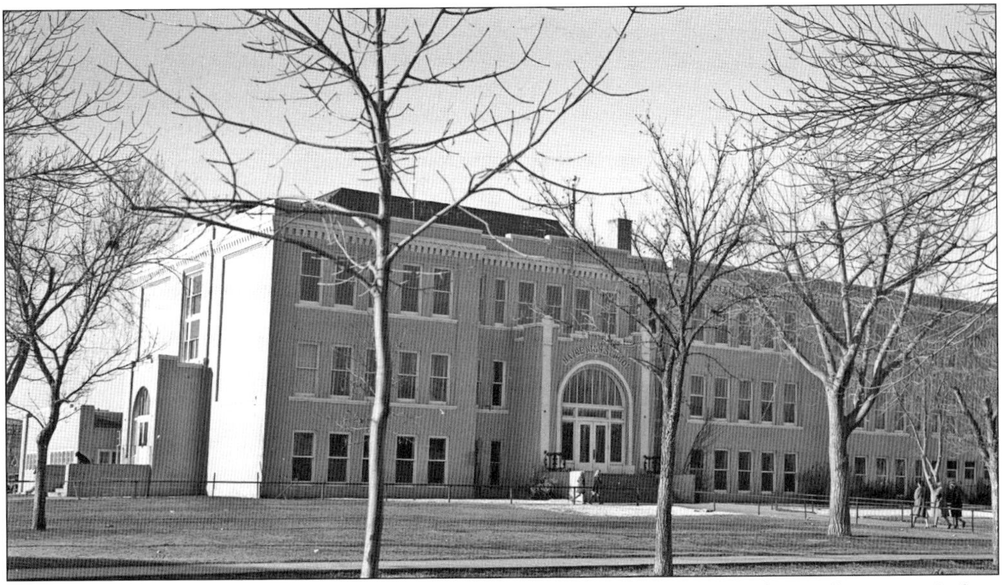

Plans for a new high school were underway when the first one burned. Frank Bossout's first design looked similar to the Hill County Courthouse, another one of his creations. The design was modified, and construction began on a new high school in 1918. It served in that capacity until 1964, when the current high school opened. The older school then became Havre Junior High until 1983, when a new school was completed. (Photograph by Frances Hulm, courtesy of Don Greytak.)

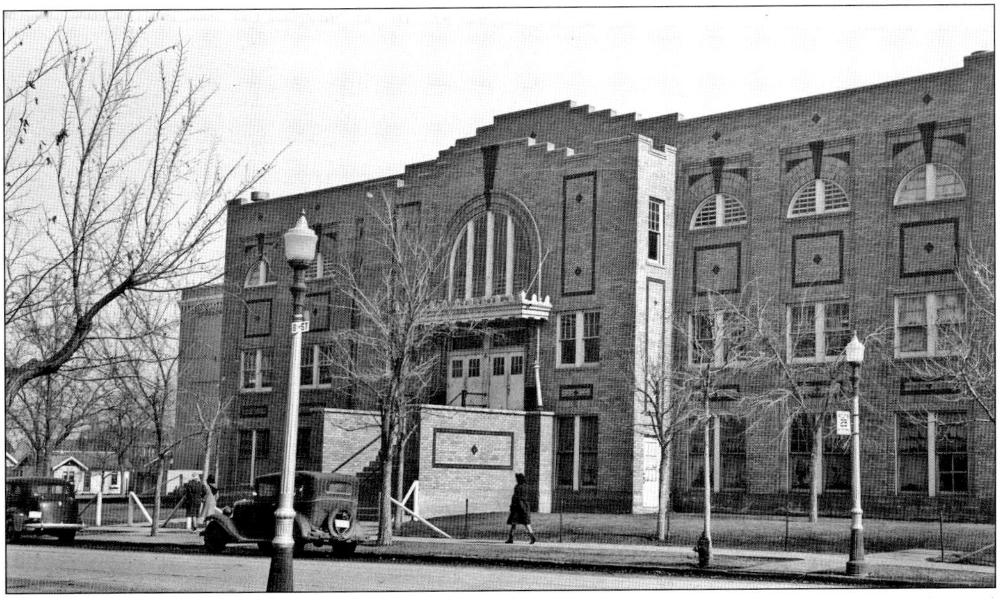

In 1928, a gymnasium was added to the second Havre High School. In addition to serving physical education classes and basketball games, a portion of the gymnasium was used for the domestic science classes. While the second high school was razed, this portion was retained in the hopes of using it as a community center. This plan did not materialize, and it was razed sometime in the 1990s. (Photograph by Frances Hulm, courtesy of Don Greytak.)

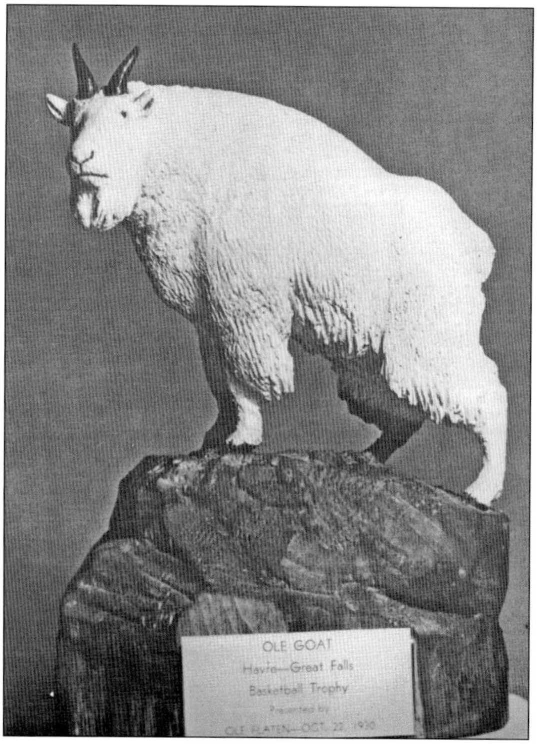

The Ole (pronounced "Oh-lee") Goat was carved by Blackfoot artist John Clarke and donated by local businessman Ole Flaten in 1930 as the trophy between the Havre and Great Falls High boys' basketball teams. Both season games must be won in order to win the trophy. The last time Havre won the Ole Goat was 1992. (Courtesy of High Line Heritage House.)

Mary Ashline served as clerk at Havre High School for many years. She also served as secretary of the Havre School Board of Trustees as part of her duties as clerk. She filled this position in the 1940s and the 1950s and was responsible for a smoothly running office for faculty, staff, students, parents, and visitors. Those who remember her speak highly of her to this day. (Photograph by Frances Hulm, courtesy of Don Greytak.)

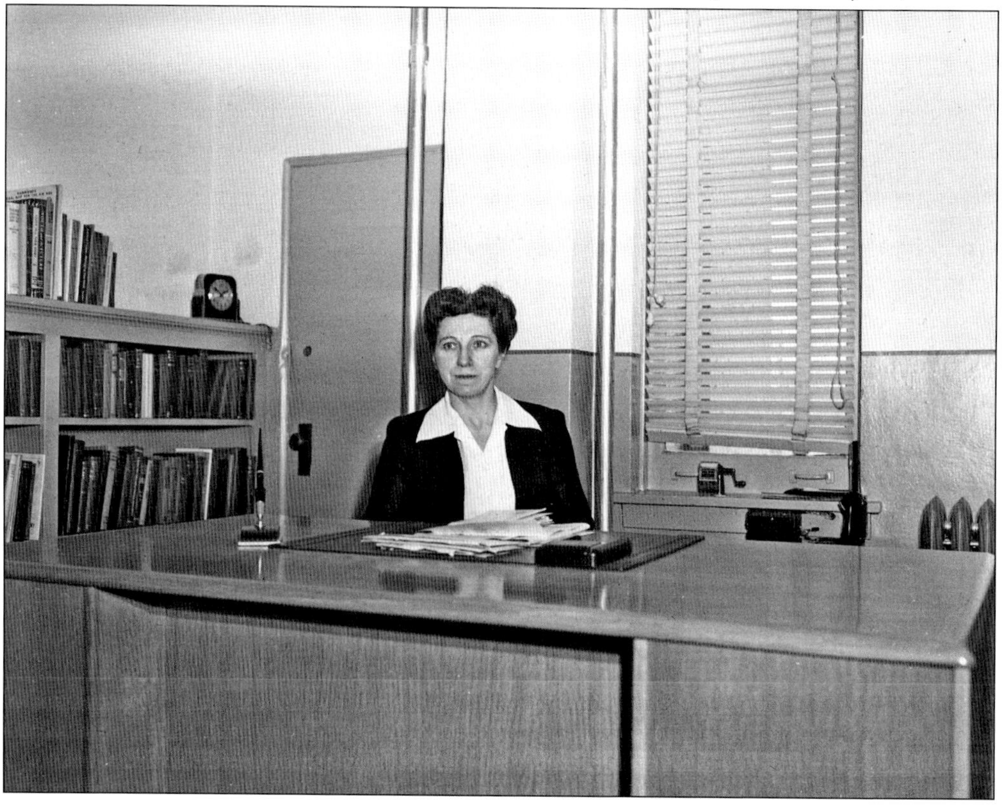

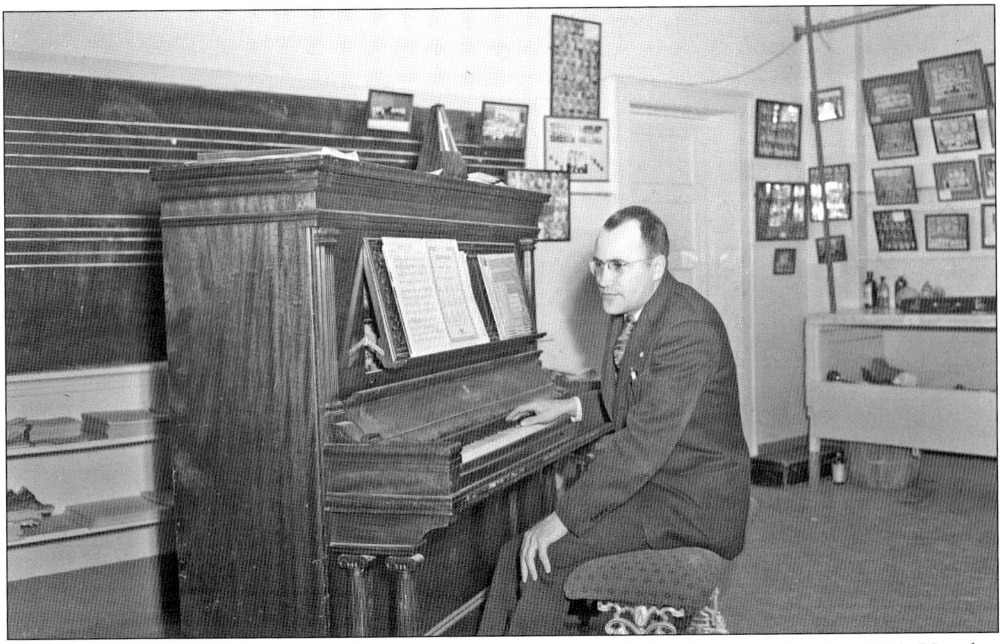

Clifford I. Carlson was the band director at Havre High School, beginning in 1946. He also served as band director of Havre Junior High School. Under his instruction, the Havre High School band became one of the best in the entire state. Carlson retired from teaching in 1973 and served the community in various capacities until his death in 1998. (Photograph by Frances Hulm, courtesy of Don Greytak.)

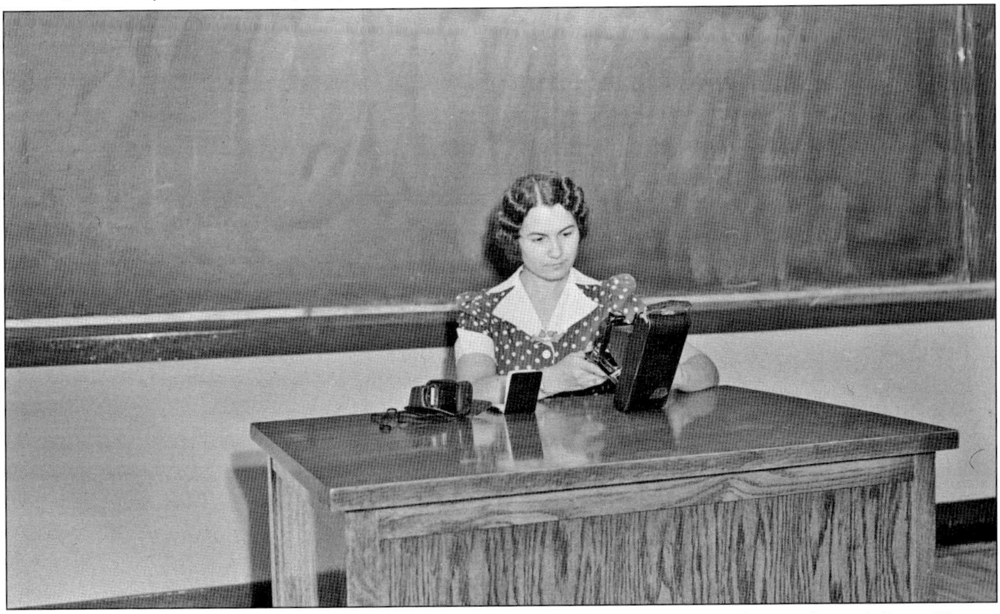

Frances Hulm was born in North Dakota and later moved to Havre. She graduated from Havre High School in 1929, taught at Havre High School for 16 years, and was responsible for the pictures in the *Blue Pony* annual, except for portraits, for 10 of those years. She also served as a mechanic during World War II. In 1956, Hulm married Walter Kralich in Great Falls, Montana. She passed away in 1997. (Photograph by Frances Hulm, courtesy of Don Greytak.)

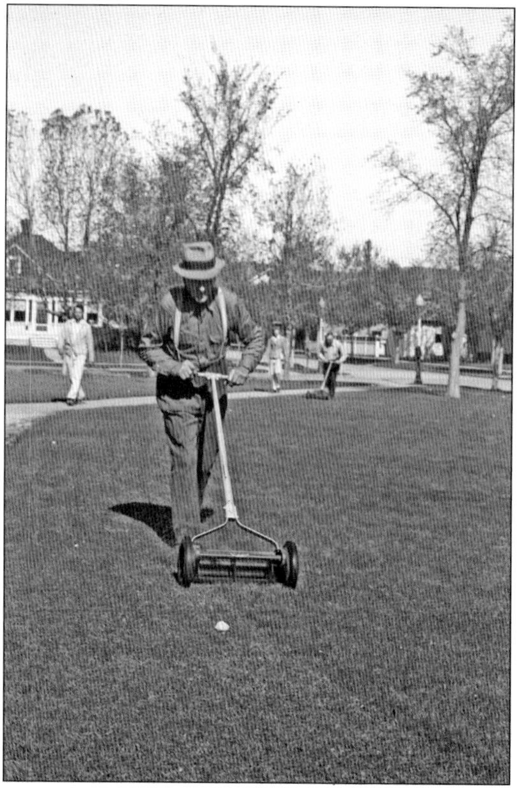

Two of Havre High School's janitorial staff mow the lawn in 1941 with reel-type mowers. The janitorial staff was responsible for the upkeep of both buildings and grounds. Duties included cleaning classrooms, offices, hallways, restrooms, the auditorium, and gymnasium, moving desks and other furnishings as needed, mowing during warm weather, and removing snow during winter. Their work helps ensure a clean and safe learning environment for students and staff. (Photograph by Frances Hulm, courtesy of Don Greytak.)

One of the home economics teachers demonstrates cooking with a double boiler at Havre High School in 1941. Gender roles were more traditional during this time, with girls required to take a certain number of credits in home economics, while boys had to take various shop classes. It was not until the latter part of the 20th century that court action on Title IX cases relaxed the rules. (Photograph by Frances Hulm, courtesy of Don Greytak.)

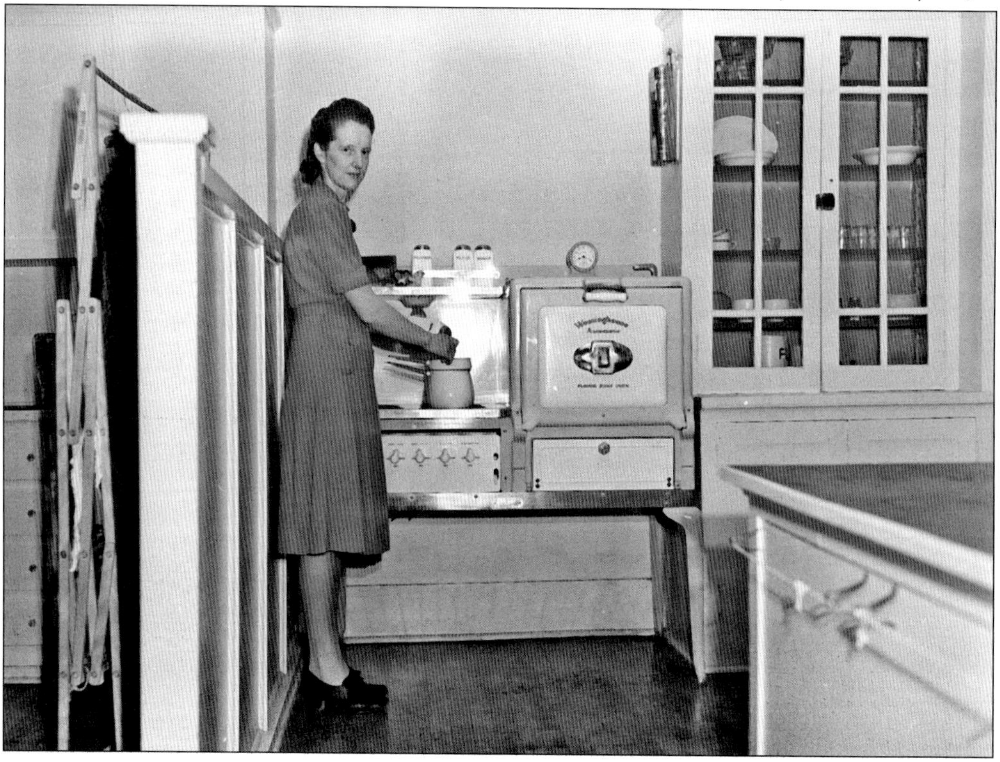

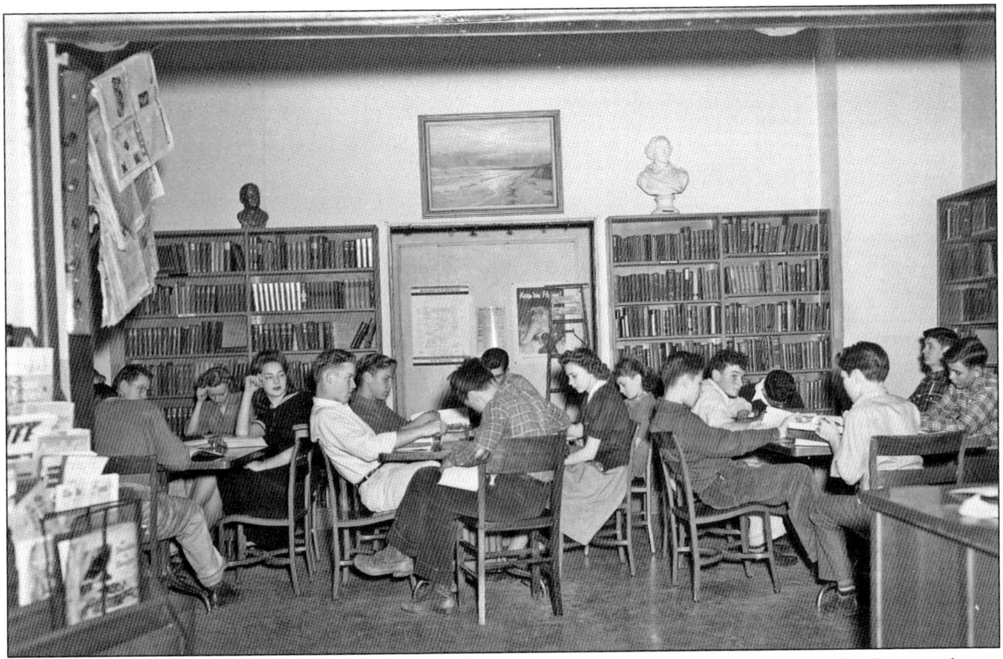

It must be test time in December 1941, as the Inner Library of Havre High School looks very busy. Libraries, both in school and in the community, were very important to parents and community members, who even during Havre's infancy stressed education and learning as an important part of Havre's offerings. (Photograph by Frances Hulm, courtesy of Don Greytak.)

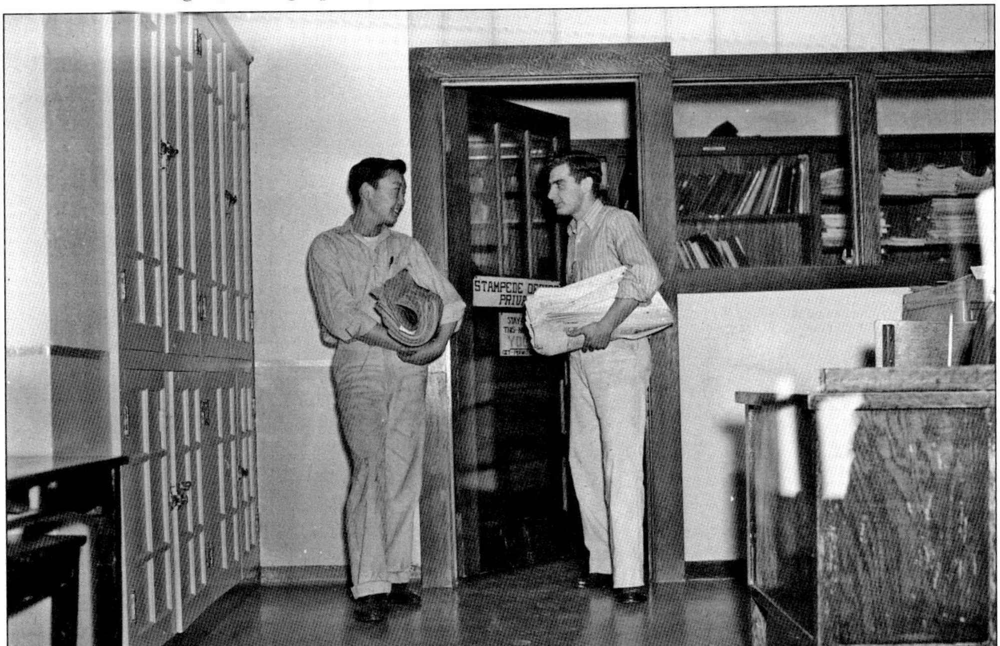

Kenneth Nepnuma (left) and Frank DeRosa are getting ready to deliver the latest edition of the *Stampede*, the student newspaper for Havre High School. The *Stampede* staff often works on the annual, and both give students the opportunity to experience what it takes to create publications and work on a deadline. (Photograph by Frances Hulm, courtesy of Don Greytak.)

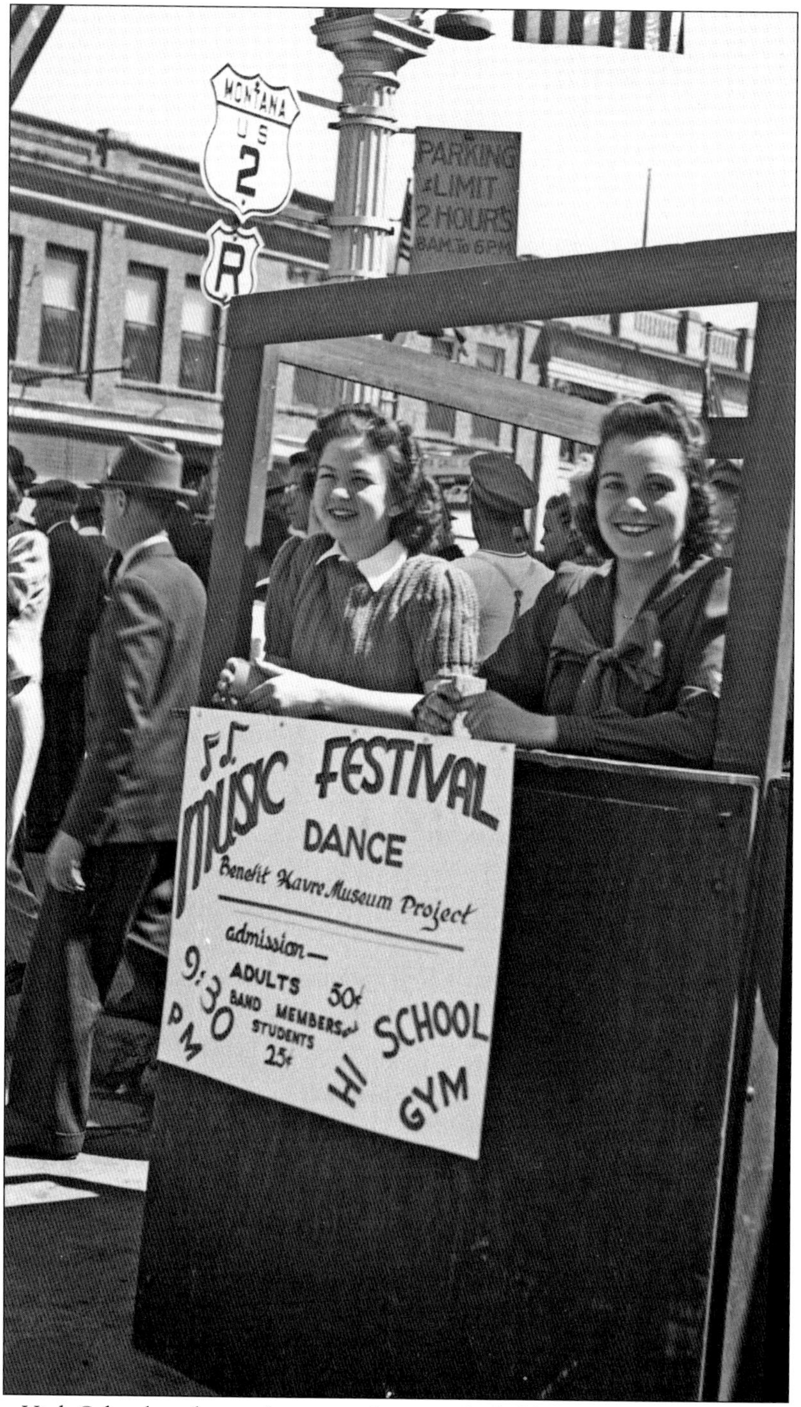

Two Havre High School students advertise a dance to be held at Havre High School during the Havre Music Festival on May 10, 1941. Dances were a popular social activity at Havre High, and several were held during the school year. Admission would raise money for class projects—in this case, a Havre Museum. This dance also happened to be for adults, students, and band members attending the festival. (Photograph by Frances Hulm, courtesy of Don Greytak.)

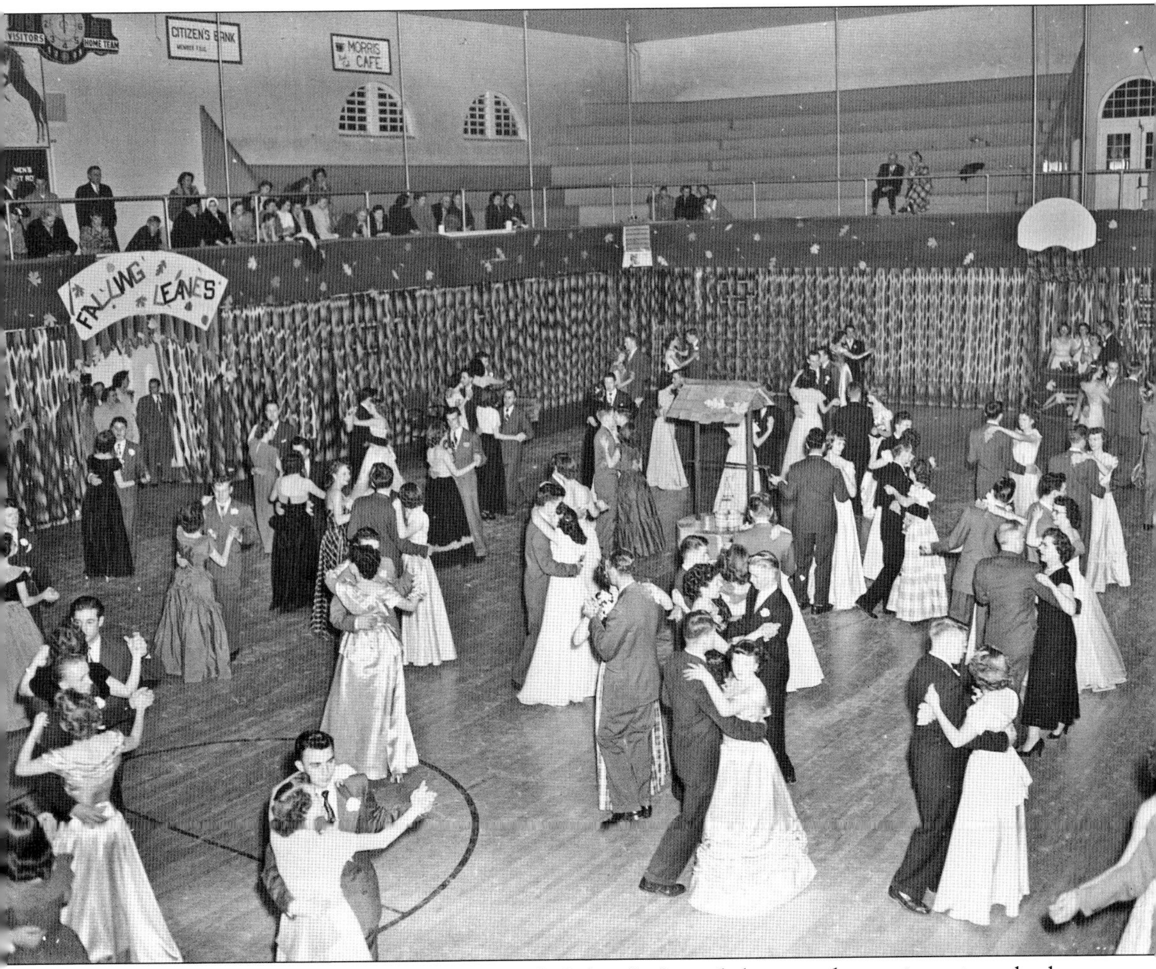

On November 19, 1949, one of Havre High School's formal dances, the senior soiree, had a theme of "Falling Leaves." Students danced with their partners under the watchful eyes of the chaperones sitting in the upper seats, carefully making sure they were adhering to social rules at the time, doing nothing untoward enough to get them removed from the celebration. (Photograph by Frances Hulm, courtesy of Don Greytak.)

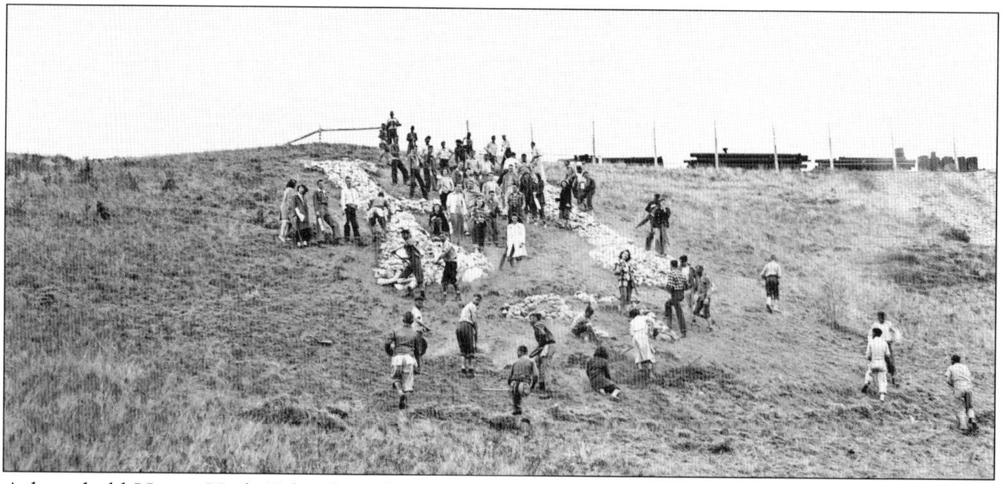

A long-held Havre High School tradition is to paint rocks that have been arranged in an "H" overlooking the football field in West Havre. Traditionally, senior students make the trek in time for the start of football season. This activity took place on September 1, 1946, as pictured here. In 1964, the tradition moved to the side of Saddle Butte, with the opening of the current Havre High School. (Photograph by Frances Hulm, courtesy of Don Greytak.)

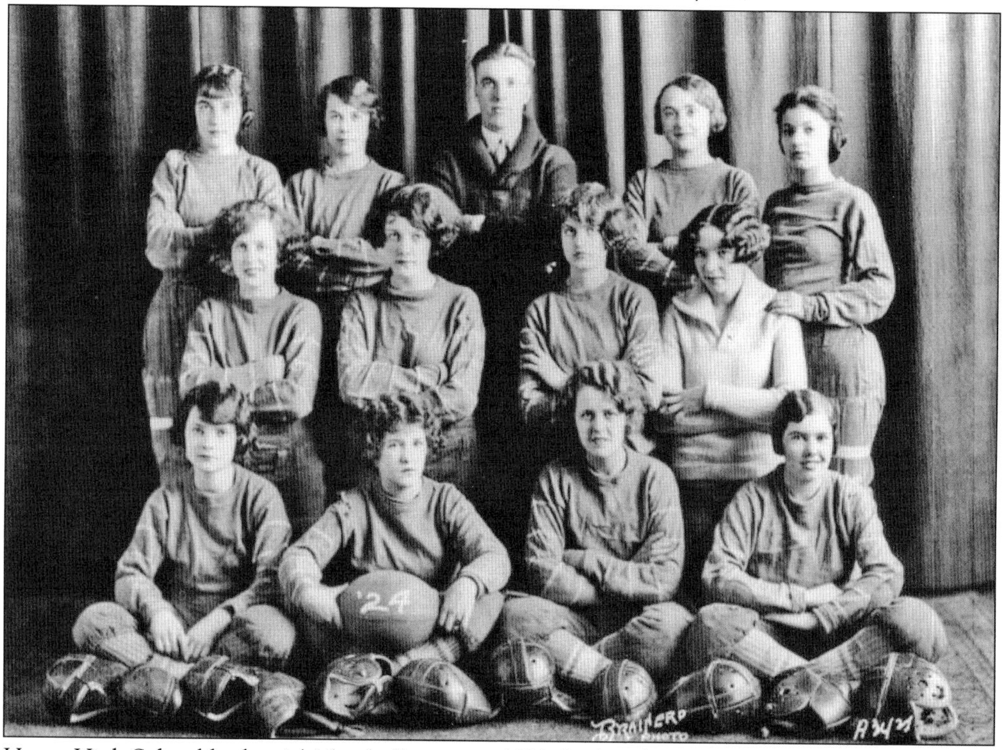

Havre High School had a girls' football team in 1924. It played one game against Big Sandy and won 7-6, but the team disbanded due to lack of local interest. Pictured here are, from left to right, (first row) Hazel Anderson, Kathryn Mathews, Virginia Olsen, and Kathleen Barrett; (second row) Corrine Loranger, Janet MacKenzie, Esther Skylstead, and Josephine Broadwater; (third row) Veva Brewer, Helen Emery, coach Dave Morris, Josie Anderson, and Alta Boynton. (Courtesy of High Line Heritage House.)

Prior to tearing down the second Havre High School in 1984, the class of 1984 had the foresight to preserve this custom-designed symbol of the school's mascot, a blue pony, by having it removed and framed, later donating it to the current high school. It hangs on the West Lobby wall. (Photograph by the author, courtesy of High Line Heritage House.)

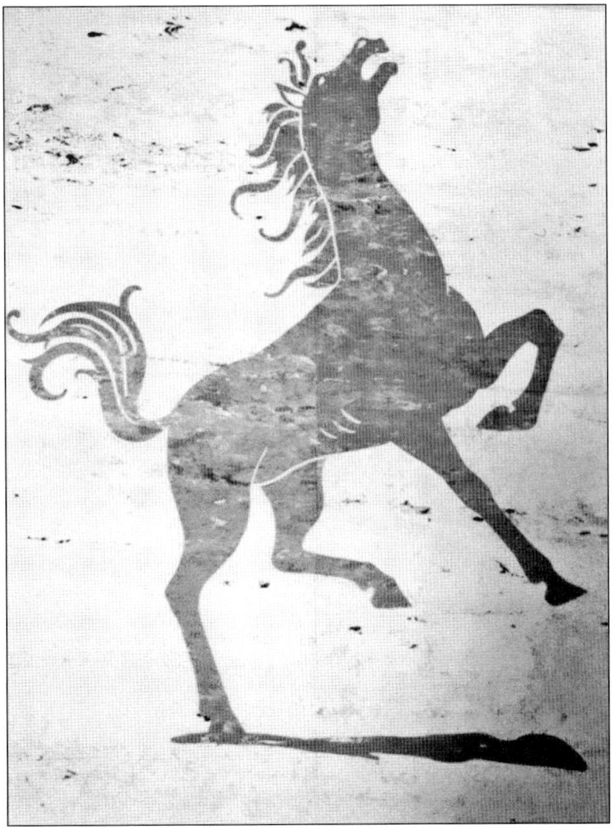

The second Havre High School also played host to the first classes of Northern Montana College. At the time this photograph of the 1947 track team was taken, Northern was a part of the University of Montana system. It was founded in 1929, and Havre's support of Northern was so strong that it operated out of different buildings until classrooms and dorms could be acquired for the fledgling college. (Photograph by Frances Hulm, courtesy of Don Greytak.)

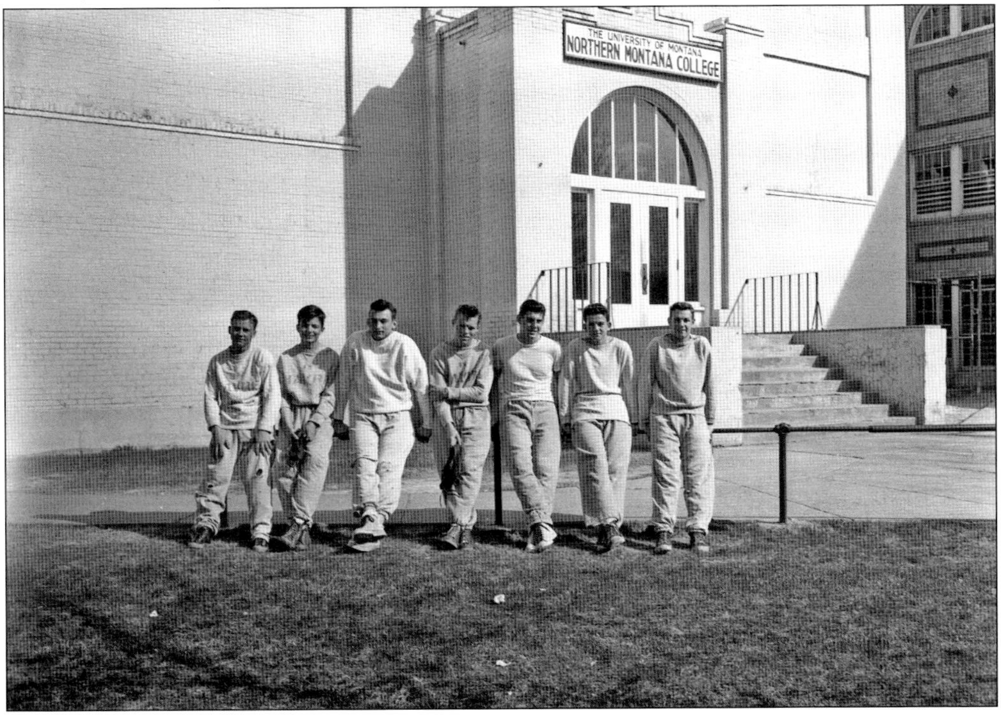

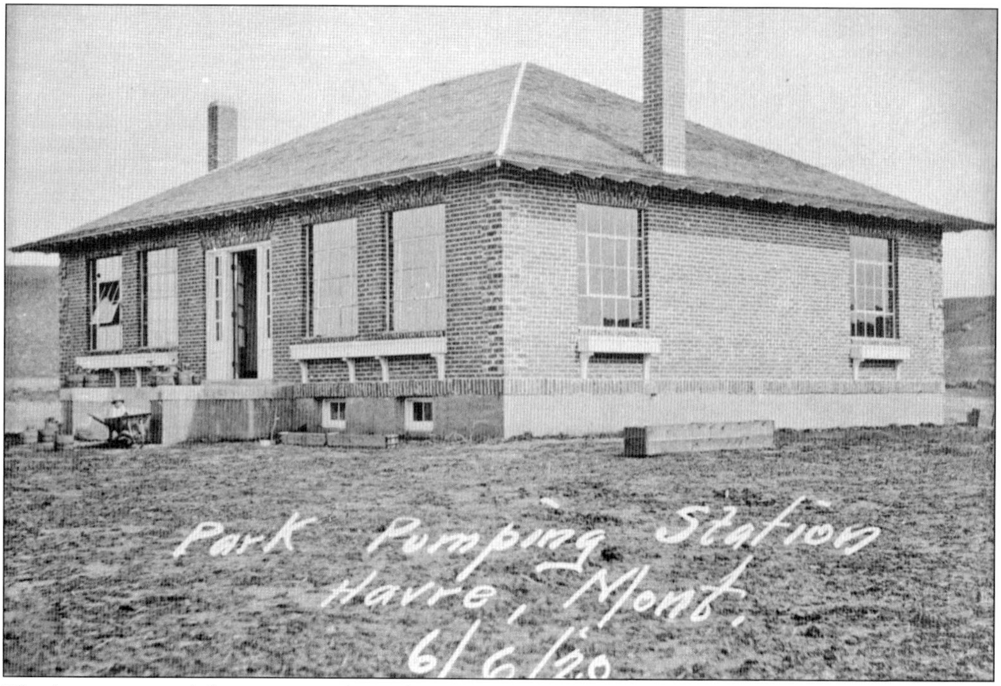

The beginnings of the campus of Northern Montana College were modest. The City of Havre had purchased a little over 44 acres that had previously been a slaughterhouse and stockyards for the Pioneer Meat Market. In 1919, the city constructed this pump house, with two levels underground and a Gould's Triplex water pump supplying water for the city's use. (Courtesy of Don Greytak.)

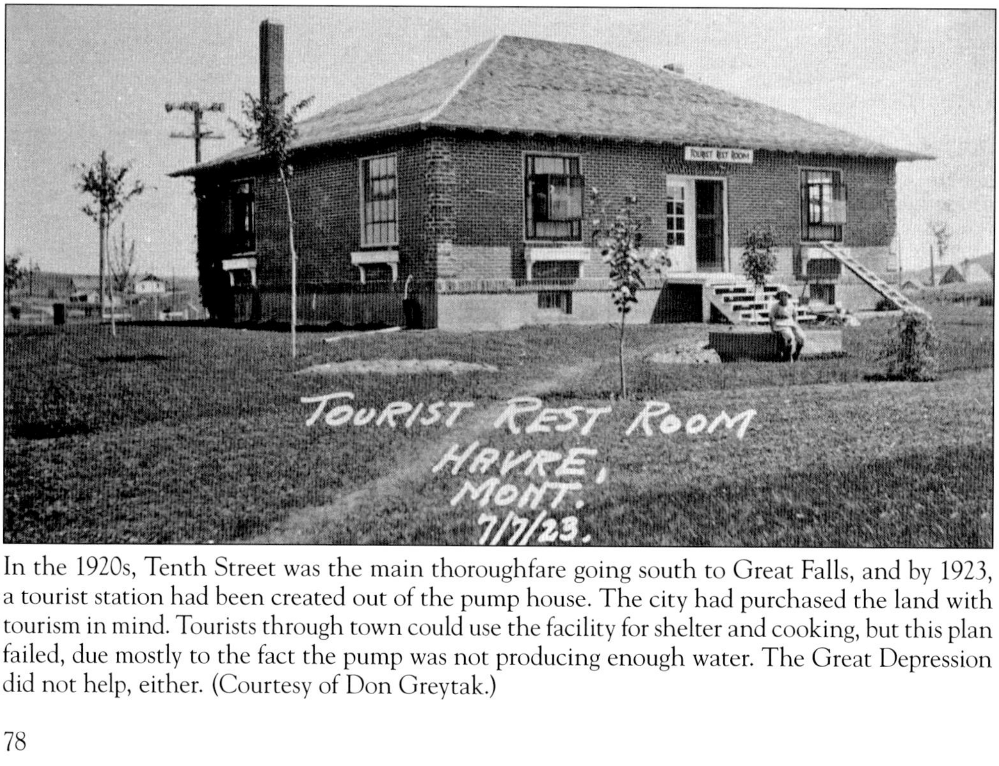

In the 1920s, Tenth Street was the main thoroughfare going south to Great Falls, and by 1923, a tourist station had been created out of the pump house. The city had purchased the land with tourism in mind. Tourists through town could use the facility for shelter and cooking, but this plan failed, due mostly to the fact the pump was not producing enough water. The Great Depression did not help, either. (Courtesy of Don Greytak.)

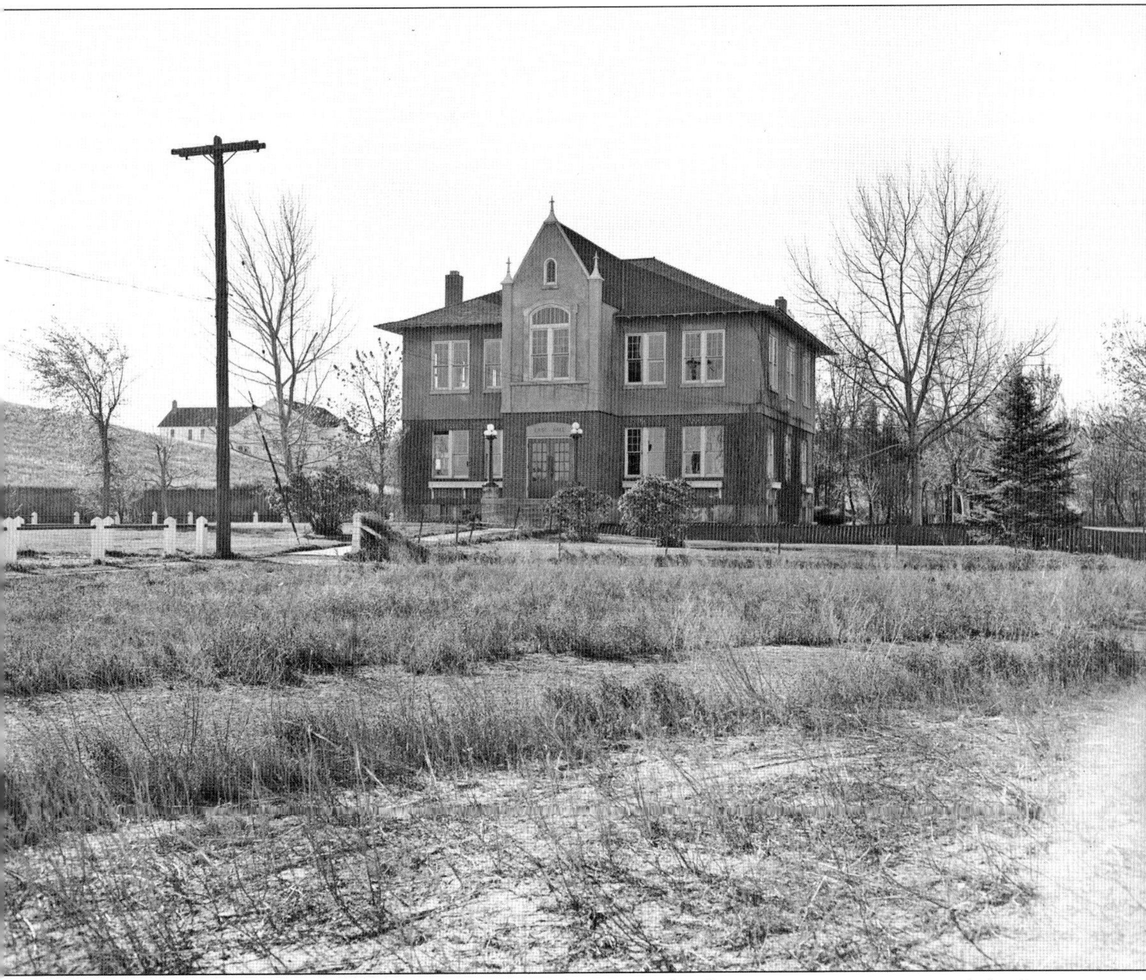

Havre architect Frank Bossout went to work redesigning the former tourist station, and the Lou Eskestrand Construction Company executed those plans. The walls were raised, new windows were added, and Northern's East Hall, the first building on campus, was ready for students in 1932. However, the building's structure began to fail over the years. It was used for storage in 1965 and razed in 1980. (Photograph by Frances Hulm, courtesy of Don Greytak.)

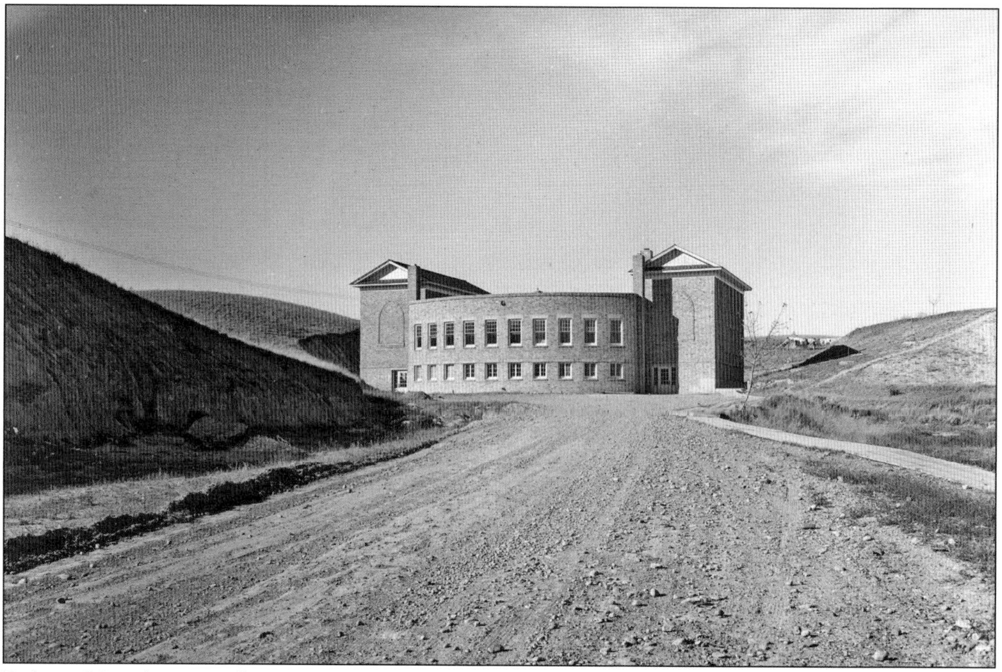

Beloved Pershing Hall, named after Gen. John Pershing, who had been stationed at Fort Assinniboine, south of Havre, was Northern's second building. It was constructed in 1933 out of brick salvaged at Fort Assinniboine and was designed by Frank Bossout. The first on-campus gradation took place in 1934 at the stage in back of Pershing Hall. In 1953, the open-air stage was enclosed to accommodate more classroom space. (Photograph by Frances Hulm, courtesy of Don Greytak.)

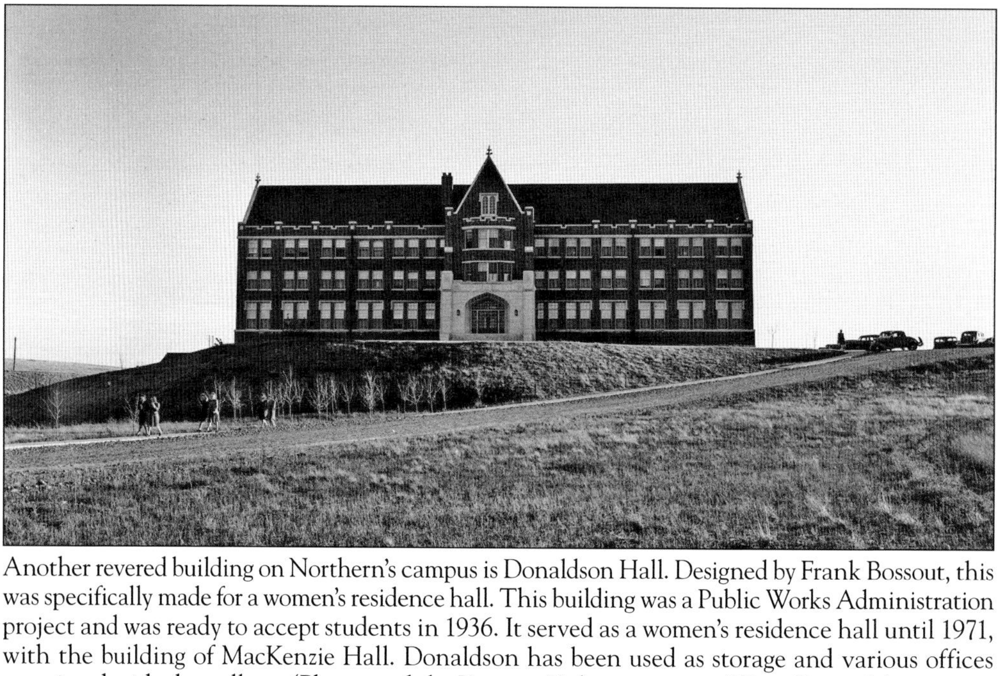

Another revered building on Northern's campus is Donaldson Hall. Designed by Frank Bossout, this was specifically made for a women's residence hall. This building was a Public Works Administration project and was ready to accept students in 1936. It served as a women's residence hall until 1971, with the building of MacKenzie Hall. Donaldson has been used as storage and various offices associated with the college. (Photograph by Frances Hulm, courtesy of Don Greytak.)

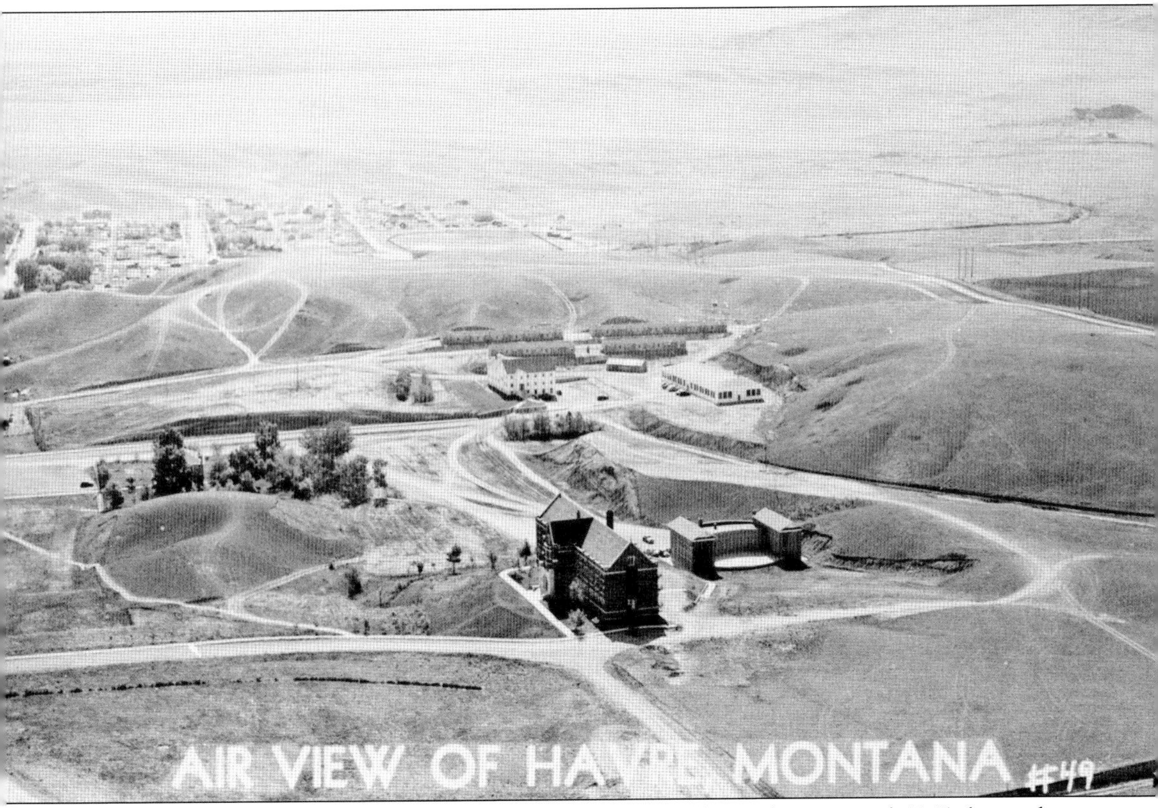

This aerial view of the campus of Northern Montana College taken around 1945 shows the proximity of the campus's buildings, as well as Pershing Hall's open stage. New buildings were added in subsequent years, but two are no longer in existence—the white, three-story men's co-op building (formerly the Hill County Poor Farm) and East Hall. (Courtesy of Don Greytak.)

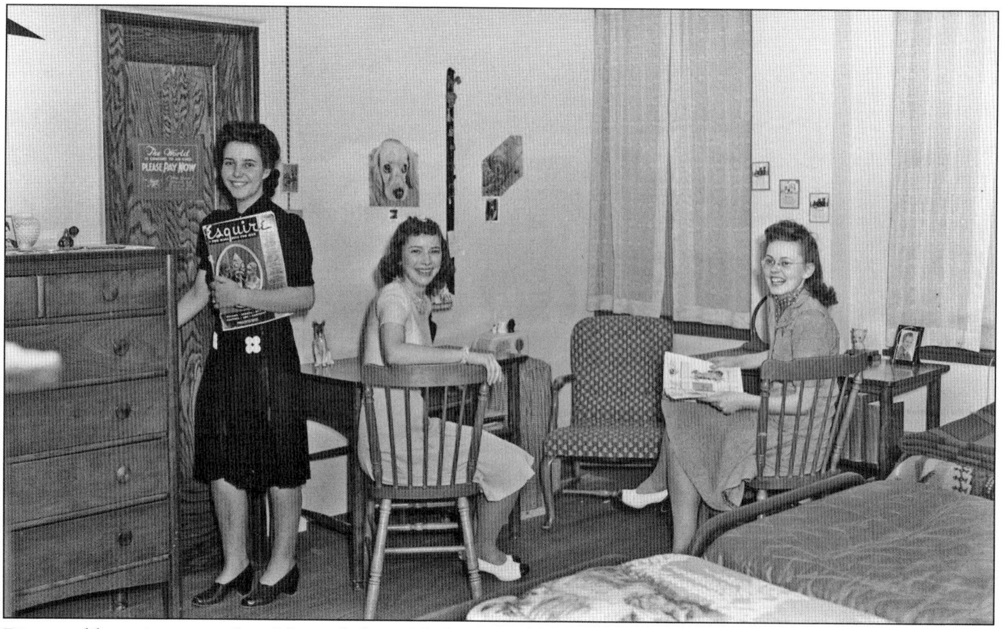

Pictured here is a sample of dorm life in 1942. Donaldson Hall provided rooms for 116 women and also had the campus's first dining hall. Few rooms, if any, were reserved for only one student. This photograph shows three twin beds in the room, allowing for very little privacy. Note the everyday dress of the students—no flip-flops or workout clothes back then. (Photograph by Frances Hulm, courtesy of Don Greytak.)

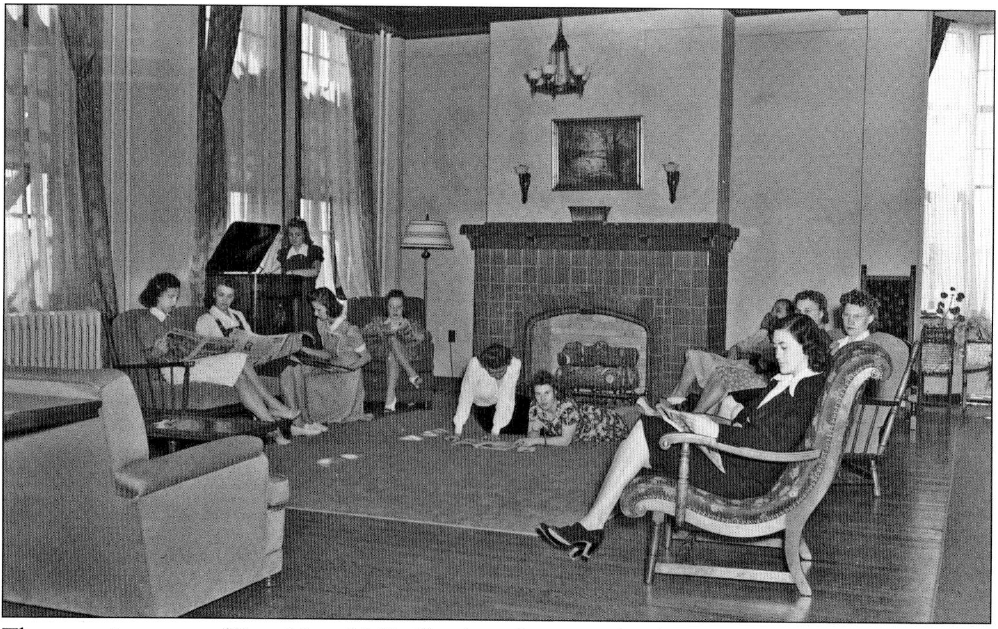

The reception room of Donaldson Hall offered an elegant and welcoming atmosphere for residents and visitors. It has also been referred to as a living room. In 1984, the alumni association raised funds to restore this room. Its renovation was successful, and the site has seen many fundraisers and retirement parties and received former president Bill Clinton on his visit to Havre in 2008. (Photograph by Frances Hulm, courtesy of Don Greytak.)

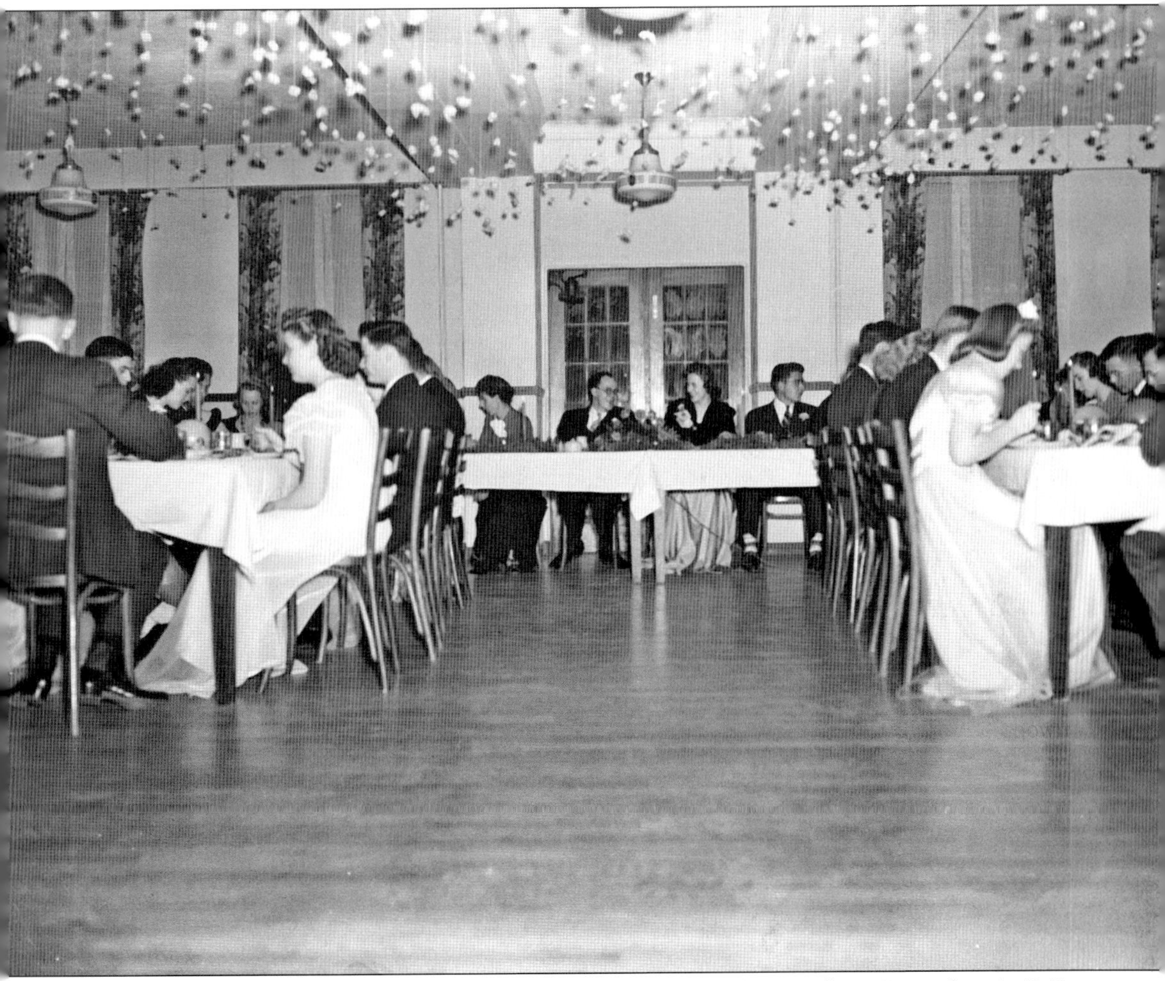

The sophomore formal dinner and dance took place in Donaldson Hall on December 6, 1941. Donaldson Hall was designed with rooms for just such occasions, which were popular during this era. Of particular note are the Art Deco lamps hanging from the ceiling. While Donaldson is a building evoking Gothic Revival–style elements, the interior contained many Art Deco trimmings, popular in the 1930s. (Photograph by Frances Hulm, courtesy of Don Greytak.)

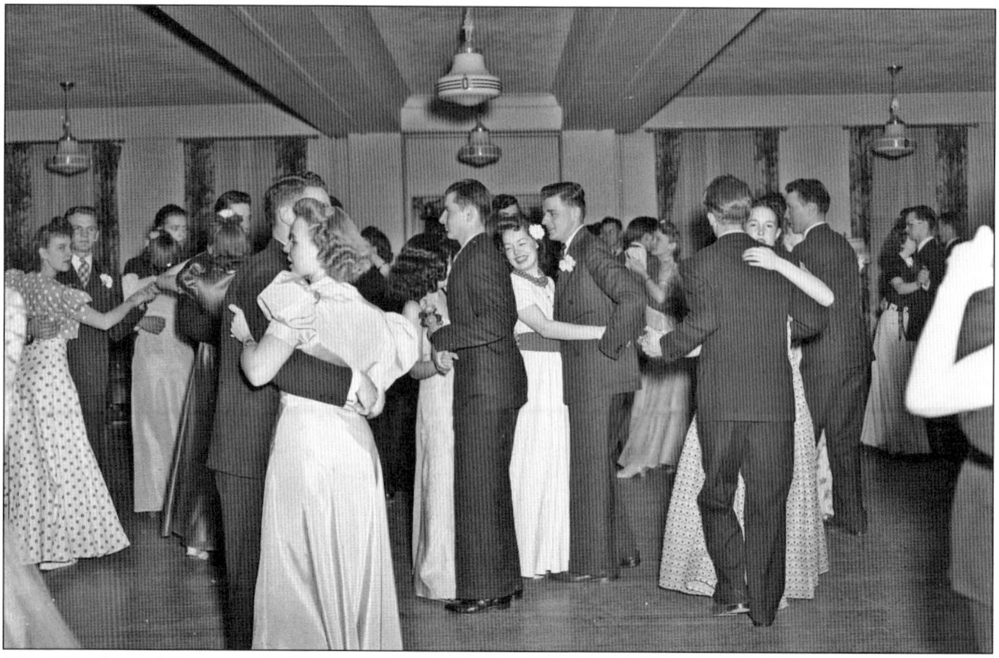

The Northern Montana College spring dorm formal took place at Donaldson Hall on April 10, 1942. These dances were a little more cozy than those of the high school, but proper decorum was still at the forefront at these functions. The large beams on the ceiling give a hint as to the construction of Donaldson Hall. (Photograph by Frances Hulm, courtesy of Don Greytak.)

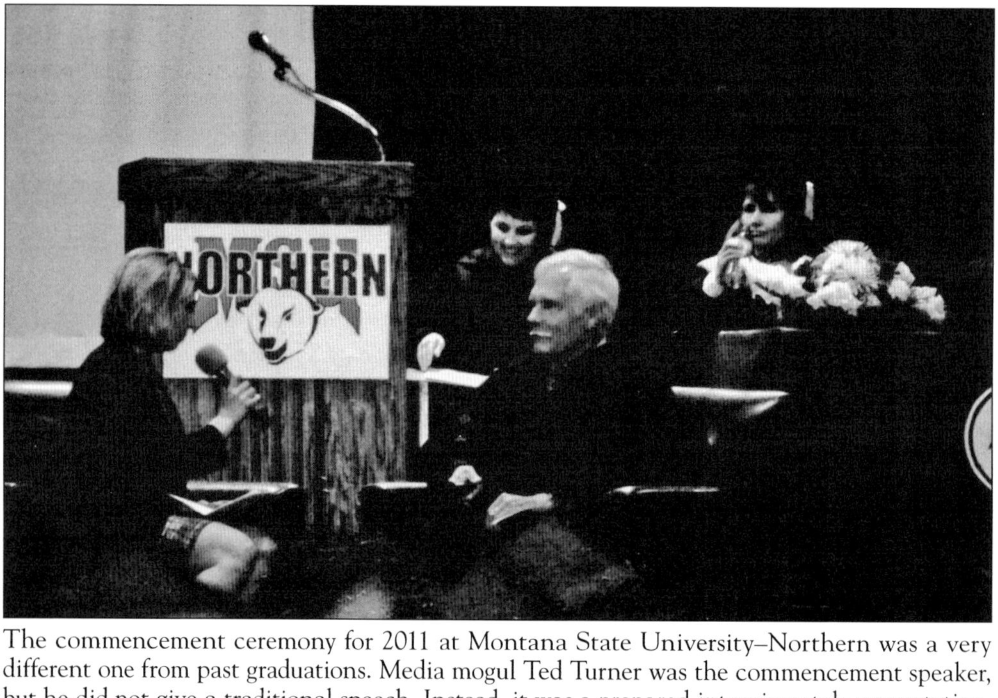

The commencement ceremony for 2011 at Montana State University–Northern was a very different one from past graduations. Media mogul Ted Turner was the commencement speaker, but he did not give a traditional speech. Instead, it was a prepared interview-style presentation, well received by the students and soon-to-be graduates. (Photograph by the author, courtesy of High Line Heritage House.)

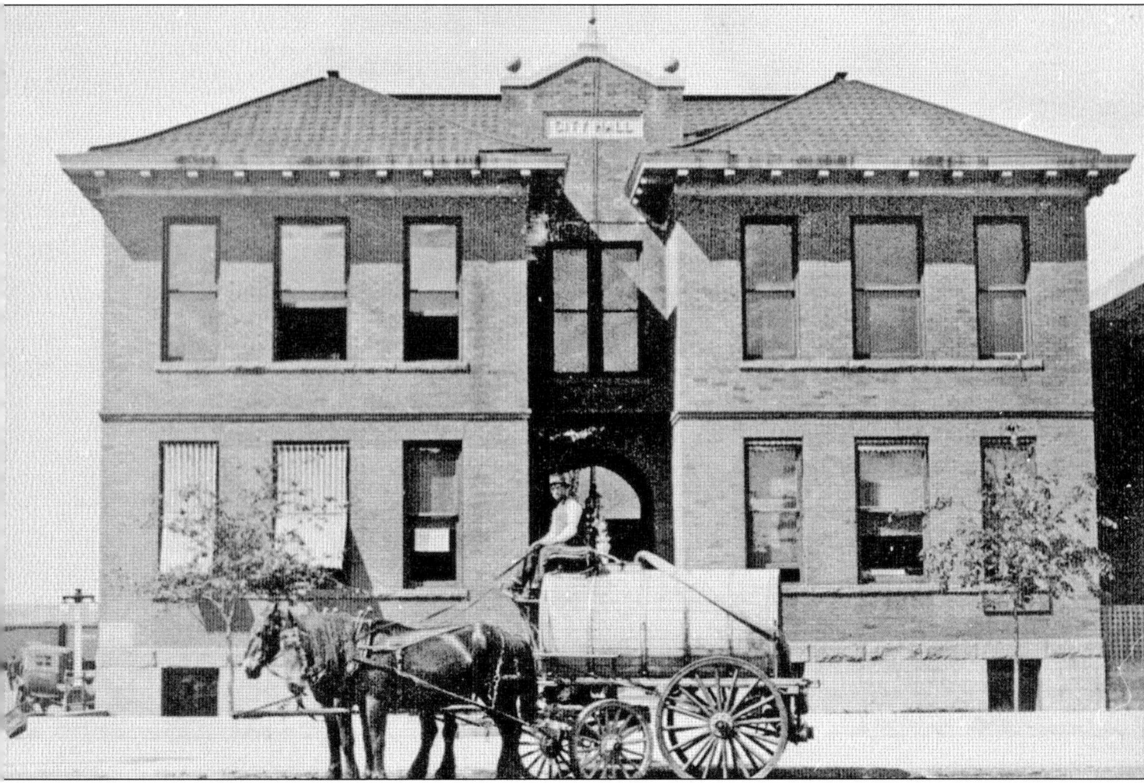

Havre was incorporated in 1893, and its meetings took place in a wooden building, razed in the 1950s. In 1907, the cornerstone of a new city hall was laid with great fanfare by the city council. It was designed by Frank Bossout and contained offices for city council, the mayor, city court, and the fire department. It was occupied from 1908 to 1971 and razed later that year. (Courtesy of Don Greytak.)

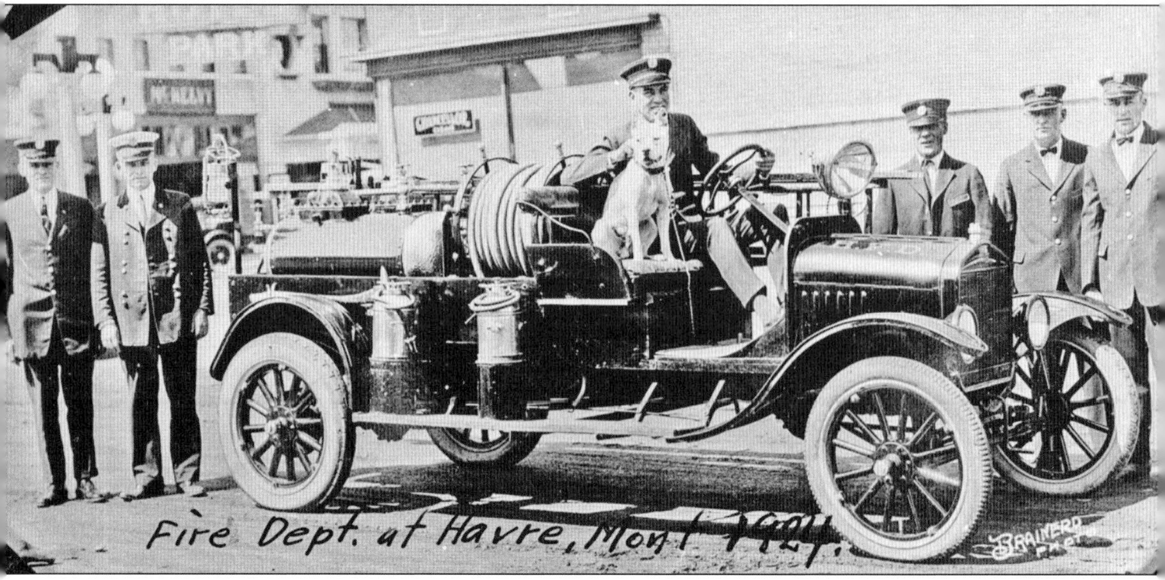

Havre's fire department was formed after the great fire of 1904. Prior to the incident, the fire department had been a volunteer one. With a professional fire department came better service. Created in 1905, the Havre Fire Department is pictured here in 1924 with its 1919 American LaFrance fire engine and the department's beloved American bull terrier, Mike. (Courtesy of Don Greytak.)

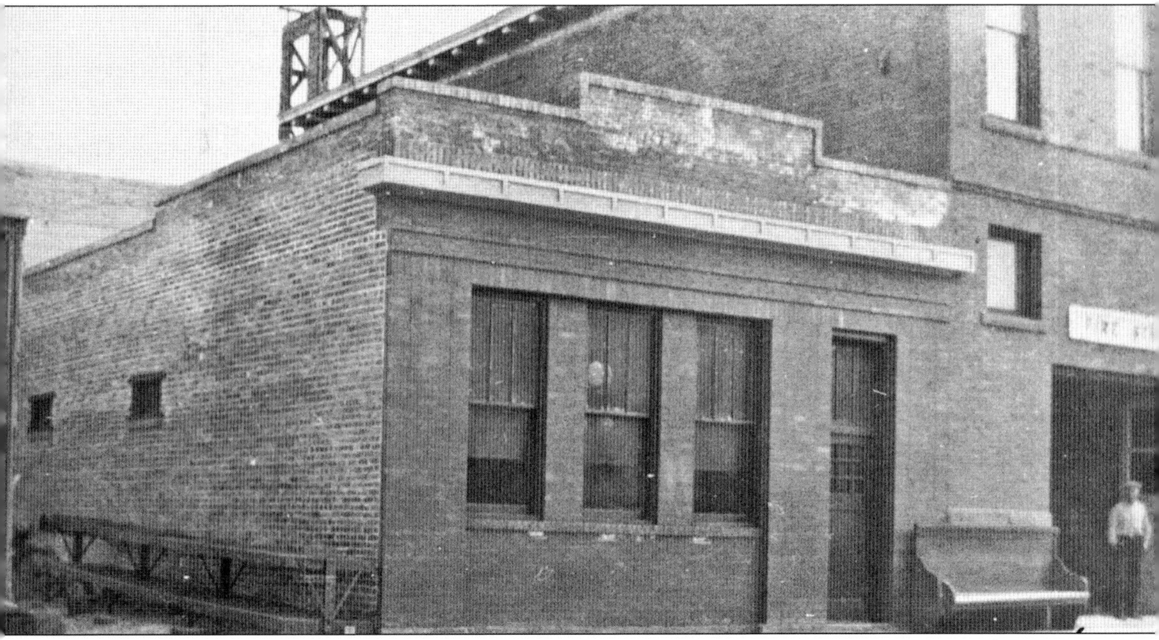

Havre's jails have long been an issue. The first was found in a wooden building, with conditions so deplorable it was described as "Hotel des Rats" by local newspapers. The 1908 city hall had plans for a four-cell jail in the basement, but it did not come to fruition. In 1916, the city leased the former DesRosier and Newman Mercantile as a jail, but in 1924, one was added to city hall (pictured). (Courtesy of Don Greytak.)

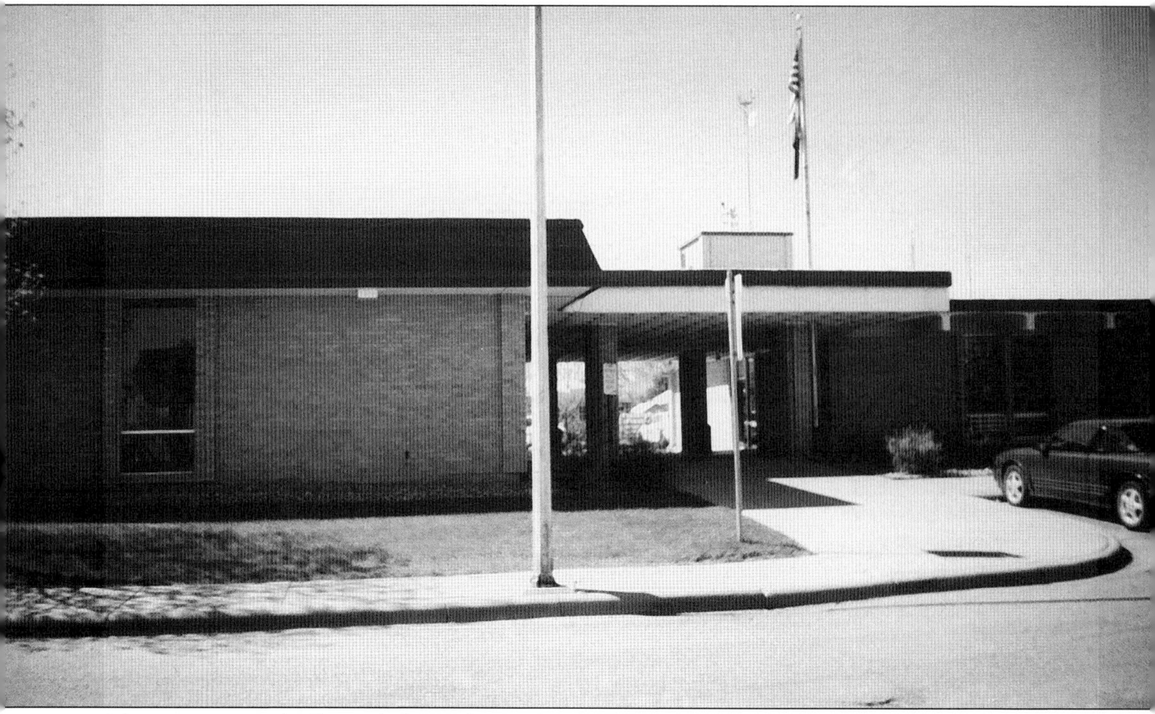

The current city hall was dedicated June 30, 1971, and includes city offices, public works, parks and recreation, the fire department, police, and a jail in one complex. It was designed by Max E. Kuhr and evokes the modernist style of architecture of its time. Interior plans included an open concept, but over time and due to security concerns, new walls have been constructed. A pitched roof was added in 2007. (Photograph by the author, courtesy of High Line Heritage House.)

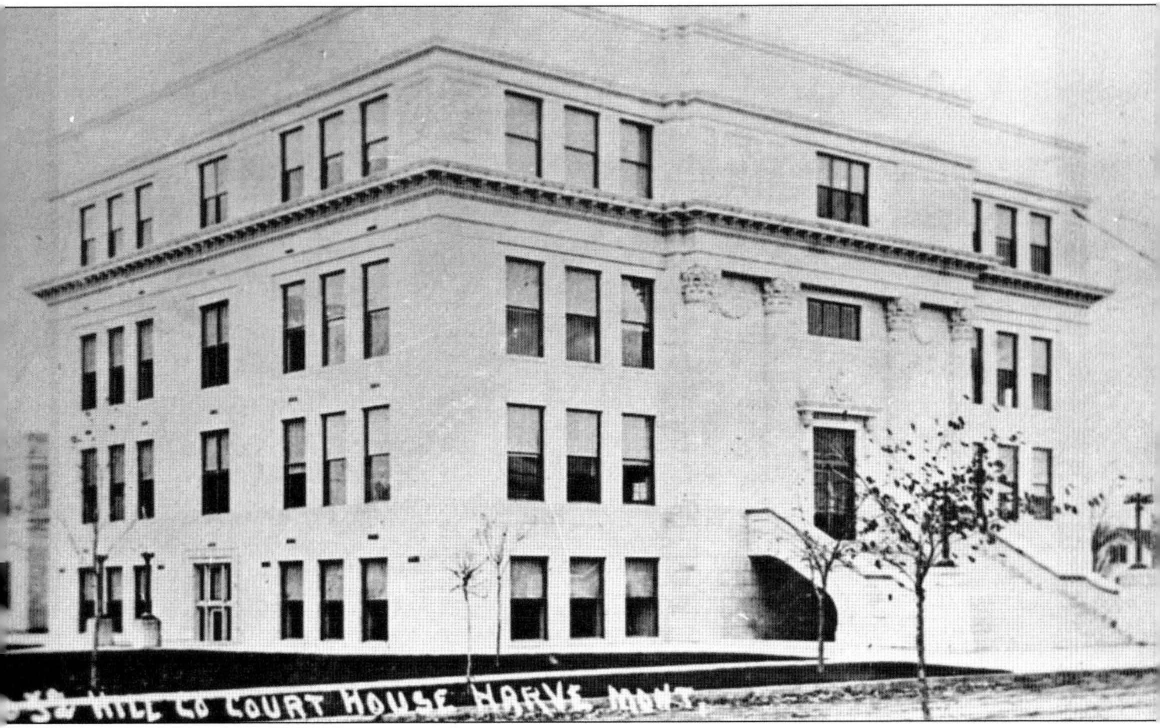

In November 1914, a bond issue to build a courthouse for Hill County passed by a mere 11 votes. Frank Bossout designed it in the Beaux-Arts style, and the courthouse is considered to be one of the best examples of this architecture in the entire state. It features Kasota stone, four levels, and an open atrium capped by a rotunda. The Oden Oyen Company from Wisconsin was hired to do interior design work. (Courtesy of Don Greytak.)

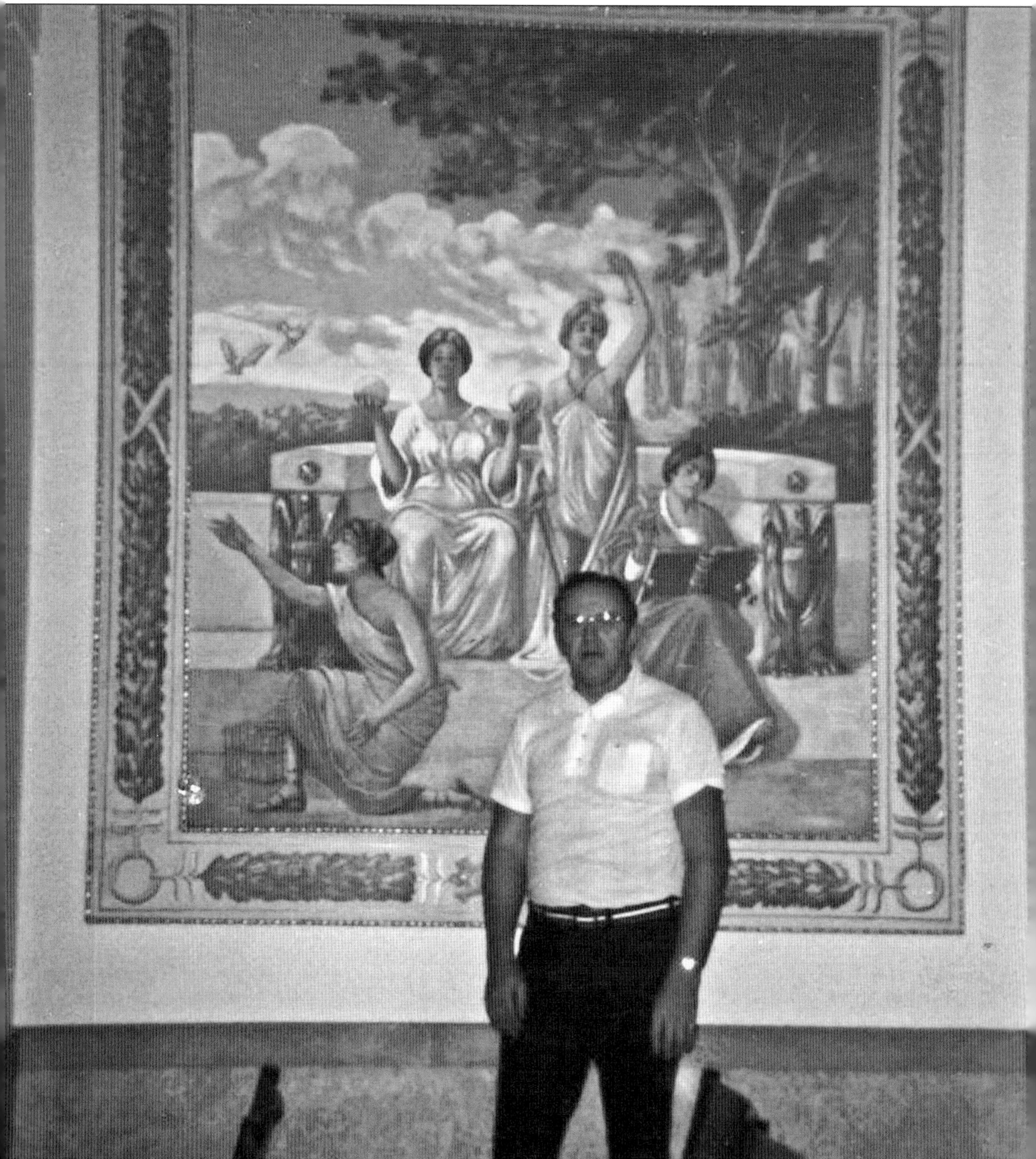

In 1963, the commissioners decided that the courthouse needed an interior face-lift. By then, the building was nearly 50 years old and showing its age. Additionally, the centennial of Montana Territory was on its way, and the commissioners wanted to do something special. Arvid "Chris" Kristoffersen was hired to paint murals and borders throughout the courthouse. He is pictured here with his mural on the third floor. (Courtesy of Arvid Kristoffersen.)

Few images exist of the Hill County Courthouse's interior prior to the 1977 remodel that took away the atrium and covered up the rotunda. This photograph gives a glimpse of what the open atrium looked like, as well as some of Kristoffersen's beautiful borders. Scaffolding was necessary for him to complete many of his designs, which took two winters and one summer to complete. (Courtesy of Arvid Kristoffersen.)

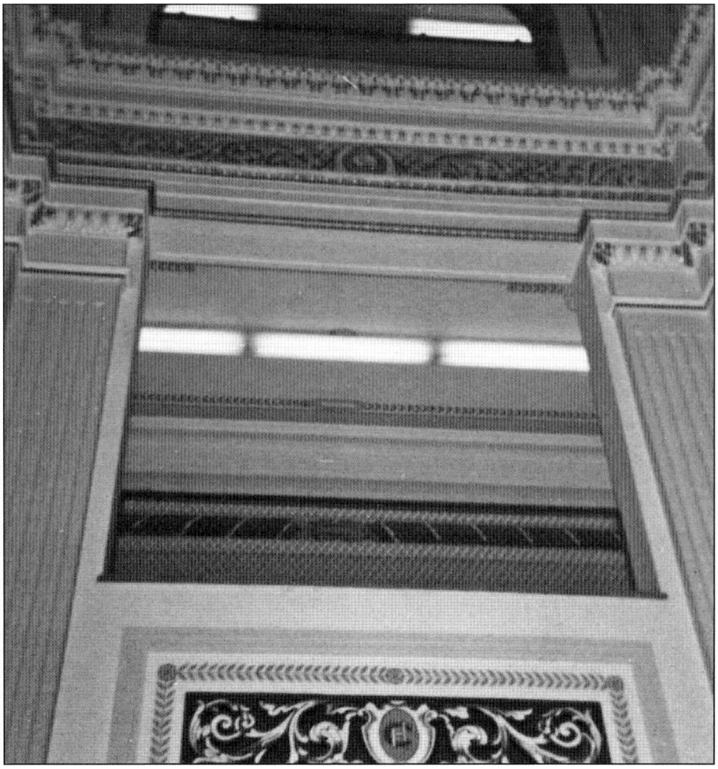

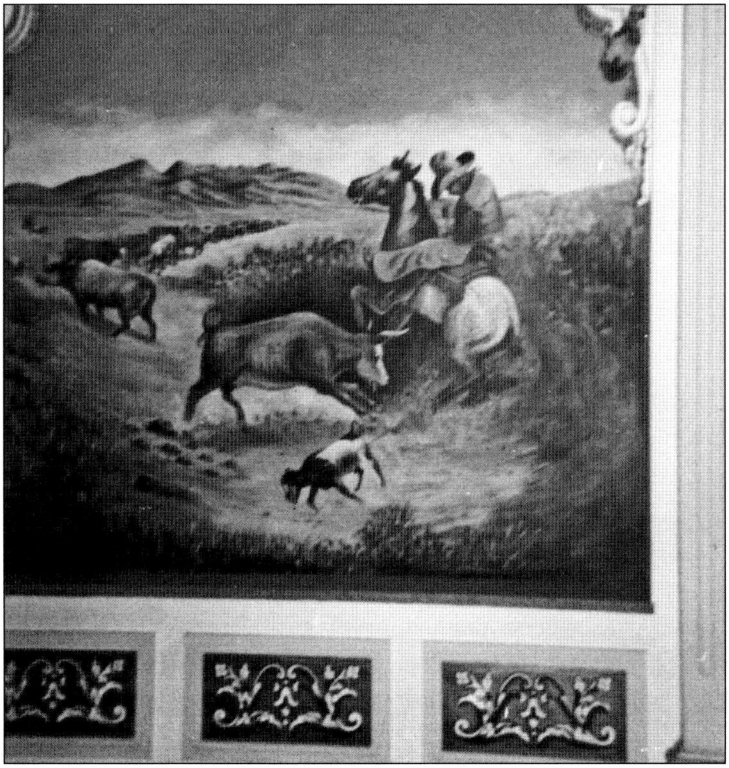

This mural depicts Havre cowboy and outlaw Long George Francis and was located on the first floor of the Courthouse. After the 1977 remodel, it was removed and went to First Bank Havre, then to the Clack Museum, where it is now part of the collections. Two of the della Robbia corbels, found throughout the courthouse, are also in the museum's collections. (Courtesy of Arvid Kristoffersen.)

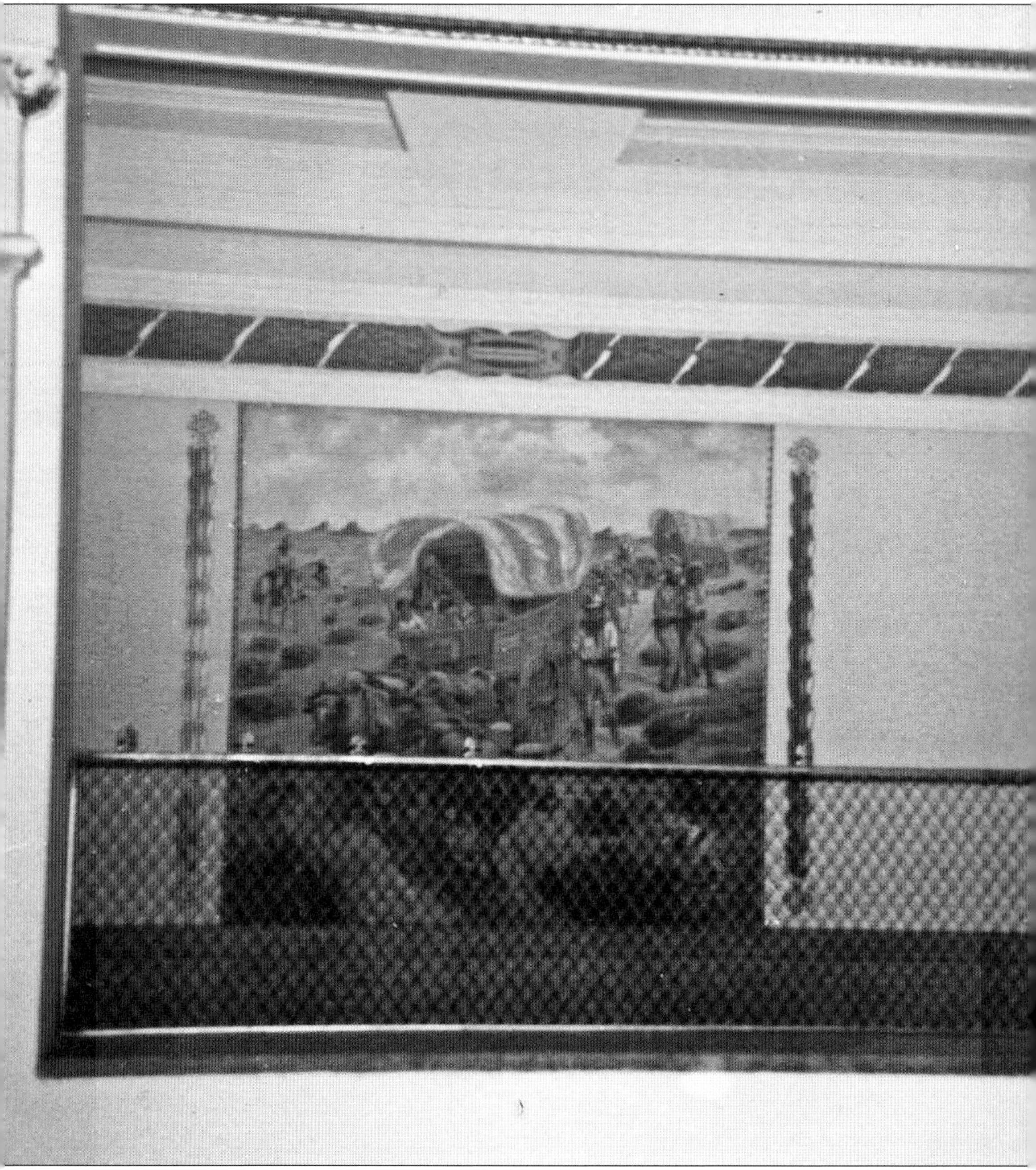

Kristoffersen stated there were murals in the courthouse when he started painting. Most were painted over, except for this one of a covered wagon. Thorweed Ronne from Chinook, Montana, painted the original murals, and the covered wagon was touched up by Kristoffersen. It is now covered over on the second floor. (Courtesy of Arvid Kristoffersen.)

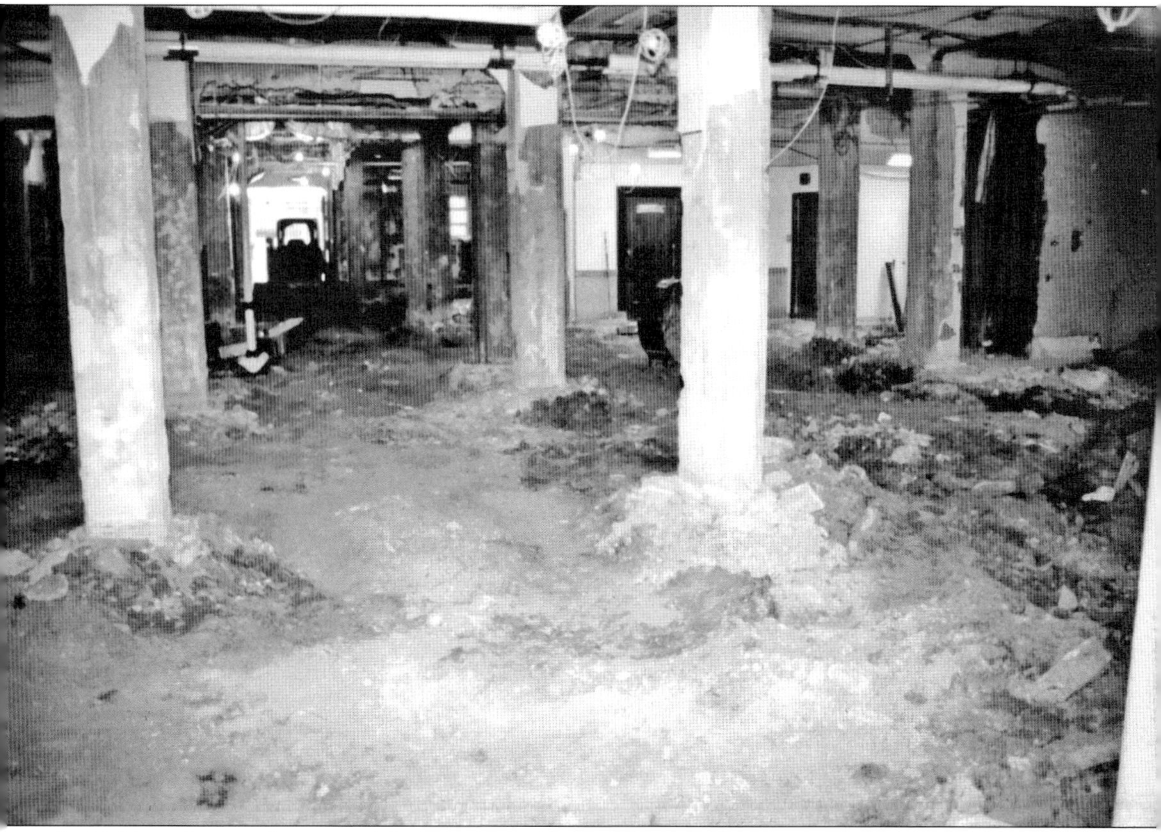

In 2007, work started on remodeling the lower level of the courthouse, mostly due to safety issues caused by the floor warping over time. The buffalo jump mural by Kristoffersen was uncovered, but it unfortunately was lost during construction. It was the only one painted on plaster and not on canvas. The entire level was gutted, which included removal of the floor. (Photograph by the author, courtesy of High Line Heritage House.)

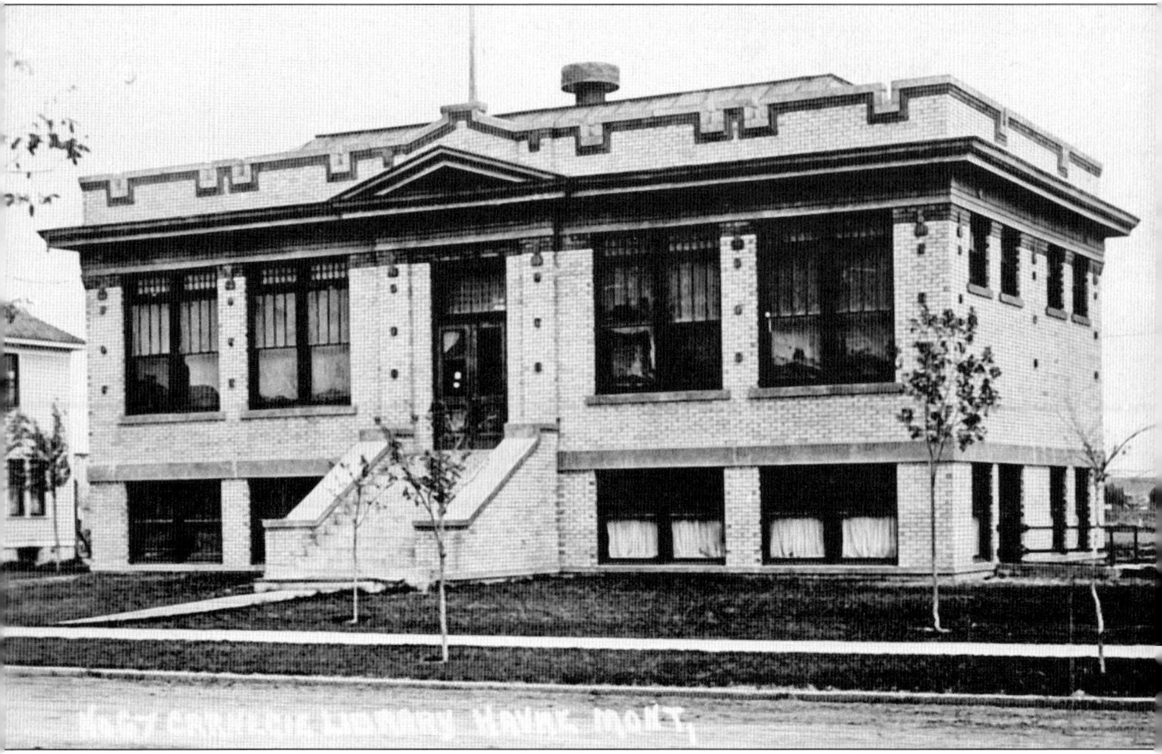

In 1904, a group of social matrons in Havre decided the young town needed a library. It was originally located in the basement of the Security State Bank, and when the city hall was finished in 1908, the library was moved there. In 1914, the Carnegie Corporation provided funds to build a freestanding library, and it was completed in January 1915. (Courtesy of Don Greytak.)

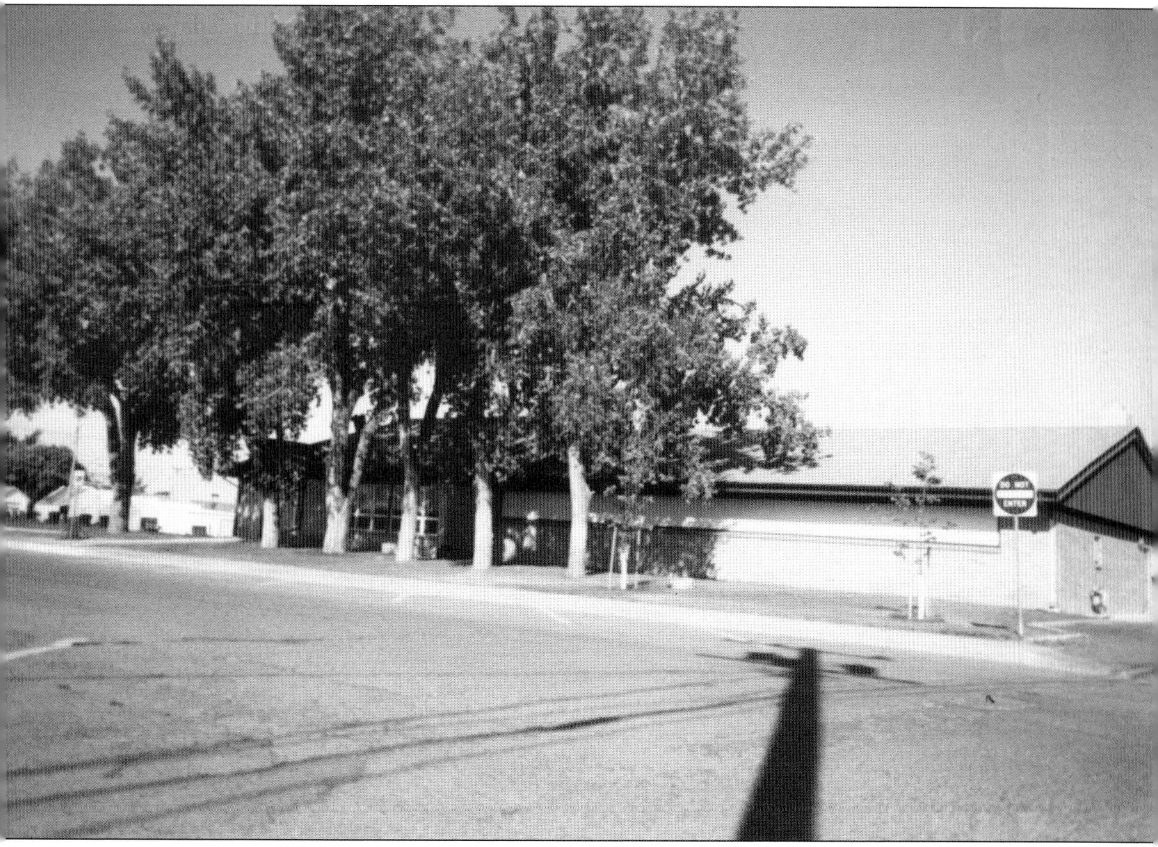

In 1981, the former Havre Clinic was offered to both the city and county libraries for a consolidated library. At the time, the county library was located where the justice of the peace courtroom is now operating, and the new Havre-Hill County Library was dedicated on April 9, 1986. The cottonwood trees are all that remain at the site of the former Pepin Mansion; there is only one tree left today. (Photograph by the author, courtesy of High Line Heritage House.)

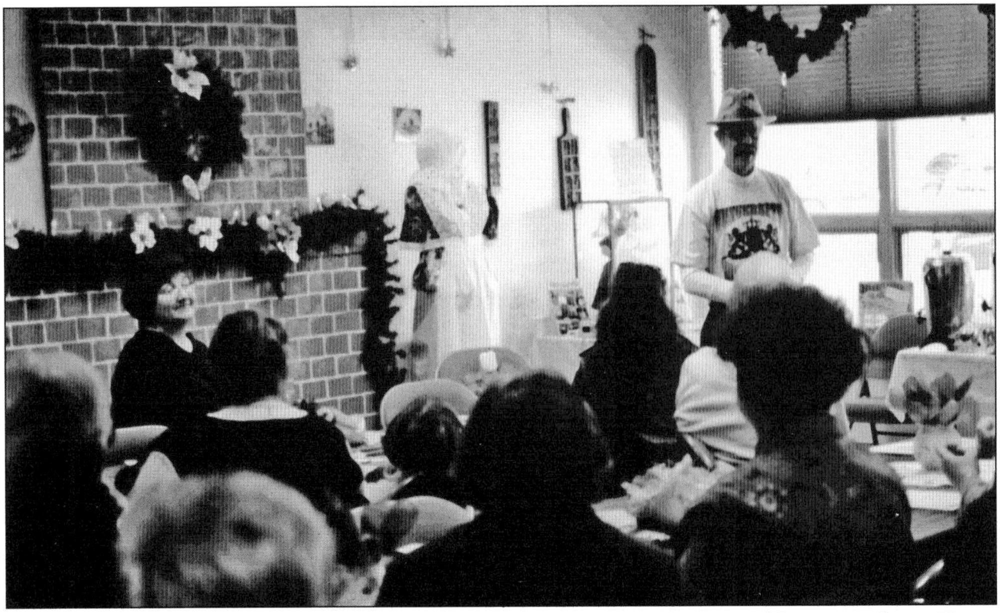

One of the most popular and beloved programs was created by longtime library employee Francine Brady, pictured here in front of a mock fireplace. Her "Christmas Around the World" series included speakers either originally born in a foreign country or those familiar with the ethnic customs of the country chosen. Genuine artifacts used for Christmas celebrations helped make the program successful. Here, Bob Nieuwenhuyse is presenting Christmas traditions from Holland in 2008. (Photograph by the author, courtesy of High Line Heritage House.)

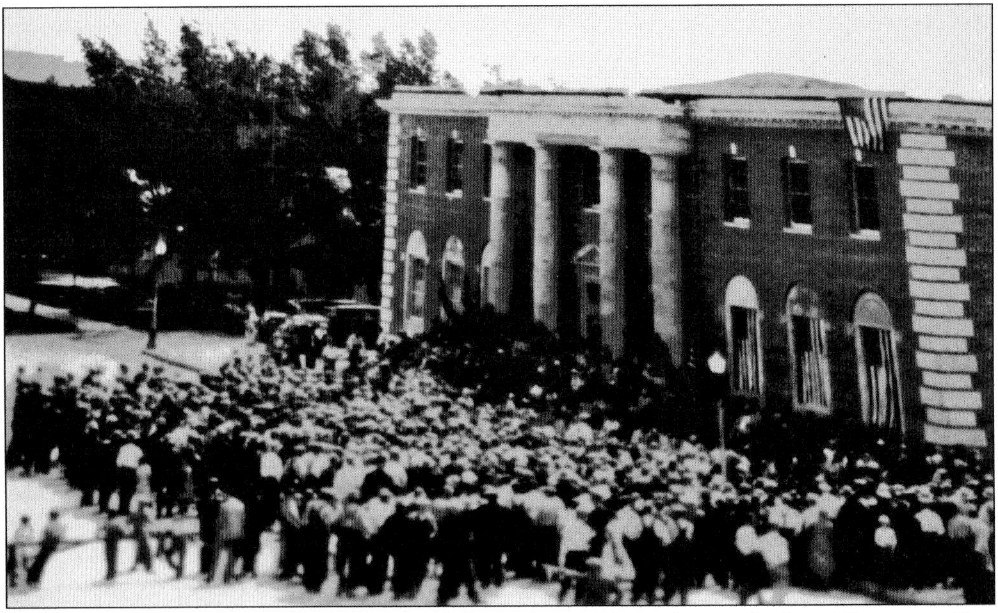

The federal building and post office was dedicated in 1932 amid great fanfare. The post office was located on the ground floor, with offices for the Internal Revenue Service, Selective Service, Social Security, the special customs agent, Navy recruiting, post office inspector, geological survey, and the Federal Housing Administration offices on the second floor. (Courtesy of High Line Heritage House.)

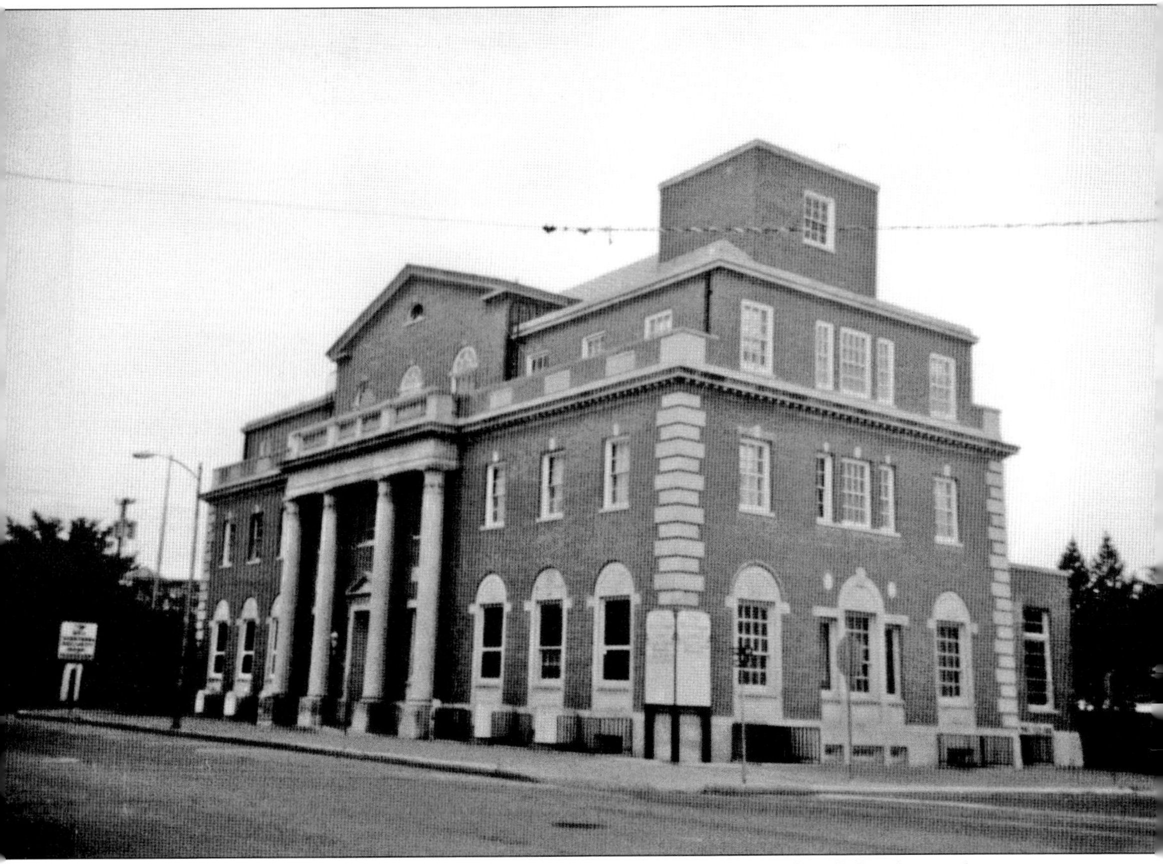

A few short years after the two-story federal building was constructed, a federal courthouse was added as a third story. This structure came into existence due to the insistence of the Havre public demanding such a building. The third story housed the federal courtroom, witness room, marshal's office and holding cell, clerk of court office, stenographer's office, and judges' chambers. (Photograph by the author, courtesy of High Line Heritage House.)

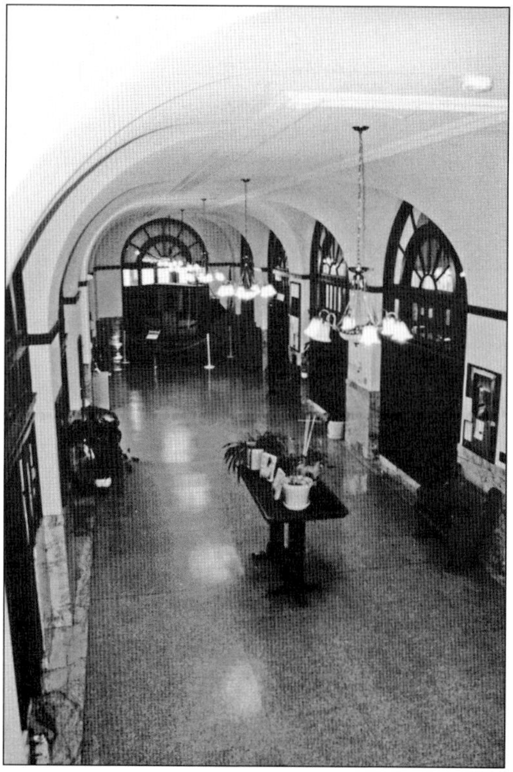

In 1995, the post office moved to a new building, and in 1996, the City of Havre, with assistance from the Clack Museum Foundation, purchased the building for use as a heritage center. The lobby was popular for a myriad of different programs. Due to a lack of community interest, the building was sold a little over 10 years later to a private party. (Photograph by the author, courtesy of High Line Heritage House.)

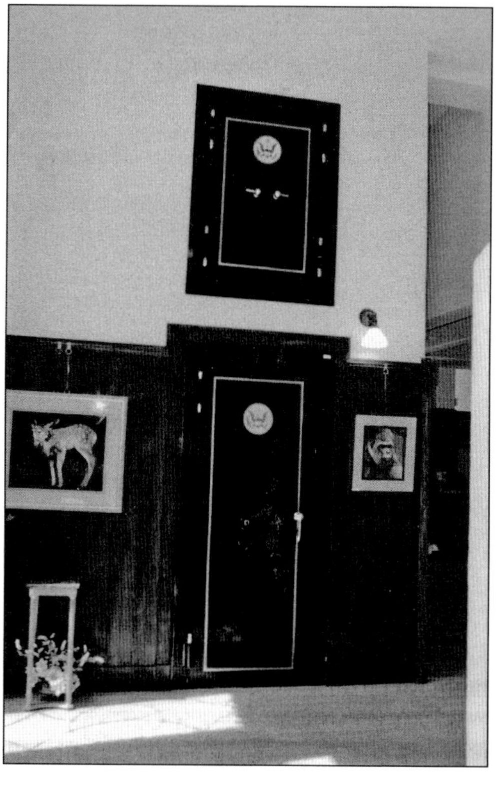

A feature of the old post office is safes used for various offices, with the smaller upper ones once being rented to the public for storage of furs, artwork, jewelry, and other valuables. Covenants put on the building by the US government due to its listing in the National Register of Historic Places are supposed to retain the historic features of the structure, including the post office boxes. (Photograph by the author, courtesy of High Line Heritage House.)

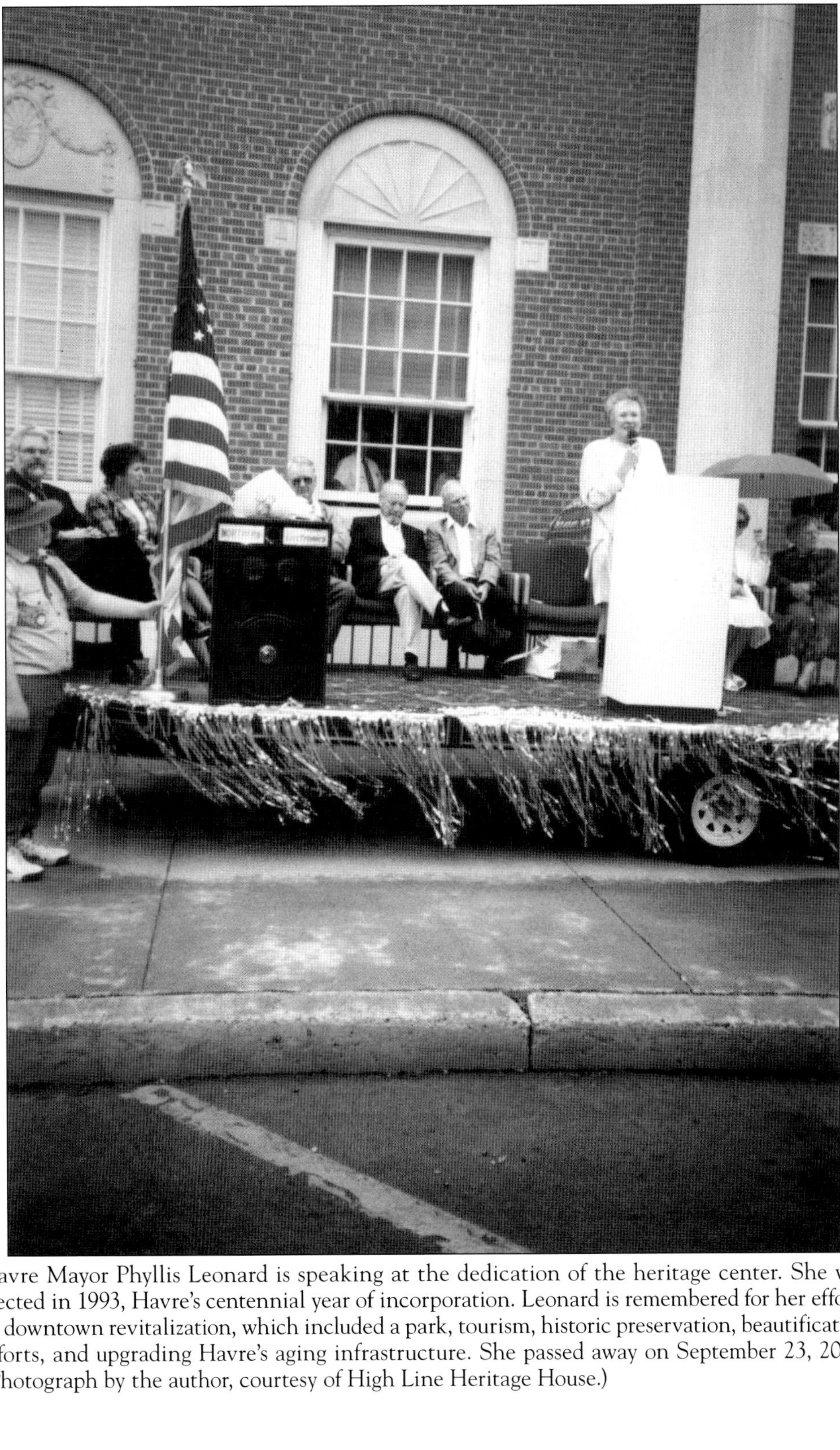

Havre Mayor Phyllis Leonard is speaking at the dedication of the heritage center. She was elected in 1993, Havre's centennial year of incorporation. Leonard is remembered for her efforts in downtown revitalization, which included a park, tourism, historic preservation, beautification efforts, and upgrading Havre's aging infrastructure. She passed away on September 23, 2003. (Photograph by the author, courtesy of High Line Heritage House.)

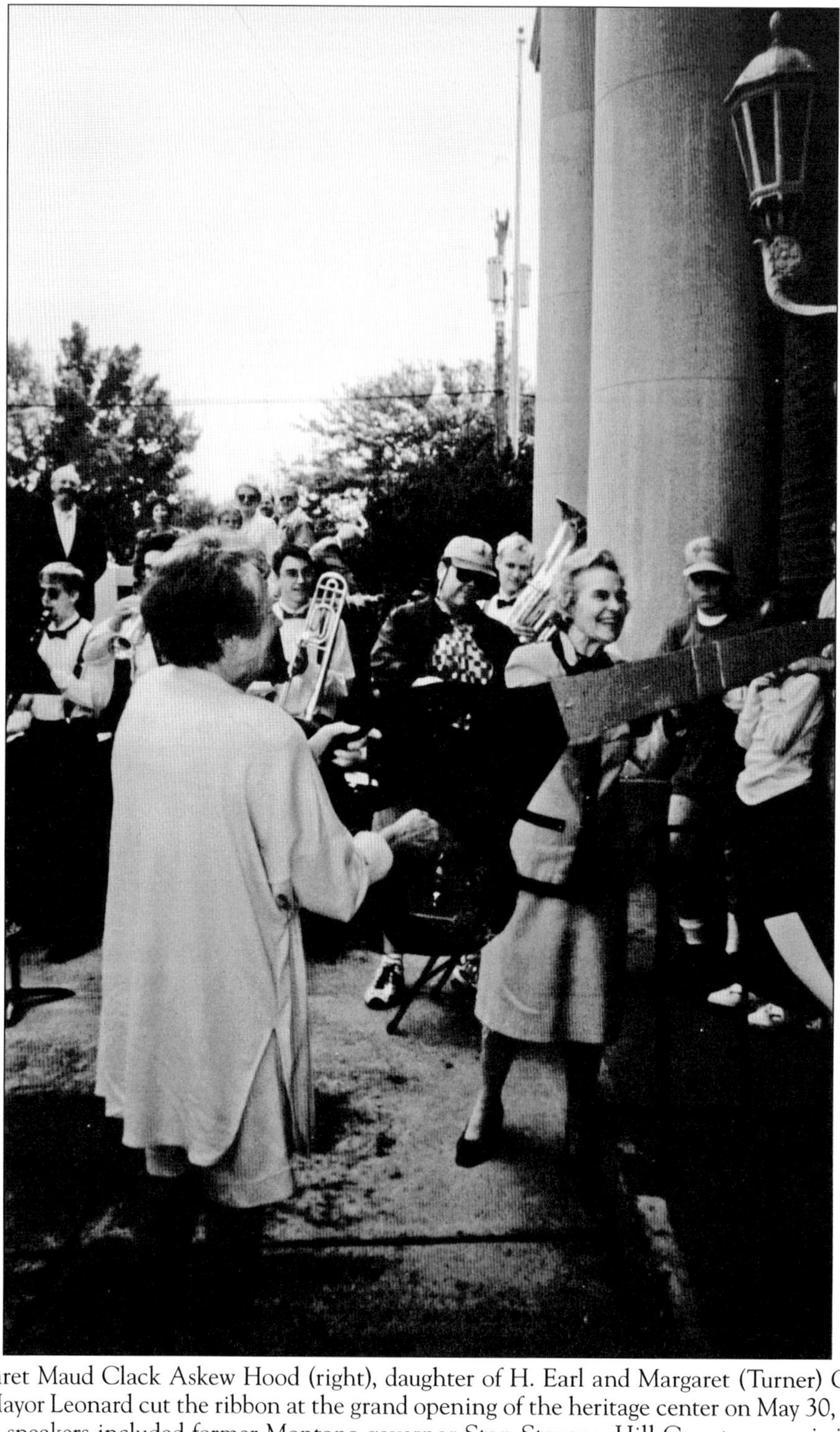

Margaret Maud Clack Askew Hood (right), daughter of H. Earl and Margaret (Turner) Clack, and Mayor Leonard cut the ribbon at the grand opening of the heritage center on May 30, 1998. Other speakers included former Montana governor Stan Stevens, Hill County commissioners Kathy Bessette and Patrick Conway, and local legend Jim Pasma. A live band played music at the ceremony. (Photograph by the author, courtesy of High Line Heritage House.)

Four

People and Their Activities

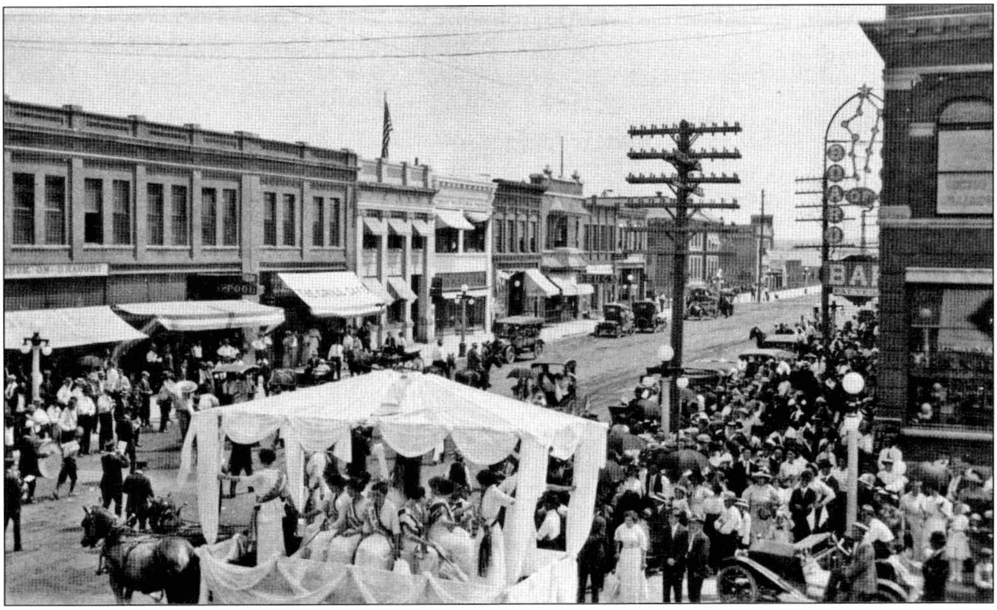

The businessmen of Havre got together in 1914 and organized a promotional parade to show off how the town had grown, that it was modern and moving forward, and that it was a great place in which to do business and live. Businesses and community organizations went all out for this parade, complete with floats that were drawn by either horses or automobiles. The celebration took place on the Fourth of July. (Courtesy of Don Greytak.)

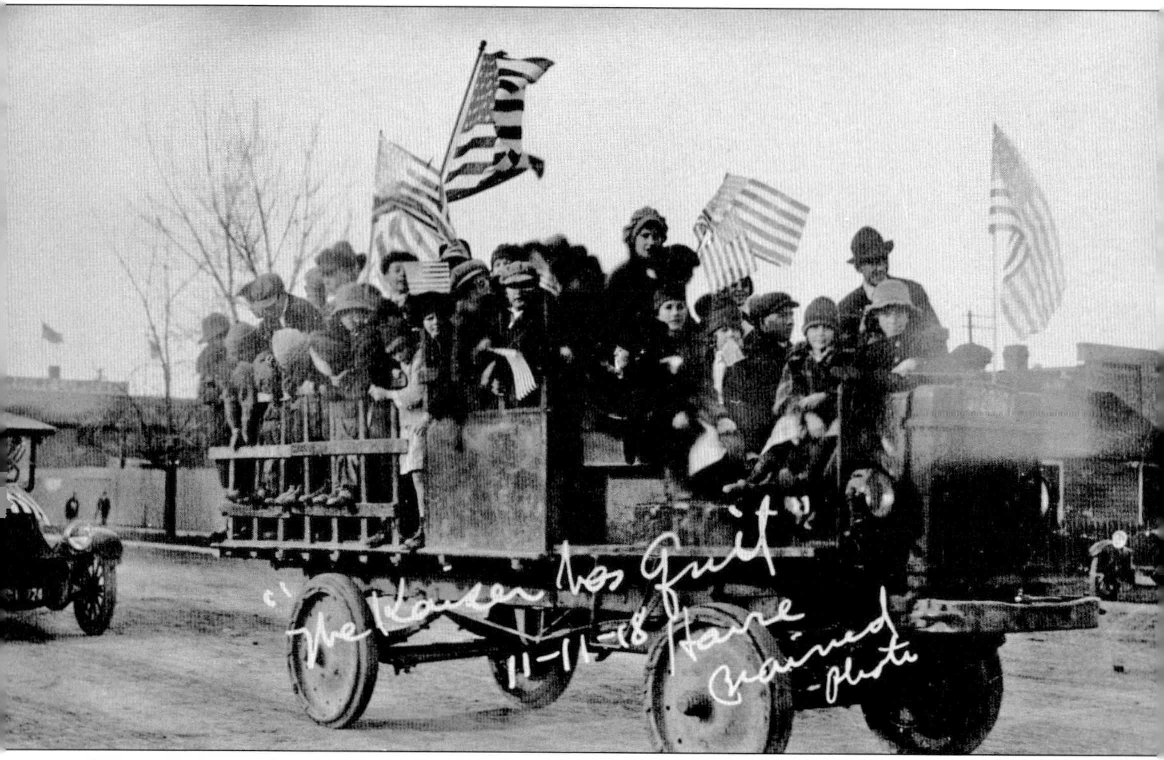

When the United States entered World War I against Germany and the Austro-Hungarian and Ottoman Empires, Montanans were among those at the forefront volunteering to fight a war on foreign soil. Local newspapers had carried news of battles since the war's beginnings. When the end of the war was announced, Havre erupted instantly into celebration. An impromptu parade was organized, church services conducted, and an effigy of the kaiser was burned. (Courtesy of Don Greytak.)

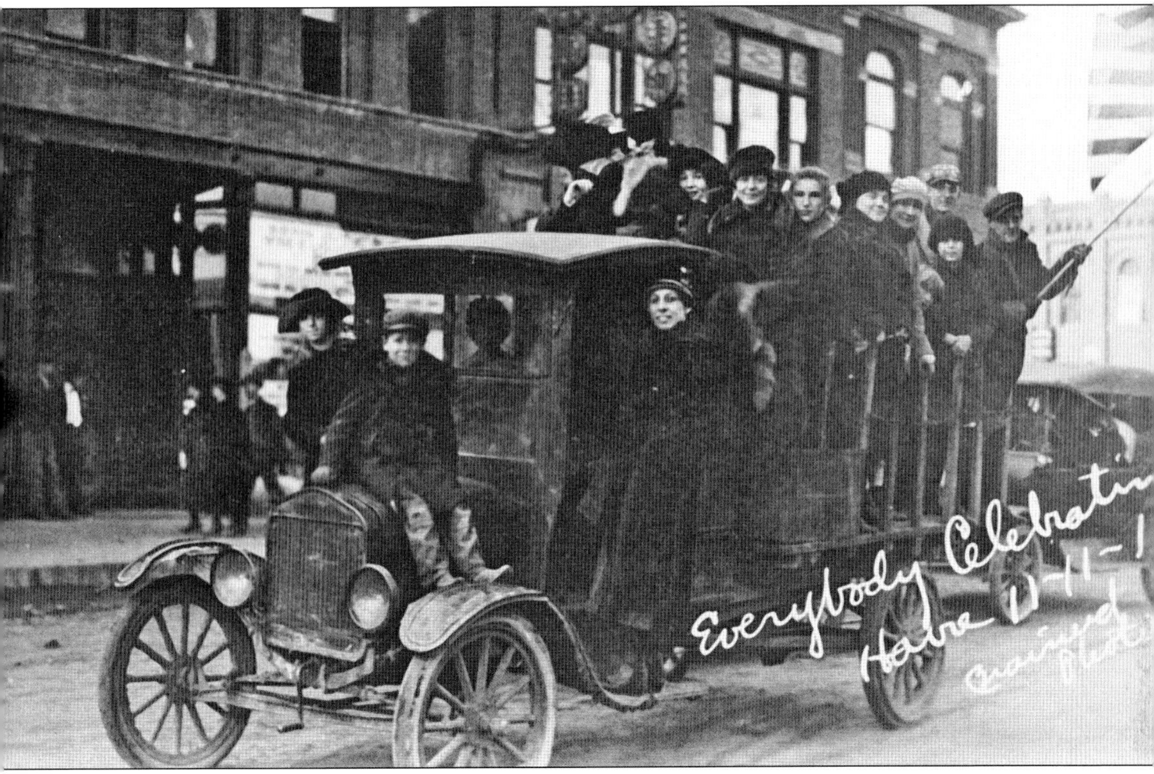

Schools let students out early, businesses closed, bands played, and almost everyone gathered in Havre's downtown to celebrate victory over the Central Powers in World War I. However, Havre did not come out of the war unscathed. Some of those from Havre who served in the war were not coming home alive, among them three Havre High students—Caleb Nystrom, Raymond Loranger, and William Cross. (Courtesy of Don Greytak.)

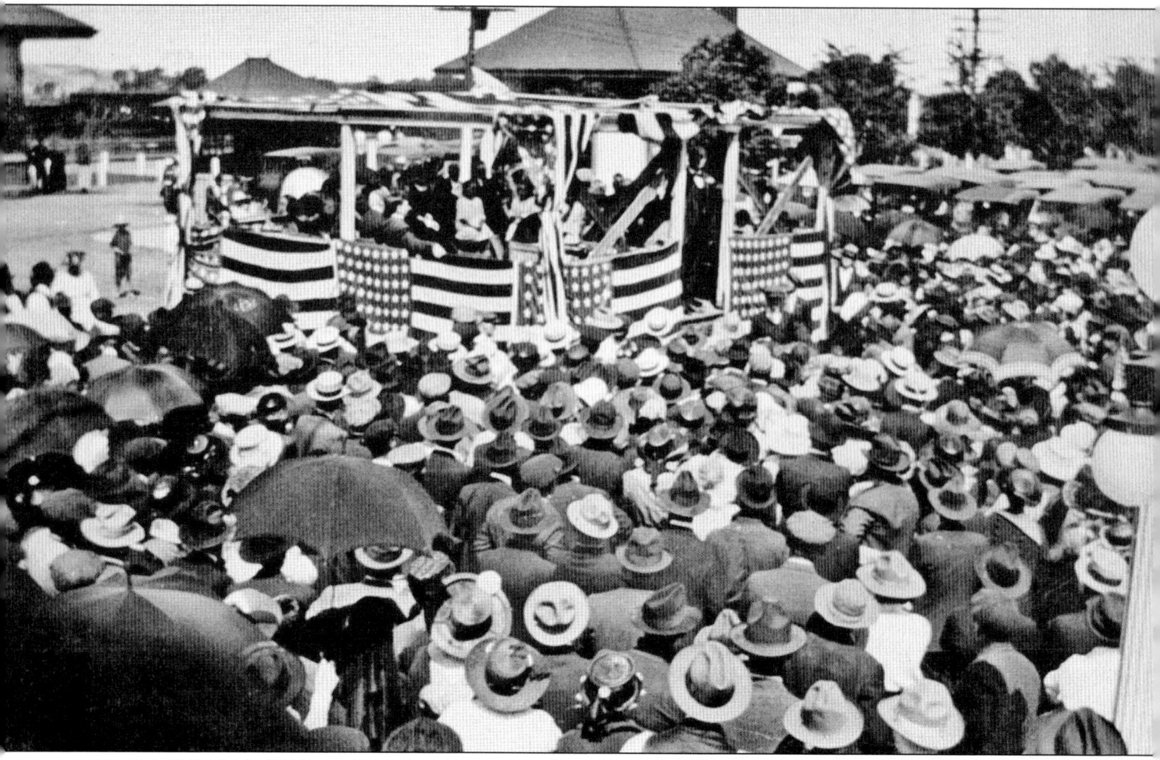

On July 22, 1922, William Jennings Bryan spoke in front of the Great Northern Depot to hundreds of people. Bryan was a three-time Democratic presidential candidate—but won none of those elections. He was known as "the Great Commoner" because of his faith in the wisdom of the common man. His message was apparently popular with people in the area, due to the number seen in this crowd. (Courtesy of Don Greytak.)

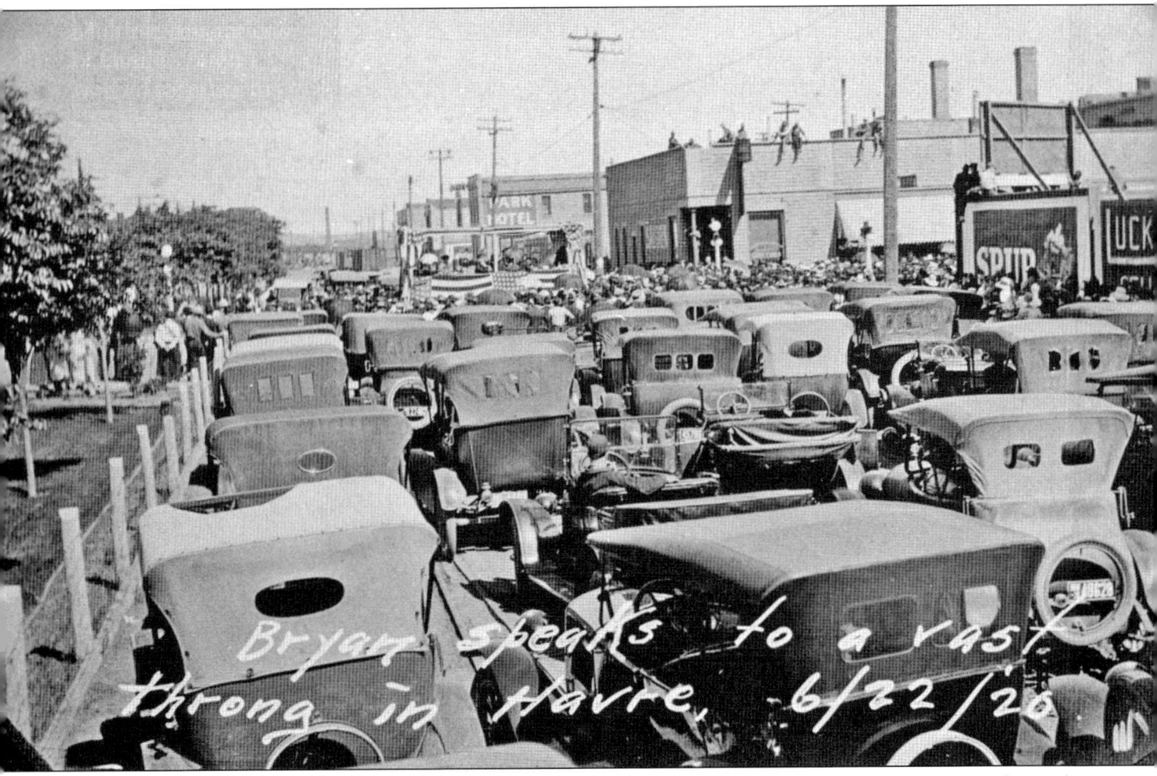

People even perched on rooftops to hear Bryan speak. The former congressman, presidential candidate, and secretary of state enjoyed the large audience. William Jennings Bryan passed away three years after his visit to Havre. His daughter Ruth Bryan Owen followed in her father's footsteps by becoming the South's first congresswoman in 1929. (Courtesy of Don Greytak.)

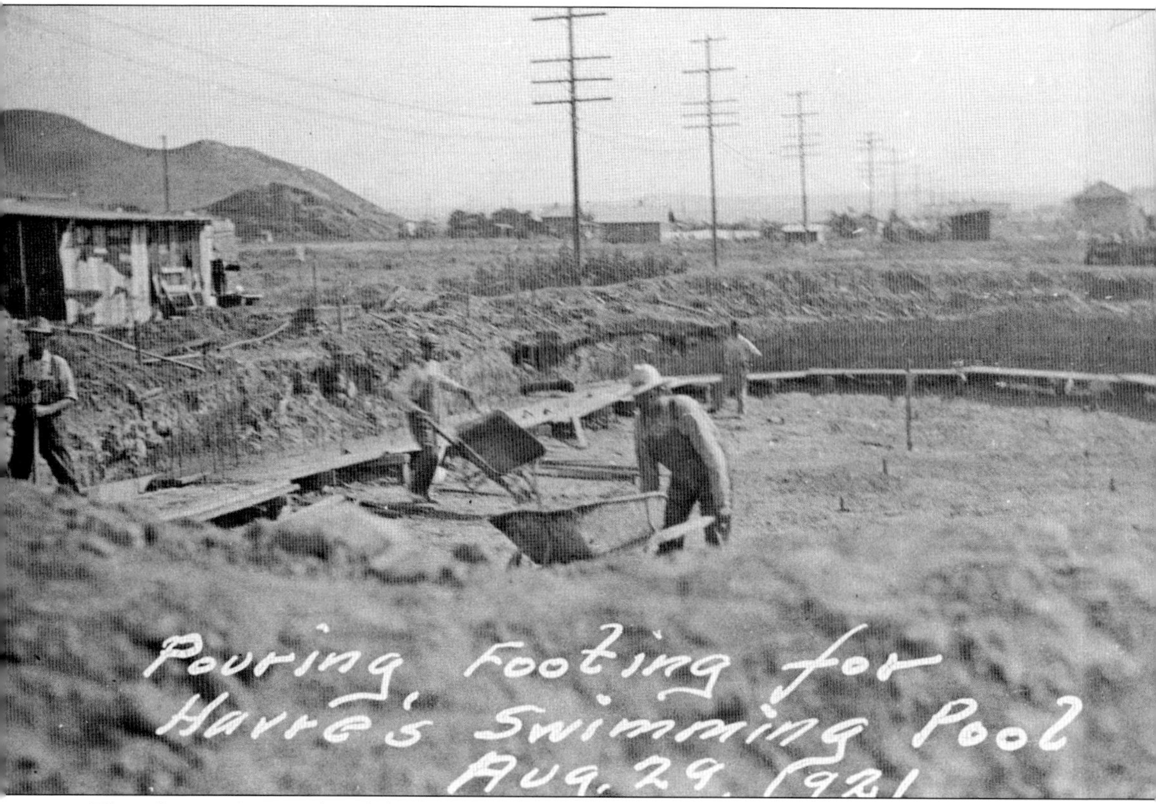

Those born in Havre already know, and it does not take long after people move to Havre for them to find out, that it gets hot in the summer. In 1921, the City of Havre decided to build an outdoor swimming pool. It was located where the current city hall is today. (Courtesy of Don Greytak.)

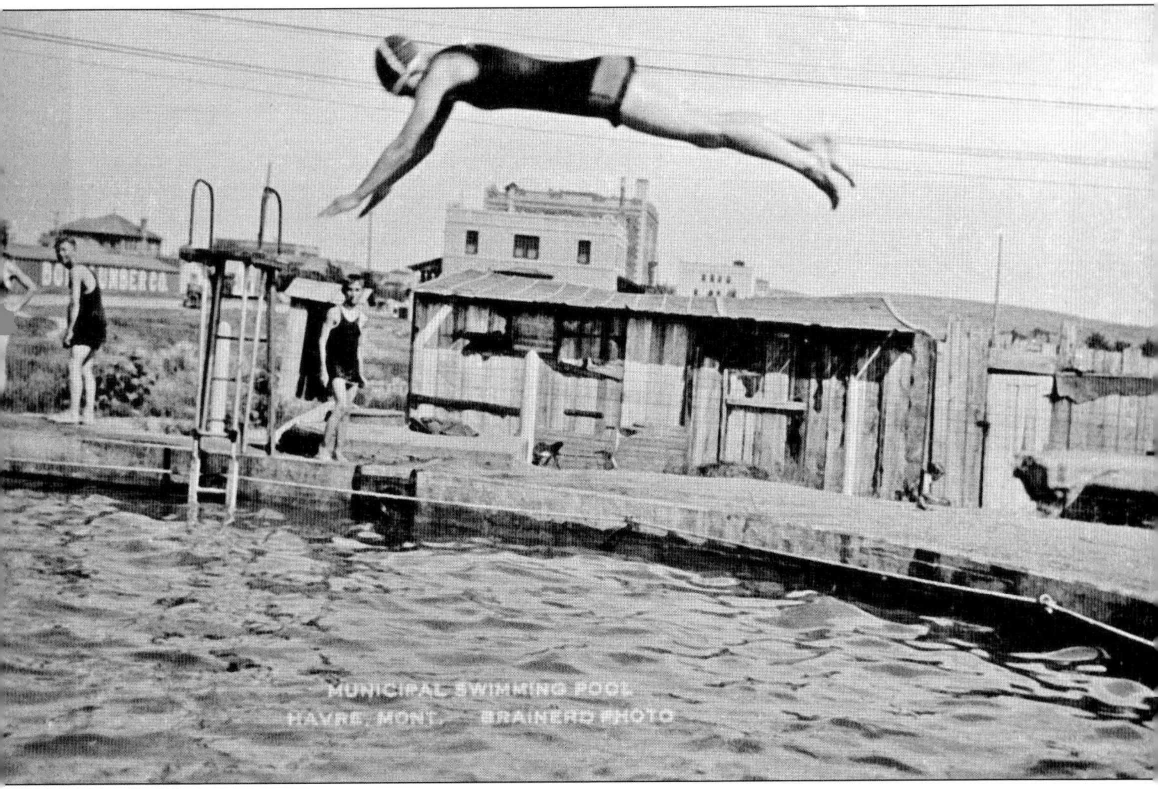

The people of Havre must have been relieved when the city swimming pool opened. It offered both respite from the heat as well as a form of great exercise. The Bond Lumber Company, Lincoln School, and the rectory and combination St. Jude Church and School can be seen in the background, as can the Sacred Heart Hospital. (Courtesy of Don Greytak.)

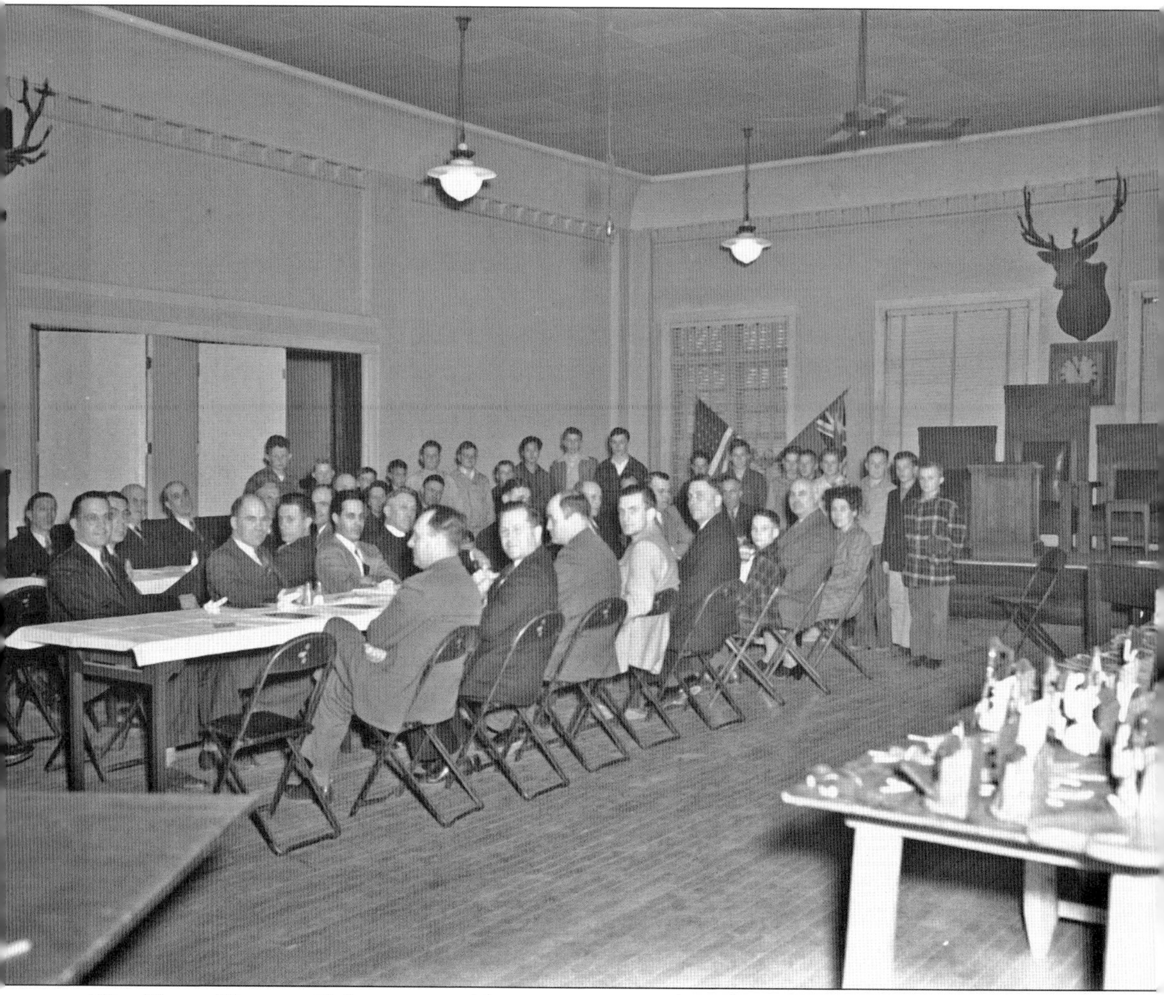

The Havre Kiwanis Club is pictured here meeting in the Elks Lodge on April 11, 1945. The Havre Kiwanis was chartered on November 23, 1923, with Victor R. Griggs serving as the first president. The group has been very active in the Havre community, notably with Camp Kiwanis in Beaver Creek Park, the largest county park in the United States, as well as assisting the Salvation Army and supporting Northern Montana College. (Photograph by Frances Hulm, courtesy of Don Greytak.)

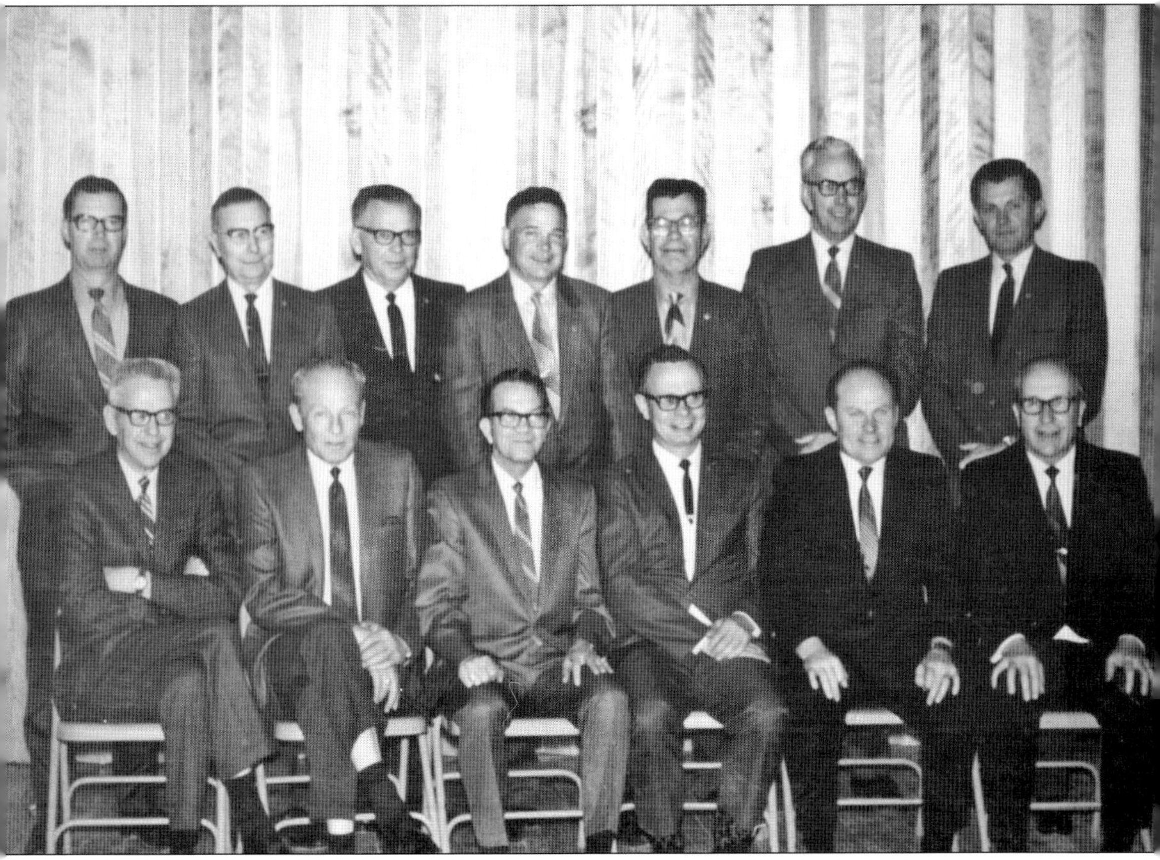

In March 1970, past presidents of the Havre Lions Club gathered for a group photograph. Pictured here are, from left to right, (first row) George Renaker, Bob Graham, Duane Swenson, Jack Norman, Floyd Witt, and Elmer Lund; (second row) Tom Wilson, Willard Paulson, Ben Decker, Ray Patrick, Bob Roush, Waldo Spangelo, and Lee Covington. The Lions Club has been active in Havre since 1927. (Courtesy of Floyd Witt.)

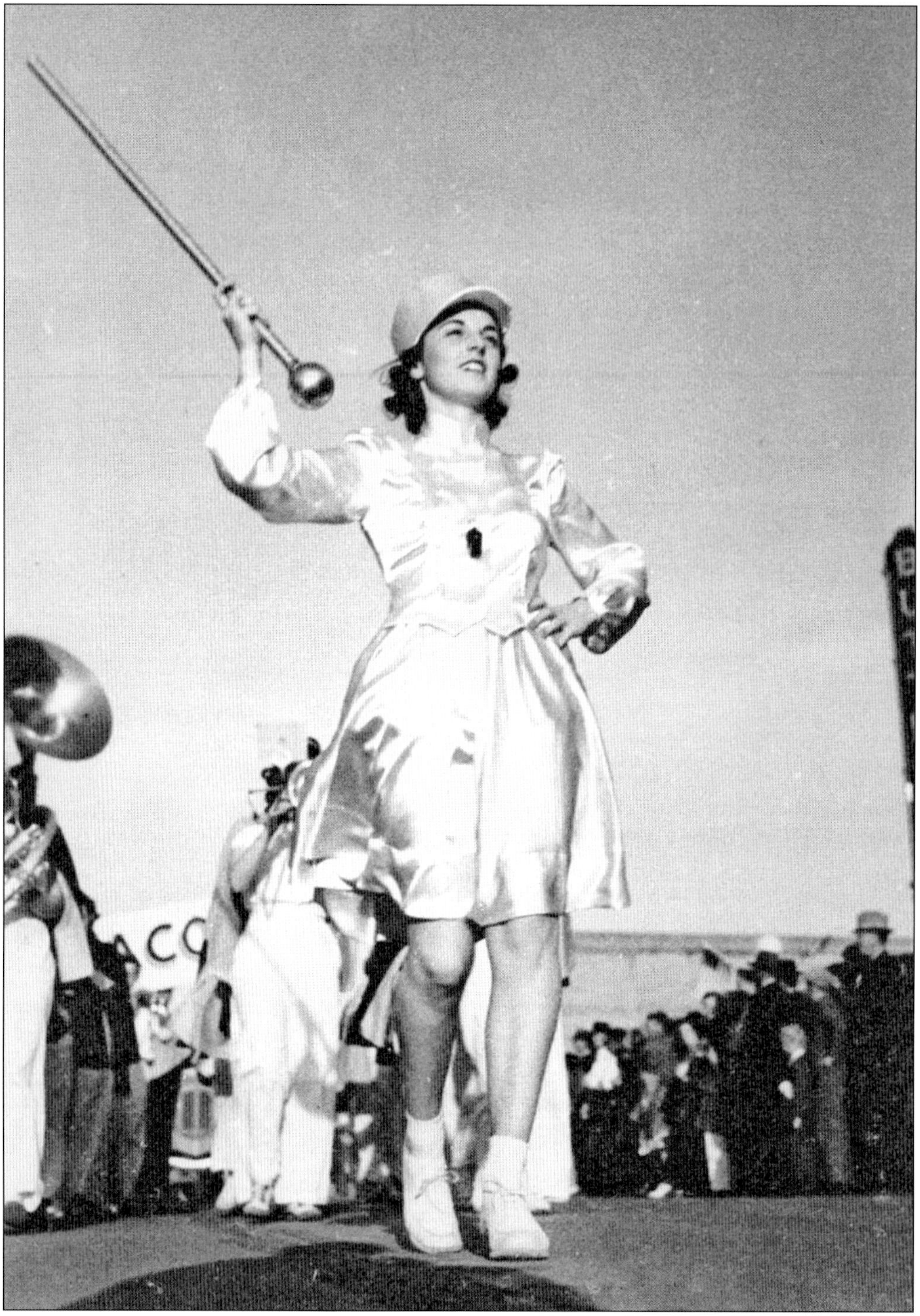

The Havre Music Festival first took place on Saturday, May 23, 1931. Bert Gourley was instrumental in getting the music festival started and, along with businesses, community groups, and the people of Havre, made it a successful event. A parade was part of the festivities, with pretty majorettes leading each band. (Courtesy of Don Greytak.)

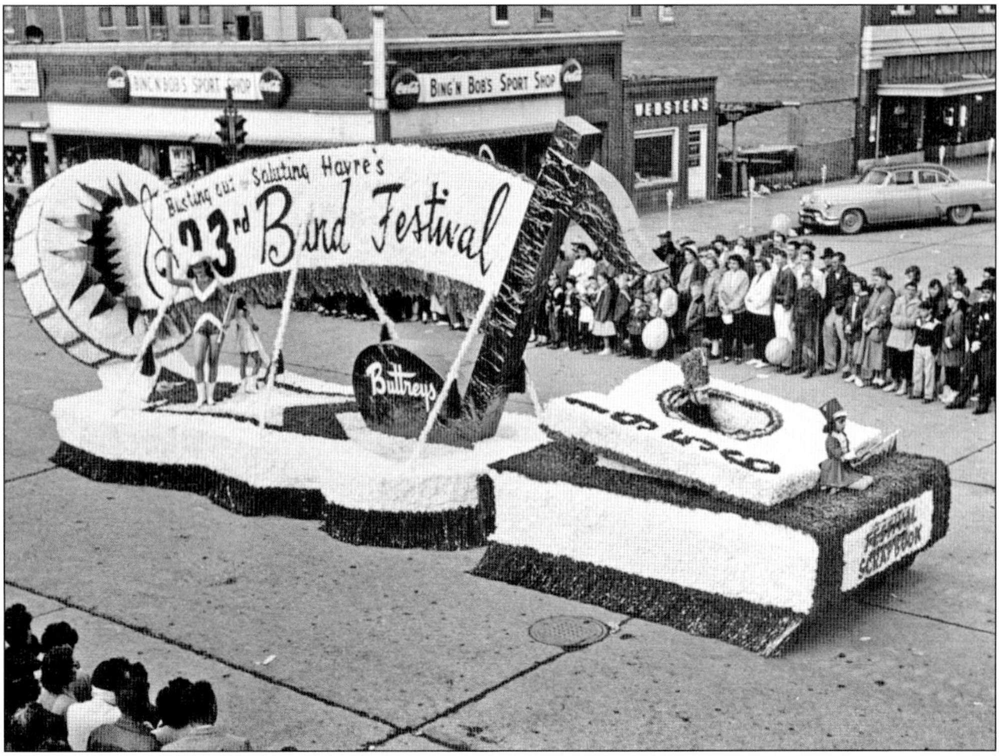

Floats sponsored by Havre businesses during the Havre Music Festival show how floats are really done. Designs for the floats were chosen months in advance, and the makers' efforts were a delight to the eye. The Buttrey's float is "Busting Out & Saluting Havre's 23rd Band Festival" in 1956. (Courtesy of Don Greytak.)

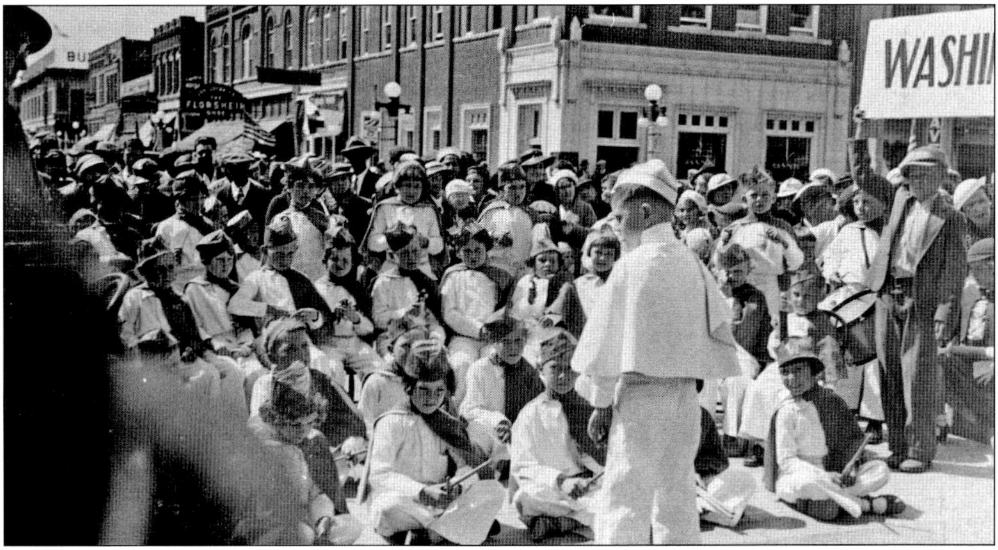

The most important part of the entire festival was the bands. Schools and organized bands each played at the festival, competing for top recognition of their music skills. No other festival in Havre has ever come close to the music festival's popularity, quality, or nostalgia. This band is from Havre's Washington School. (Courtesy of Don Greytak.)

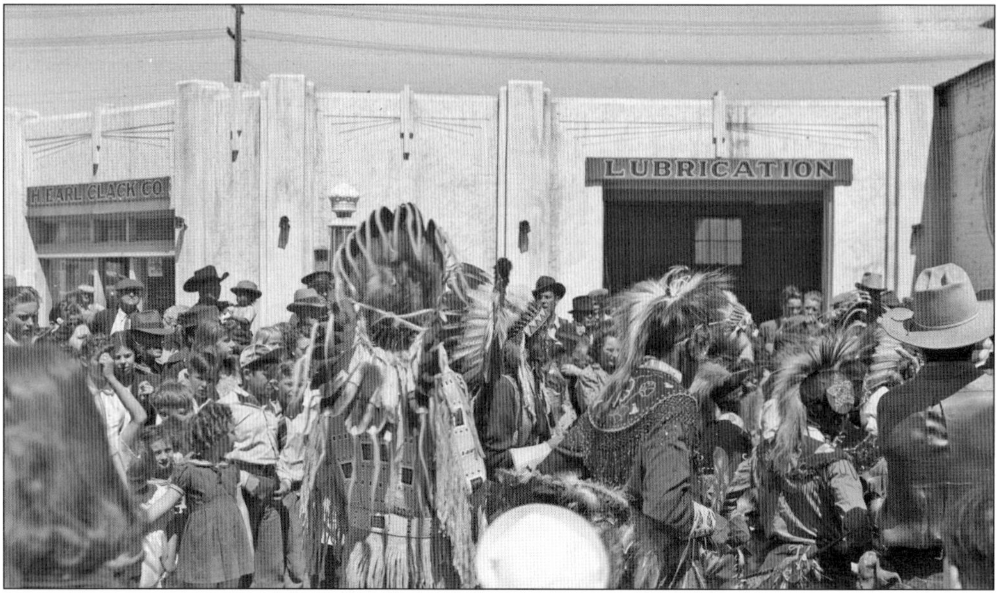

Members of the Rocky Boy Indian Reservation also participated in the Havre Music Festival's activities on May 10, 1941. They are performing a traditional dance in front of the H. Earl Clack Co. station on the northwest corner of Fifth Avenue and First Street. Rocky Boy Reservation was founded in 1916 and is home to the Chippewa and Cree tribes of Montana. (Photograph by Frances Hulm, courtesy of Don Greytak.)

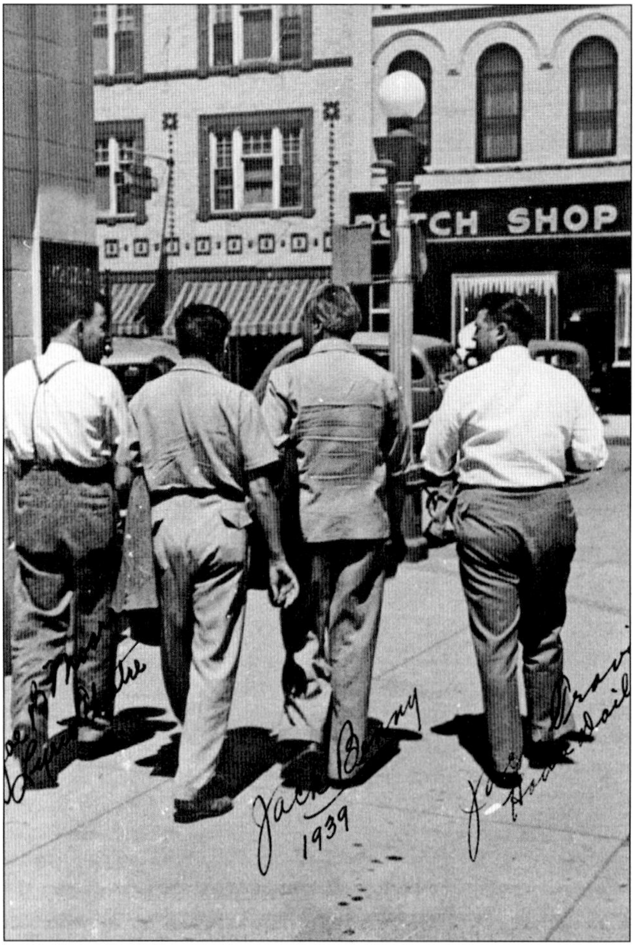

In 1939, radio personality Jack Benny paid a visit to Havre and caused a stir. He took some time to speak with Jack Travis of the *Havre Daily News* and Joe Moore of the Lyric Theatre, as well as to shop at the Lou Lucke Company. Benny left holding a package with traditional packaging—green tissue tied with red string. He did business with the Lucke Company for many years. (Courtesy of Don Greytak.)

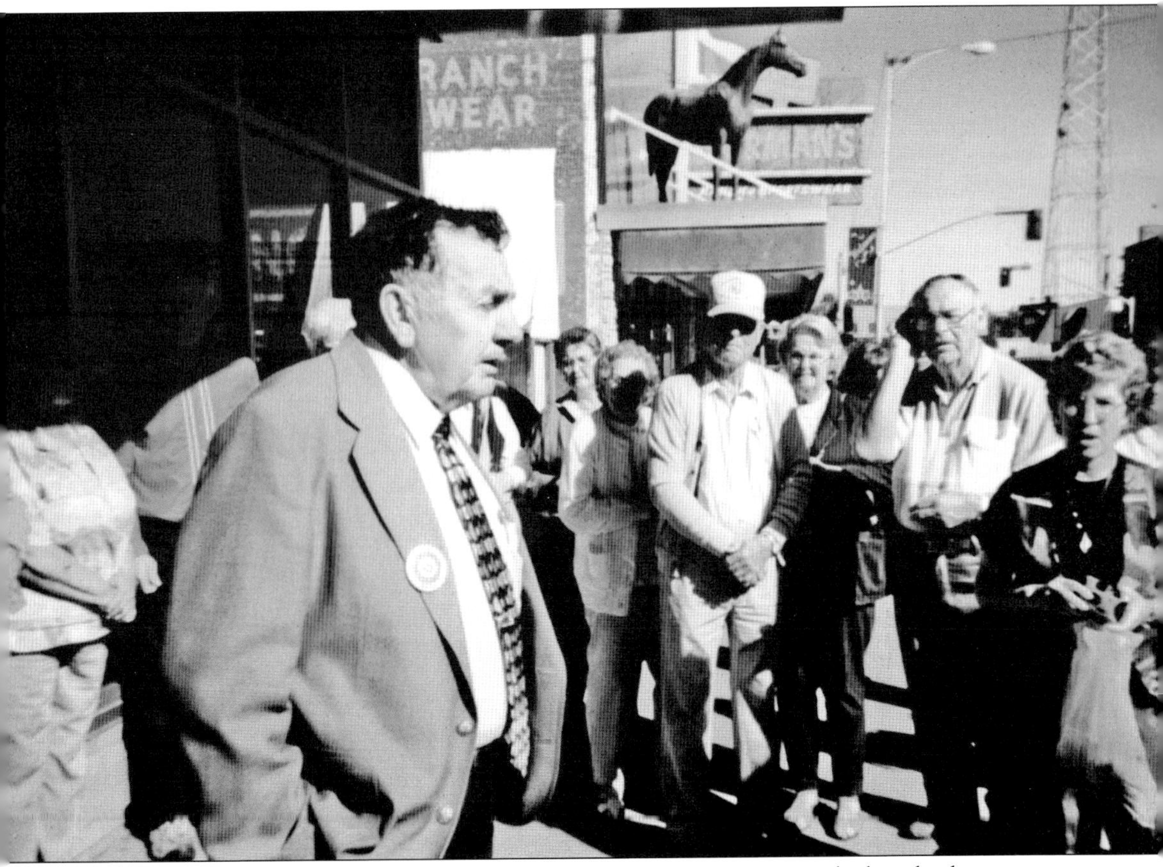

Former railroad employee and noted Havre historian Frank DeRosa worked tirelessly to create both Havre Beneath the Streets and the Railroad Museum. He is pictured here on September 17, 1999, at the dedication of the Railroad Museum, which would later be named after him due to his untimely death in 2005. The Railroad Museum is located in the former Hub Clothing building on Third Avenue. (Photograph by the author, courtesy of High Line Heritage House.)

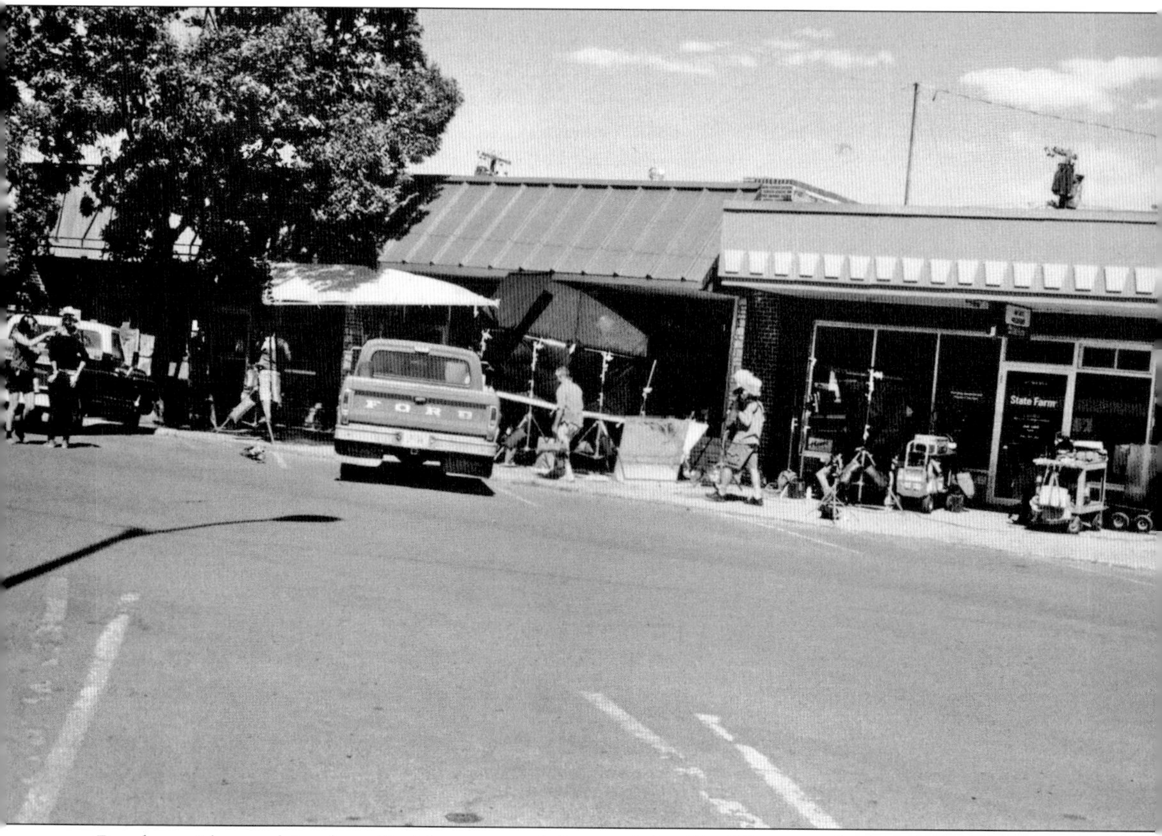

Brothers Alex and Andrew Smith wrote and directed the film *Winter in the Blood*, based on James Welch's novel of the same name. In August 2011, shooting took place for the film in downtown Havre. The film crew is pictured here on the north side of the 300 block of Third Street where Cavalier's is located. (Photograph by the author, courtesy of High Line Heritage House.)

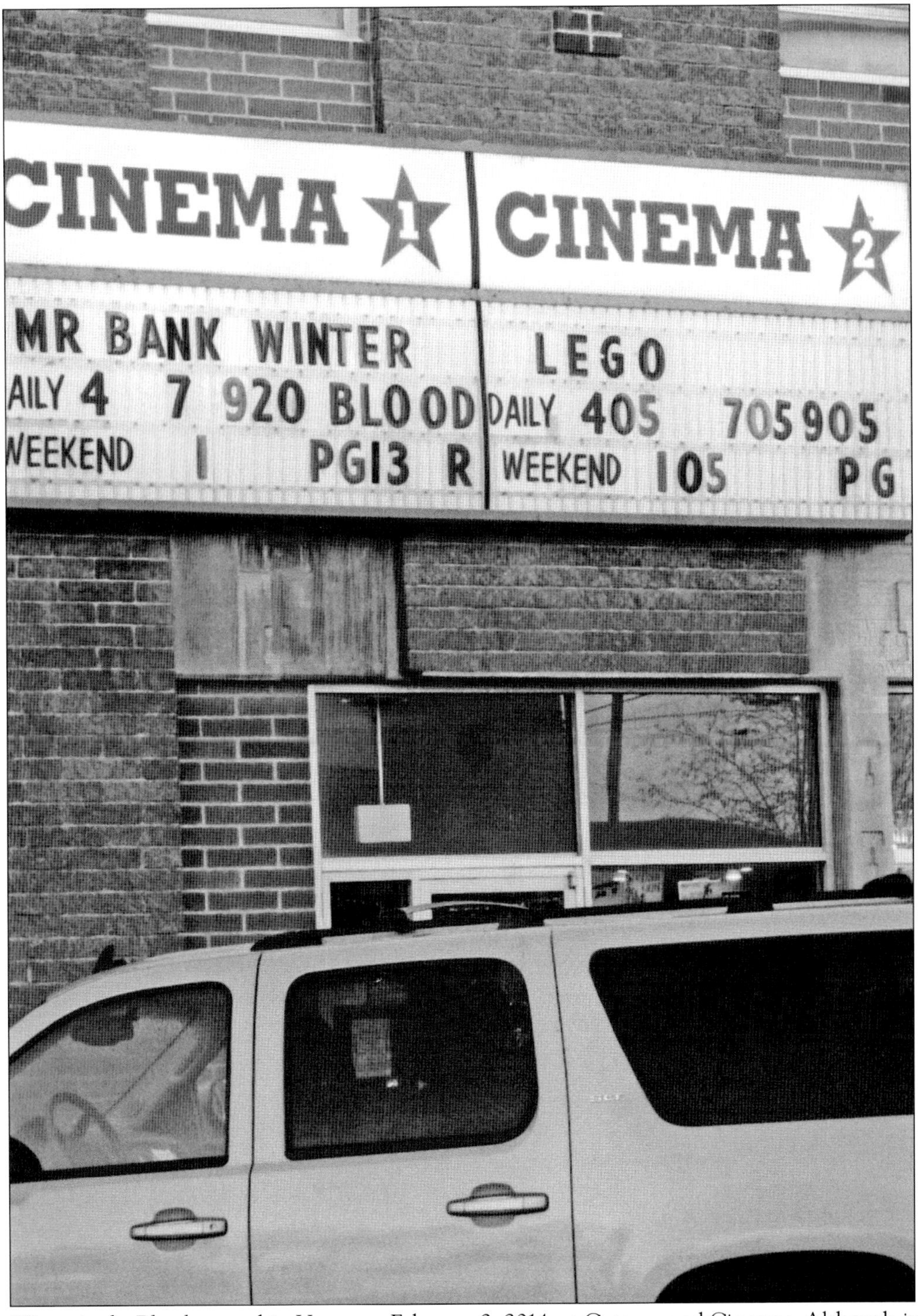

Winter in the Blood opened in Havre on February 2, 2014, at Cottonwood Cinemas. Although it was Super Bowl Sunday, the movie was well attended and favorably received. A reception was held the following evening at the historic post office, which is under the ownership of Drs. Erica Farmer and Marc Whitacre. (Photograph by the author, courtesy of High Line Heritage House.)

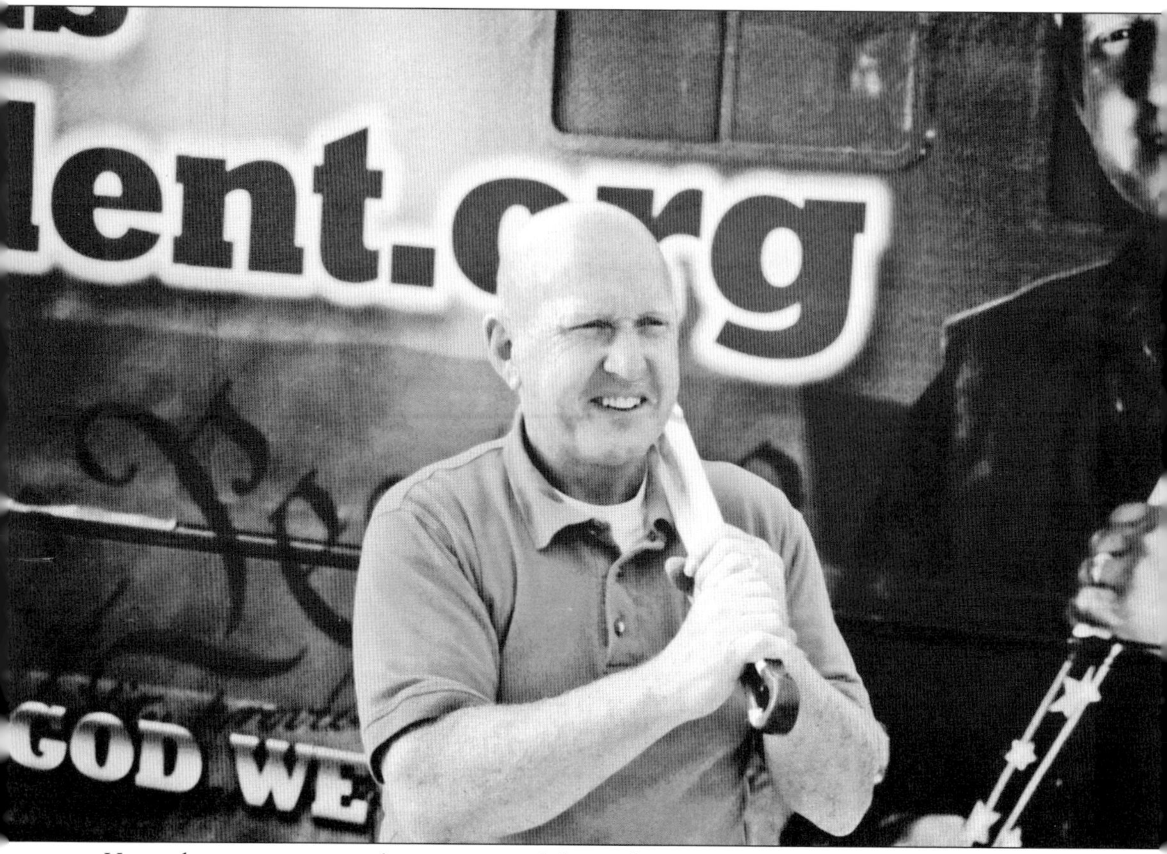

Havre does not get a visit from many candidates who running for president. On September 15, 2011, John Davis, presidential candidate under the Republican ticket, visited the Hill County Courthouse. His goal was to visit every courthouse in the country, delivering his message about getting to work solving the nation's problems. He is carrying his trademark wrench and was warmly welcomed by the few Hill County employees and press who came to see him. (Photograph by the author, courtesy of High Line Heritage House.)

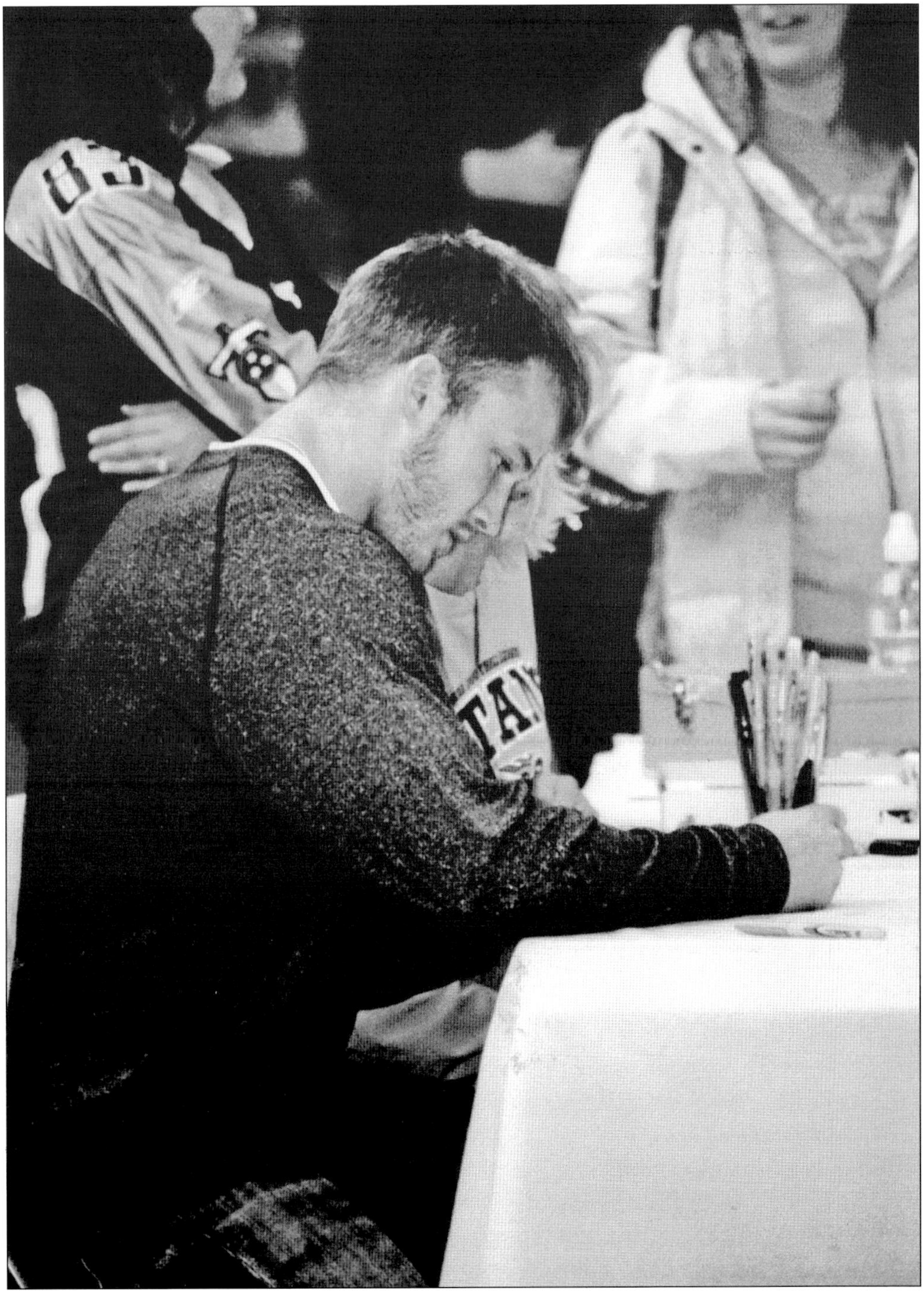

Marc Mariani is a graduate of Havre High and the University of Montana and a standout football player. He was drafted by the Tennessee Titans in 2010 and is a two-time Pro Bowl player. Mariani broke his leg playing against the Arizona Cardinals in 2012 and was released by the Titans in 2014. In November of that year, he signed a two-year contract with the Chicago Bears. (Photograph by the author, courtesy of High Line Heritage House.)

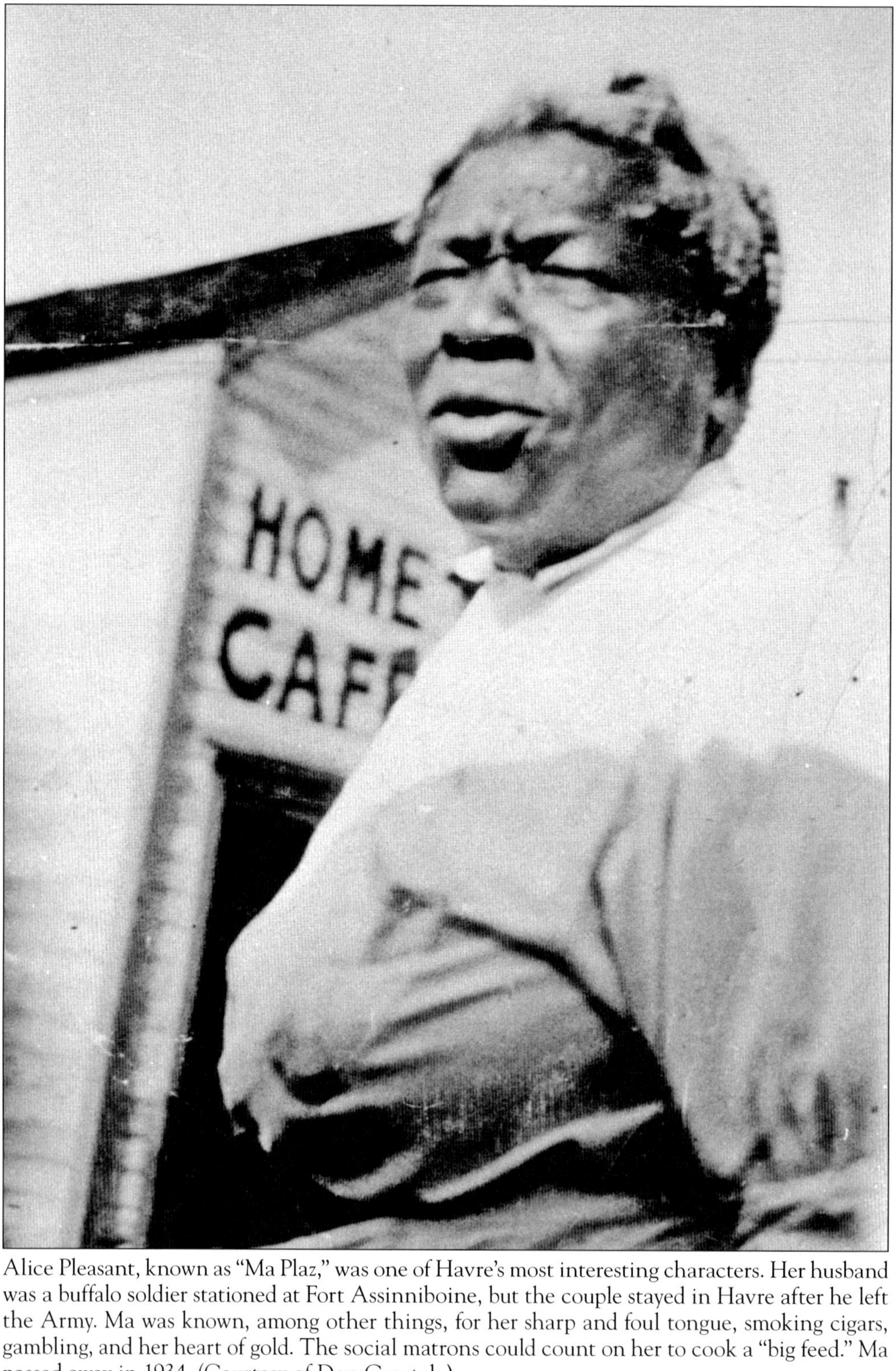

Alice Pleasant, known as "Ma Plaz," was one of Havre's most interesting characters. Her husband was a buffalo soldier stationed at Fort Assinniboine, but the couple stayed in Havre after he left the Army. Ma was known, among other things, for her sharp and foul tongue, smoking cigars, gambling, and her heart of gold. The social matrons could count on her to cook a "big feed." Ma passed away in 1934. (Courtesy of Don Greytak.)

Five

In the Halls of History

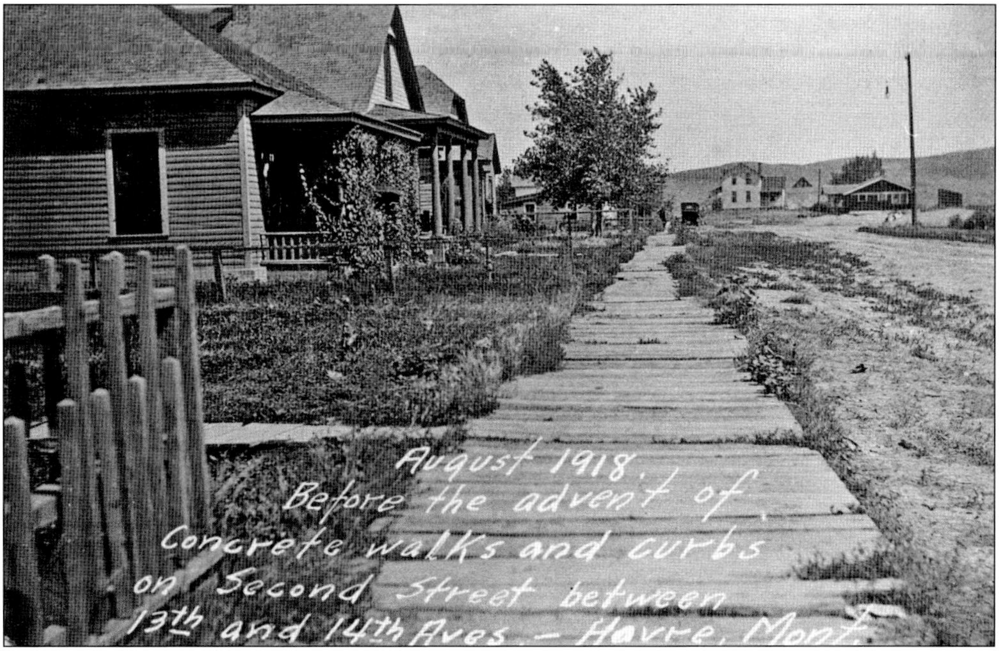

Dirt roads and boardwalks were common fixtures of newly formed towns, and it took a while for modern roads and pedestrian walkways to become a reality. The downtown area and residences in the original townsite were the first to receive concrete sidewalks. Havre's east end would get them later, and this photograph reveals this side of town still had boardwalks in 1918. (Courtesy of Don Greytak.)

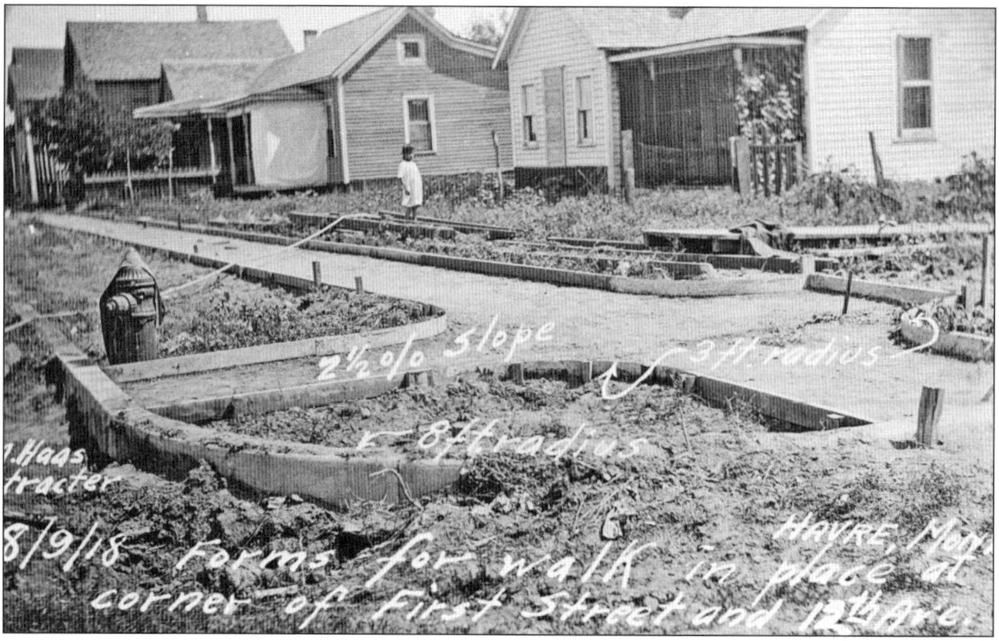

Forms were being put into place at the corner of First Street and Twelfth Avenue in 1918 for new curbs and sidewalks. The photograph also shows the slope degrees and other measurements, as well as the boulevards. Boulevards were an important part of towns, because they provided not only a buffer between the street and sidewalks but also gave an image of a progressive and cultured community. (Courtesy of Don Greytak.)

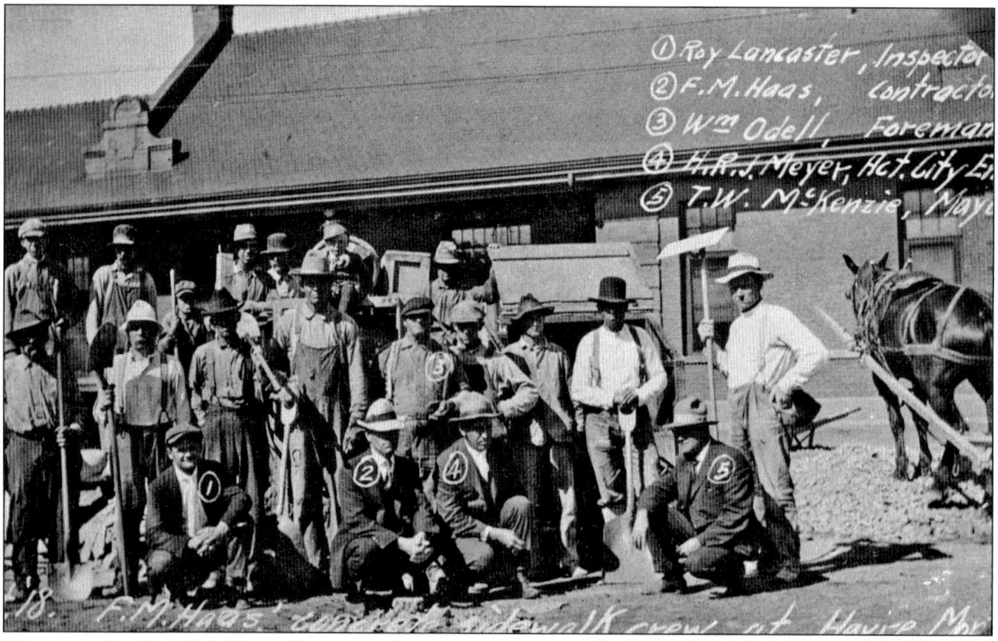

The crew for the F.M. Haas Concrete Company is pictured here in 1918 along with City of Havre officials. The F.M. Haas Concrete Company was from Minot, North Dakota. It received the winning bid to construct sidewalks mostly on Havre's east end and in the railroad depot area. The photograph was taken in front of the Great Northern Depot. (Courtesy of Don Greytak.)

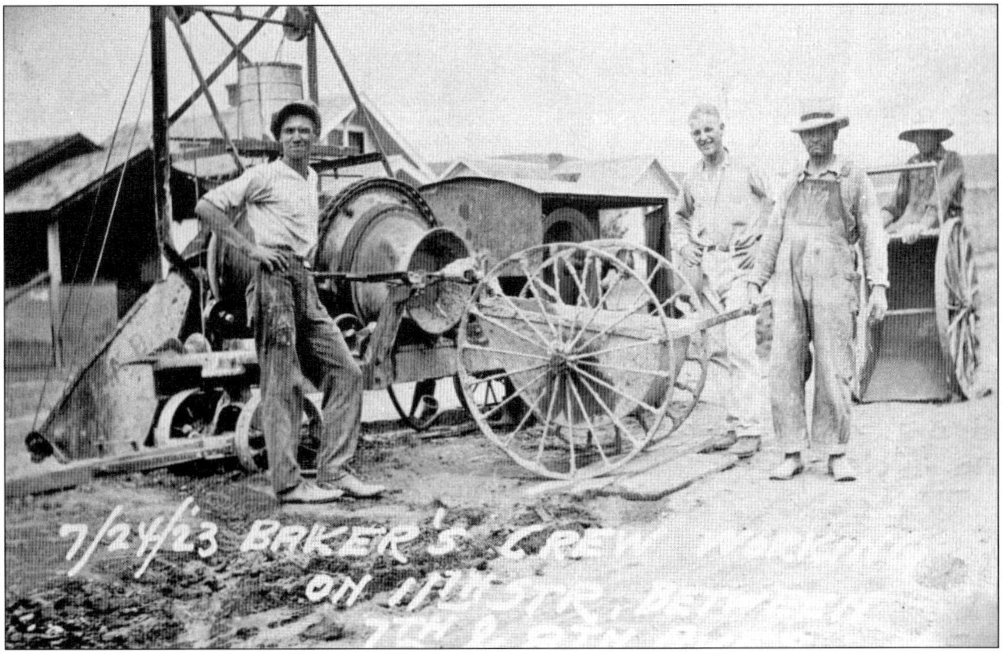

Another concrete contracting company that built sidewalks in Havre was the F.A. Baker Company. Stamps bearing its name can be found in the Havre Residential Historic District dating from 1914 to 1923. The crew is pictured here in 1923. (Courtesy of Don Greytak.)

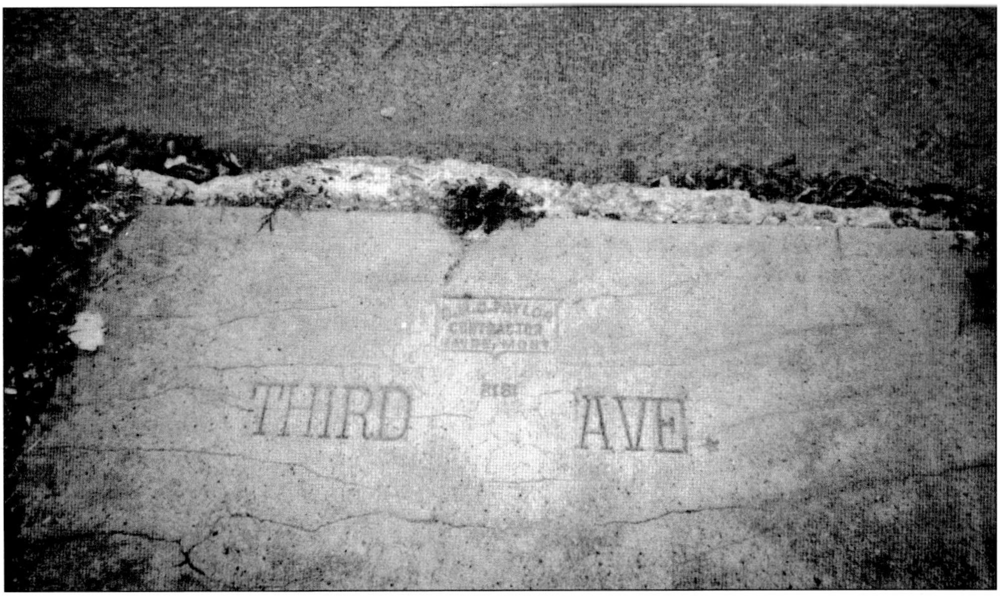

One of Havre's most prolific concrete contractors was Cassius Marcellus Clay "Cash" Taylor. His C.M.C. Taylor sidewalk stamps featuring a shield can be seen throughout the Havre Residential Historic District and into the east end. Taylor also built houses in the Taylor-Lucke subdivision, including his home located at 805 Third Avenue, constructed in 1914. (Photograph by the author, courtesy of High Line Heritage House.)

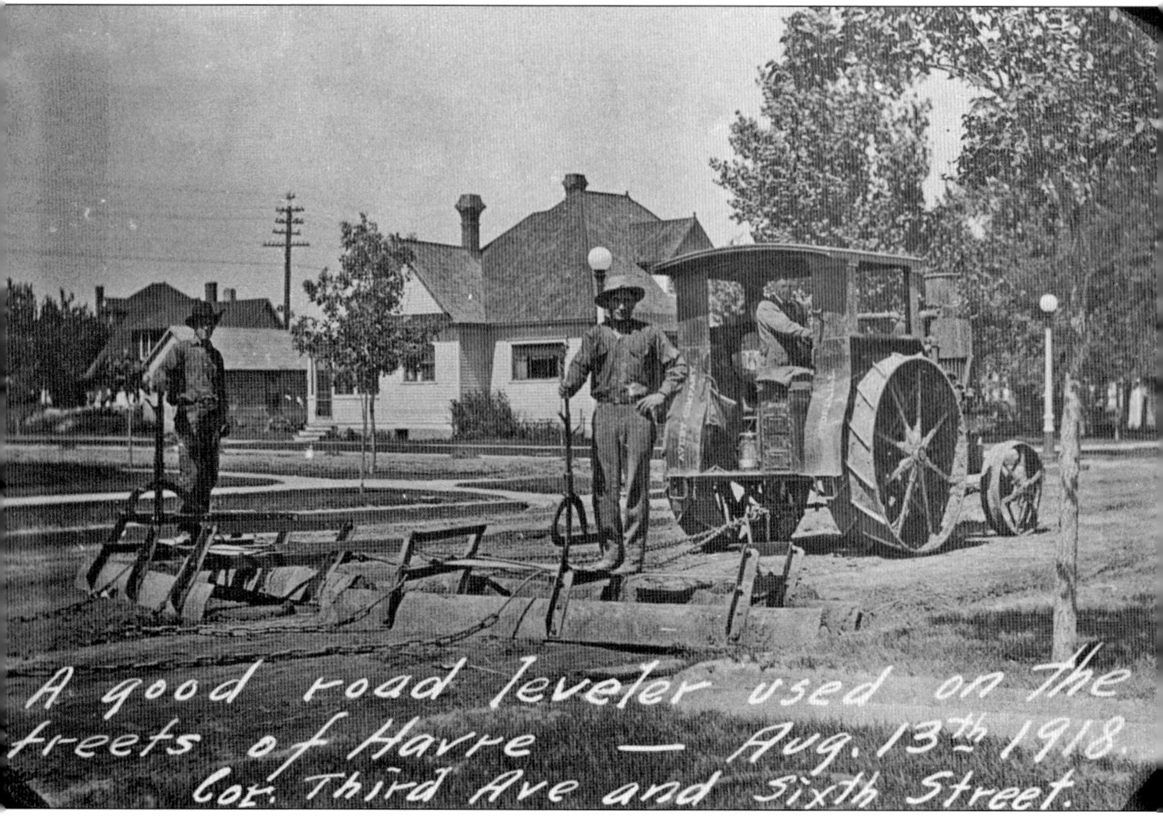

While Havre's streets remained dirt, it was necessary to level the ruts out of the road both for comfort and safety. Behind the road leveling crew and its machine is the James Carnal home, located at 536 Third Avenue. He was a cashier at the Citizens National Bank in 1909 and brother of Havre lawyer and politician Florian Carnal. "J.S. Carnal" is stamped on the sidewalk leading to the home. (Courtesy of Don Greytak.)

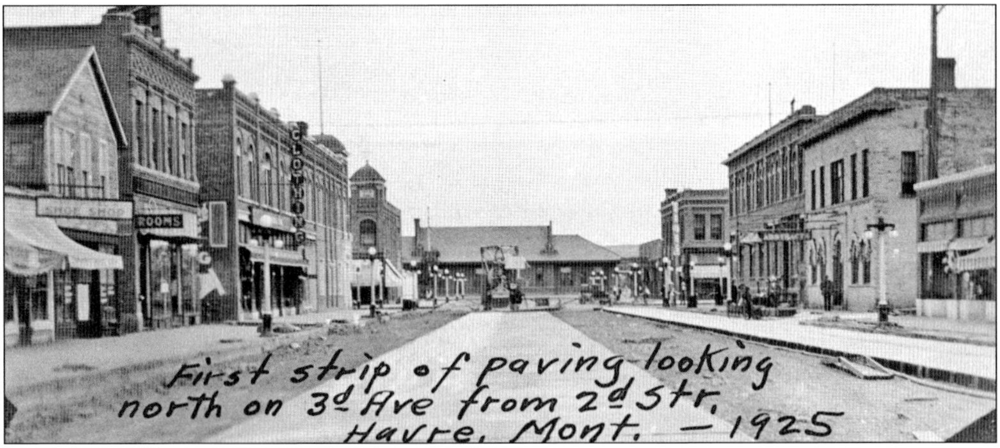

Third Avenue was the first to be paved, in 1925. Back then, Third Avenue and Tenth Street were the main thoroughfares into and out of Havre from the south. It only made sense that this would be the first to be paved. This paving can still be seen today in the downtown part of Havre. (Courtesy of Don Greytak.)

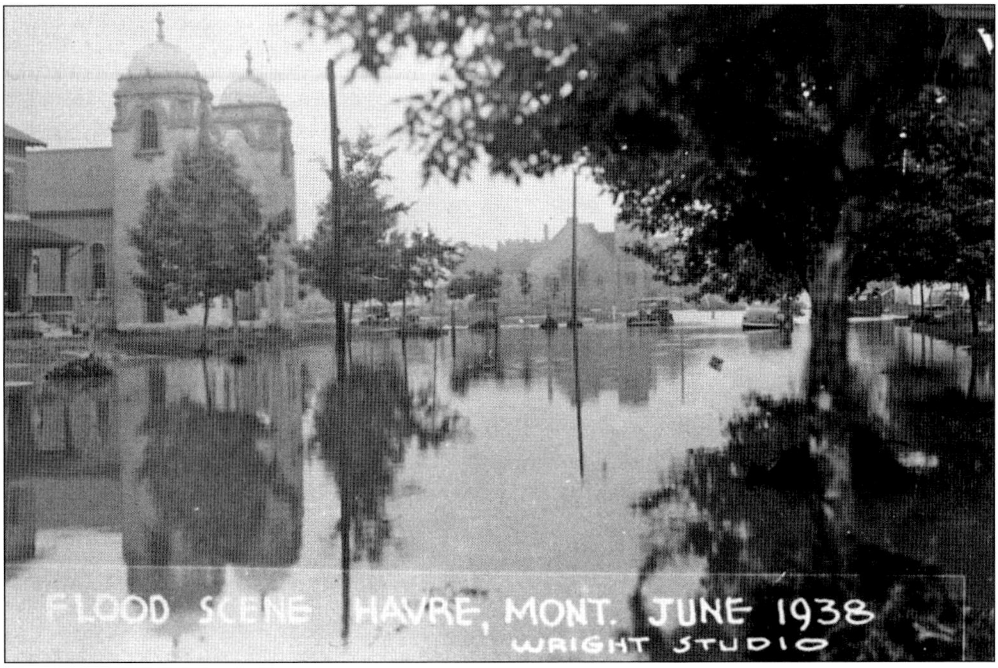

The deadly flood of 1938 wreaked havoc on Havre, the small town of Laredo, and the Bear Paw Mountains to the south. On June 22, a cloudburst in the Bear Paw Mountains dropped heavy rains. In Havre, it rained 1.20 inches within a half hour and measured 1.75 inches within an hour. Water from the Bear Paws joined what was falling in Havre, flooding businesses, government buildings, and homes. (Courtesy of Don Greytak.)

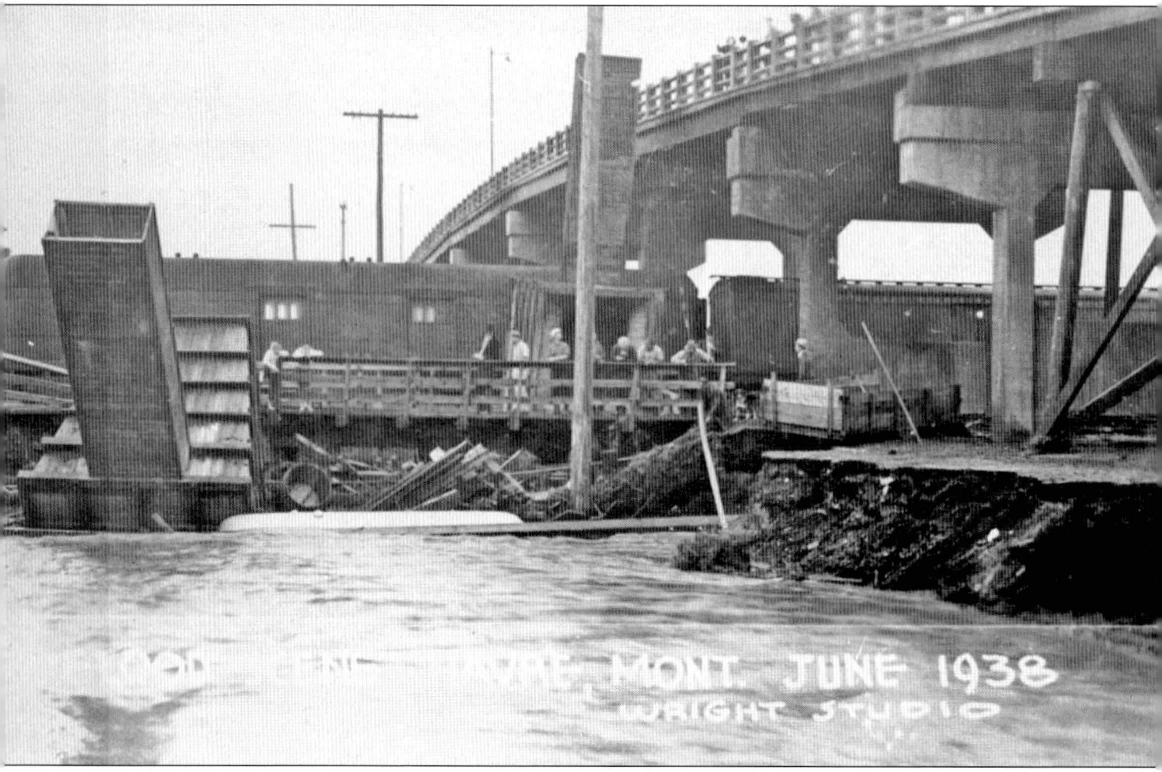

The Great Northern Railroad was also affected by the flood of 1938. The railyard in Havre was a shambles, and track south was pushed off course due to the strong current. It would take a few weeks before rail traffic was back to normal. (Courtesy of Don Greytak.)

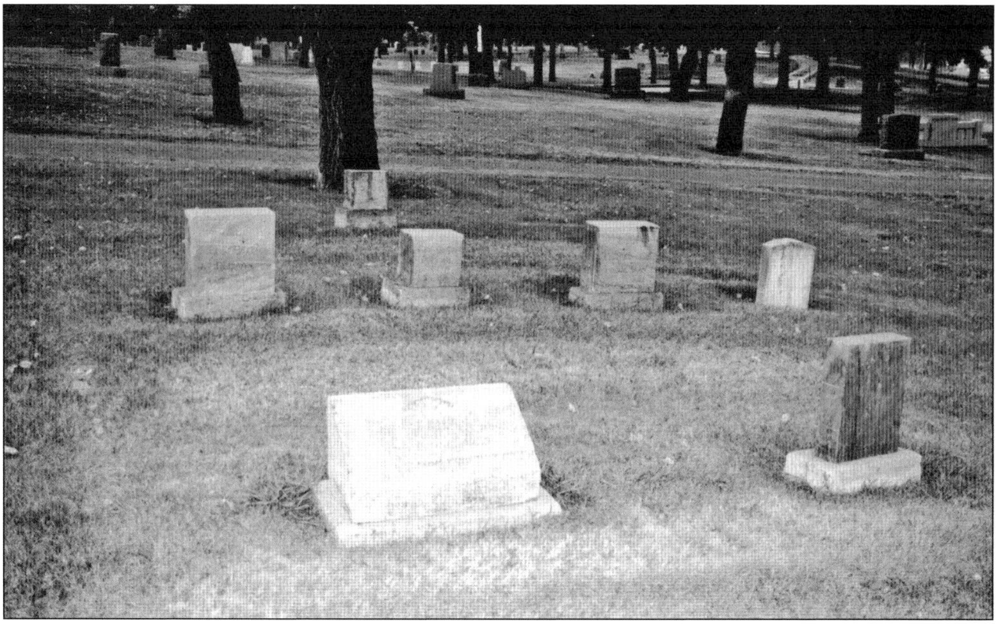

The flood turned deadly in Laredo, with the entire Emil DeHaan family of six perishing, along with Charles Pratt, Herman Wendt, and James Brown. The DeHaan gravesites seen here are located at Highland Cemetery, and Charles Pratt and James Brown are interred a short distance away. Wendt had no relatives in Montana, so his body was sent to his home state of Wisconsin for burial. (Photograph by the author, courtesy of High Line Heritage House.)

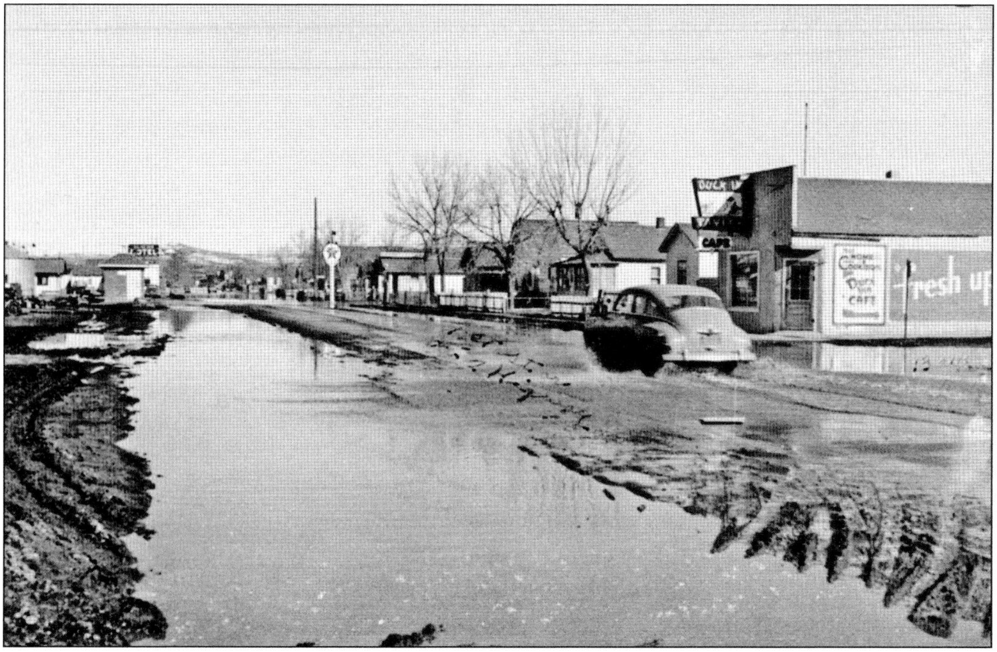

Flooding occurred in Havre quite frequently, due to the Milk River to the north, the Bear Paw Mountains to the south, and Havre's being situated in a valley. While not fatal to human life, the flood of 1952 caused a great deal of damage to homes and businesses. This photograph was taken on Havre's east end. (Courtesy of Elsie K. Nelson.)

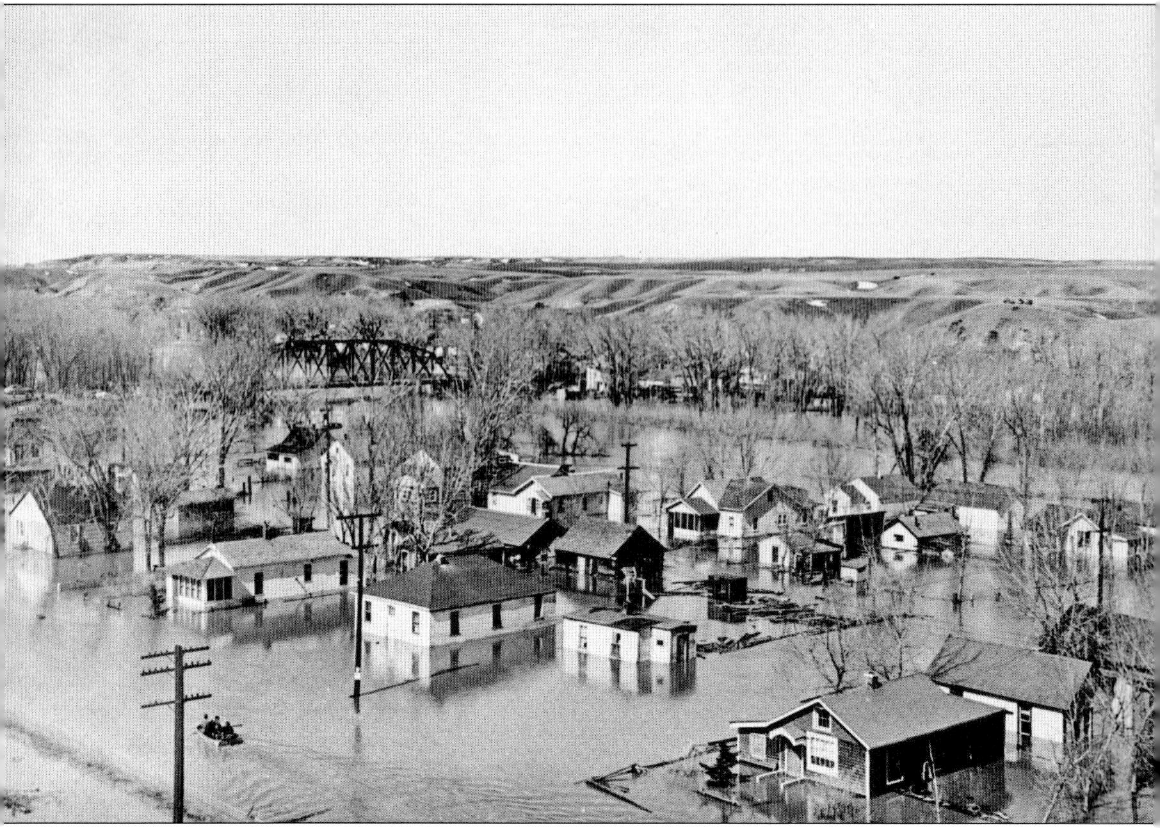

It was almost always Havre's unincorporated north side that received the brunt of flooding. It was located north of the railroad tracks, with the Milk River bisecting the two sides, and any considerable rise of the river would cause residents grief. The flood of 1952 was the worst. Flood control efforts later that decade still benefit the community today. (Courtesy of Don Greytak.)

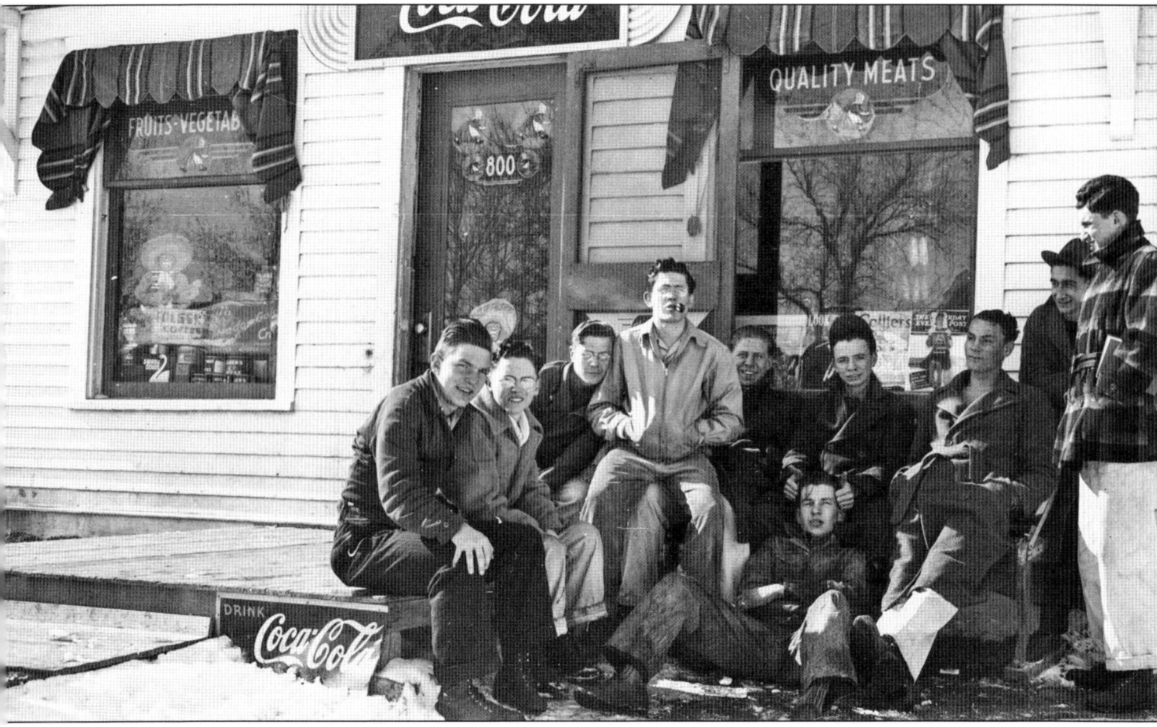

Havre was once dotted with several neighborhood grocery stores. It was a wonderful convenience to the homeowner and helped define neighborhood life. Over time, however, these stores have closed. Pictured here is a group of young men in front of the South Side Grocery on March 1, 1941. (Photograph by Frances Hulm, courtesy of Don Greytak.)